This book is available for special purchases in bulk by organizations and institutions, not for resale, at special discounts. Please direct your inquiries to Random House Premium Sales, fax 212-572-4961.

Please address inquiries about electronic licensing of reference products, for use on a network or in software or on CD-ROM, to the Subsidiary Rights Department, Random House Reference, fax 212-572-6003.

Visit the Random House Reference Web site: www.randomwords.com

Typeset and printed in the United States of America.

Library of Congress Cataloging-in-Publication Data is available.

First Edition
0 9 8 7 6 5 4 3 2 1
November 2003

ISBN: 0-375-72041-3

Vicious Vocabulary

Phil Eisenhower

Random House Reference

New York   Toronto   London   Sydney   Auckland

ACKNOWLEDGMENTS

My most heartfelt thanks to my brother Will,
to Stella and her daughter Nicole
to my students at San Fernando Senior High and LACHSA
to my mother, Laura,
and sisters Christel and Lauralyn for their support,
and to Elise, Mark, Arthur, and Alexandra for their prayers.

INTRODUCTION

"I'm going to cut you."

It was my first day on the job as a teacher in one of the toughest Los Angeles high schools, and I stood face to face with an angry teen holding a broken bottle up to my neck. I had just broken up a fight and tossed one kid behind a locked door to protect him. Turning, I faced the other, only to find the jagged edge of a broken bottle pressed against my throat. If I challenged the kid, it would be testosterone city, male toe-to-toe, lock-horns time, and the kid would feel he had to follow through on his threat.

On the other hand, I couldn't let him eviscerate the other kid behind the door, either. Besides, the door was locked and the rest of the staff was huddled safe and sound behind it. I was alone, with no safety net, staring down this teenage menace in a school for emotionally troubled youth.

"Well, you can cut me," I offered coolly, "but you still won't get through that door."

The boy looked a tad confused, his eyes shifted back and forth as he weighed his options: I hadn't locked horns with him, but he still wasn't getting what he wanted. He dropped his hands, cursed, and walked away. As I strutted through the office, I was slapped on the back many times by other teachers and administrators for this composed diplomacy. Reaching the bathroom, I calmly shut the door.

"They didn't mention this in the teacher manual," I reflected.

That about sums it up for me. In my years of teaching in the classroom, I, like many other teachers, have had to be "creative" when faced with unusual circumstances: disinterested students, diminished supplies, and violent and/or chaotic surroundings—sometimes dodging bullets.

The lessons compiled in *Vicious Vocabulary* are those that I conjured up after watching a Monty Python episode in which some bloke accidentally wanders into the Office for Verbal Abuse. I'd racked my brain to think of a way to teach college-level vocabulary to gangsters, students afraid of the gangsters, kids from the barrio, and kids just off the boat. When I saw the Monty Python episode, it hit me: Why not teach them to insult each other? I came up with an initial list of 20 insults, went over it in class, and then promptly forgot about the whole affair until five weeks later, when an irate female student plodded in on a bleary Monday morning, plopped her books on her desk, and said, "Men," trying to stifle the tears trapped in her throat. "They're nothing but lying sycophants!"

Could I believe my ears? Did she correctly use one of the insults I had taught her five weeks before? I hadn't done any review. My concept must have worked!

I began to test my theory that people in all walks of life are more prone to remember an insult than to recall random vocabulary. Perhaps this concept works because insults are easily stored in our primitive brains. This is true of aphasia patients; they can hurl out a cussword when they can't pronounce the word they want to say. Whatever the reason, insults seem to stick in our heads.

I didn't write this book to create more strife in the world, but to give students (and others) an alternative to the usual four-letter words that make up their scatological vernacular.

An effort has been made to make this book as politically correct as possible but still have an edge. Racist, sexist, religious, and sexual-preference slurs were avoided. This was done not out of concern for censorship, but out of a sense of direction. The purpose of this book is education—everyone's! I made a few exceptions to this rule in cases where I feel culture or time has extracted the inflammatory value of a particular slur. If you feel insulted by a slur that I've included, then I invite you to thumb through the book, find the right vicious vocabulary with which to insult me, and spew it out as you shake your fist in the air.

Though the pejoratives may seem to be the unique aspect of this book, it's the quotes that truly set it apart from any other vocabulary book. Once I began to put the quotes in, I noticed people were far more likely to pore over the book and pass it around to their friends.

Now I offer it to you: to the gangsters, secretaries, students, and housewives out there, to bosses and workers, old and young. This book is for all you irate folks who, with repressed rage, grit your teeth searching for that perfect comeback, that salient slur, that ribald retort for your most diabolical foes.

HOW TO USE THIS BOOK

There are two major differences between this book and any other vocabulary book. The first difference is that words are grouped together in a slur, as in *mendacious dog* or *duplicitous cad* or *traducing pile of tripe*. The premise of this is that the reader will more likely remember a phrase than a single word, and will more likely remember a slur than a random phrase.

Why? When you read the meaning behind the slur *mendacious dog*, every prevaricating putz who ever lied to you pops into your memory. You now have the word associated with someone you already have in your long-term memory. If you had merely memorized the word *mendacious*, it would have been forgotten. After all, what is the word *mendacious*? It's a concept, an abstraction. But if you hear the two words grouped together, as in the slur "mendacious dog," you'll remember that jerk that did you dirty and thereby remember that the definition of *mendacious* is "lying."

There is a strong emphasis on adjectives in the book, as in *mendacious dog*. Obviously I want you to study the word *mendacious*, not *dog*. In almost every case, the adjective is the word I want you to emphasize in your study, but sometimes you'll see the second word italicized, as in lying *sycophant*. In this case, it is the second italicized word that you should learn.

Occasionally, words grouped together may sound redundant, as in *archaic gaffer*. This is done to help embed the meaning into the gray matter between your ears. *Archaic* means "ancient" or "old-fashioned," and a *gaffer* is an old man; hence, *gaffer* should reinforce the meaning of *archaic*.

The second unique quality of this book is the quotations. There are plenty of quotation anthologies and gobs of vocabulary books, but this is the only one that has a quote for virtually every word. The quotes rarely include the word. Each quote is simply germane to the topic. Their purpose is to entertain, and their importance can't be overstated. If the book is entertaining, you'll be more apt to thumb through it; furthermore, the more entertaining it is, the more likely you'll remember the definitions of the words.

Each chapter in *Vicious Vocabulary* follows the same structure: the intro, a list of words, a story, a few quizzes, and a review.

The Intro. Each chapter has an intro in which I make suggestions on how you should study. If your purpose is to engross yourself in this material, then I suggest you follow my suggestions. If, however, you merely want to breeze through, take the tests, and then scan the definitions for only the words you miss, that's fine. Use the book as you see fit. If you're the breezy type, you're probably not bothering to read this part anyway.

The Words. Most of the words in these lists have been culled from lists of words most likely to be on the SAT or GRE. However, sprinkled throughout the book is arcane verbiage for the word sleuths out there. These are words that might seem new to even the most erudite pedant, such as *potvaliant* and *mussitate*. It won't kill you to add these to your lexicon of slurs. Remember, most of the words are used as adjectives, but occasionally you'll see a word used as a noun, in which case it will be italicized—for example, lying *sycophant*.

The Story. Each word list is accompanied by a short and vicious story that features the words in context.

The Quizzes. I suggest you take each quiz, writing the answer on the left and, when you finish the book, go back and take each test again as a review. First, cover the answers on the left and then draw a line from a word to its definition. Sometimes, one definition will fit two or more words. Don't get flustered by this. Simply mark each answer with the appropriate letter. And don't be confused when you get to a quiz and find a different word form than the one you saw before. I've done this deliberately so you can learn two words for the price of one!

Review. For some, this section might be difficult. Don't sweat it. Do your best. Some of the matched quotes and words may seem obvious and others obscure. Pick the best possible choice.

I leafed through the introductions of the other vocabulary books that fill the shelves of bookstores and saw that many authors emphasize why their book is better than the competition's. The implication is that you should buy their book and not another. What a bunch of bumptious, obstipated tripe! If you want to improve your vocabulary, you should buy all of them. But in the spirit of competition, my argument for *Vicious Vocabulary* is this: If you like sardonic humor, if you like waggish wit, if you're tempted at times to spice up your boss's, coworker's, or employee's tea with a little arsenic, then you might want to buy my book before you blow your dough on the others.

PRONUNCIATION KEY

STRESS

Pronunciations are marked for stress to reveal the relative differences in emphasis between syllables. In words of two or more syllables, a primary stress mark (′) follows the syllable having greatest stress, as the first syllable of **rabbit** (rab′it). A secondary stress mark (′) follows a syllable having slightly less stress than primary but more stress than an unmarked syllable, as the second syllable of **jackrabbit** (jak′rab′it).

ENGLISH SOUNDS

a act, bat, marry
ā age, paid, say
âr air, Mary, dare
ä ah, balm, star
b back, cabin, cab
ch child, pitcher, beach
d do, madder, bed
e edge, set, merry
ē equal, bee, pretty
ēr earring, cheerful, appear
f fit, differ, puff
g give, trigger, beg
h hit, behave
hw which, nowhere
i if, big, mirror
ī ice, bite, deny
j just, tragic, fudge
k keep, token, make

l low, mellow, bottle (bot′l)
m my, summer, him
n now, sinner, button (but′n)
ng sing, Washington
o ox, bomb, wasp
ō over, boat, no
ô order, ball, raw
oi oil, joint, joy
o͝o oomph, book, tour
o͞o ooze, fool, too
ou out, loud, cow
p pot, supper, stop
r read, hurry, near
s see, passing, miss
sh shoe, fashion, push
t ten, matter, bit
th thin, ether, path

th̸ that, either, smooth
u up, sun
ûr urge, burn, cur
v voice, river, live
w witch, away
y yes, onion
z zoo, lazy, those
zh treasure, mirage
ə used in unaccented syllables to indicate the sound of the reduced vowel in alone, system, easily, gallop, circus
ᵊ used between i and r and between ou and r to show triphthongal quality, as in fire (fīᵊr), hour (ouᵊr)

NON-ENGLISH SOUNDS

A as in French **ami** (A mē′)
KH as in Scottish **loch** (lôKH)
N as in French **bon** (bôN) [used to indicate that the preceding vowel is nasalized]

Œ as in French **feu** (fŒ)
R [a symbol for any non-english r sound, including a trill or flap in Italian and Spanish and a sound in French and German

similar to KH but pronounced with voice]
Y as in French **tu** (tY)
ᵊ as in French **bastogne** (ba stôn′yᵊ)

TABLE OF CONTENTS

Chapter 1

*The first human to hurl an insult
was the founder of civilization.*
—Sigmund Freud

WHAT IS A BARB? It's a thorn, something you can prick your finger on, but it's also a slang term for an insult, a slur, a slight. The barbs in *Vicious Vocabulary* are selected from lists of words that are most likely to be on the SAT and GRE exams (the offensive ones, mind you). Usually they're adjectives and I've coupled them with words you probably already know.

The most important way to approach learning these lofty (albeit acerbic) words is to not take the process too seriously. After all, everyone hates a bore . . . no. Think of this as a steam valve, something to help you blow off some hot air. When some abrasive, abhorrent idiot cuts you off on the freeway, these words will help you rise above the situation and sneer with contempt.

To remember these words you must visualize them, so I suggest you doodle. Yes, you read this right. Doodle! Pick words you don't know and draw a cartoon (nothing fancy) of something or someone that depicts the essence of each word. In doing so, you'll firmly place the definition in your long-term memory.

GRISLY LIST 1

"The play was an **abysmal** failure!" the critic wrote. Tom, feeling a bit **abased**, read the **abrasive** words carefully. "**Abysmal** failure?" he thought, "Really?"

"The cast moped about the stage like an **acephalous** bunch of **abject** sheep," the review went.

"But that was the point!" Tom thought. "Macbeth was a sheep. Doesn't he get it?"

Tom read on.

"If you're going to do Shakespeare in drag, and do it in such an **abhorrent** and **abominable** fashion, you might as well allow the audience to shoot the cast after the show and serve mutton."

"Hey, now, that's low!" Tom thought. "I've had some pretty **acerbic** reviews before, but this takes the cake! What do I have to do to get a good review?"

Tom dropped the **acidulous** review and eyed the Mustang in front of him.

"Yup. This is his. Nice paint job. Well, Mom always told me not to quit my night job." He slipped the slim jim into the door and quietly **absconded** with the critic's car.

1. **abased** reject ə-bāst′ To be abased is to be humbled, belittled, humiliated, or lowered. From Latin, *abassare* = to lower, to bring down.

   > *It is a bitter dose to be taught obedience after you have learned to rule.*
   > —*Publilius Syrus*

2. **abhorrent** monstrosity ab-hôr′ənt Provoking fear or disgust. Anything abhorrent is worthy of hate. From Latin, *ab* = away + *horrere* = to shudder.

   > *I captured some of the people who tried to assassinate me.*
   > *I ate them before they ate me.*
   > —*Idi Amin*

3. **abject** wretch ab′ject Anyone abject is completely miserable and degraded. From Latin, *abjectus* = to throw away.

   > *It makes no difference whether you win or lose until you lose.*
   > —*Unknown*

4. **abominable** freak ə-bom′ə-nə-bəl Anything abominable is vile or disgusting. From Latin, *ab homin* = away from man; hence, inhuman.

   > *When men are inhuman,*
   > *take care not to feel towards them*
   > *as they do towards other humans.*
   > —*Marcus Aurelius*

5. **abrasive** she-devil ə-brā′siv One who is abrasive is irritating and rude. From Latin, *ab* = away + *radere* = to scrape.

   > *It's like kissing Hitler.*
   > —*Tony Curtis, about Marilyn Monroe*

6. **absconding** fugitive ab-skon′ding To abscond is to depart in a secret manner, especially to avoid capture. From Latin, *ab* = from, away + *candere* = to hide.

   > *The thief is sorry that he is to be hanged,*
   > *not that he is a thief.*
   > —*English proverb*

7. **abysmal** flop ə-biz′məl An abysmal person or thing is truly wretched—hopelessly bad. From Greek, *abyssos* = without bottom.

   > *I have a new philosophy.*
   > *I'm only going to dread one day at a time.*
   > —*Charles Schulz*

8. **acephalous** lynch mob ə-sef′ə-ləs Anything acephalous is without a head or without a leader. From Greek, *a* = without + *kephale* = head.

   > *A mob has many heads, but no brains.*
   > —*Thomas Fuller*

9. **acerbic** **sourpuss** ə-sûr'bĭk Acerbic means sharp, sour, or bitter. From Latin, *acerbus* = bitter.

> *Blame someone else and get on with your life.*
> —Alan Woods

10. **acidulous** **critic** ə-sij'ə-ləs Acidulous means faintly sour or acidic in taste . It can also mean extremely sarcastic. From Latin, *acidus* = sour.

> *Folk whose own behavior is ridiculous are always first to slander others.*
> —Molière, Tartuffe

QUIZ 1

Match the definitions with the words on the left.

_____ 1. abased
_____ 2. abhorrent
_____ 3. abject
_____ 4. abominable
_____ 5. abrasive
_____ 6. abscond
_____ 7. abysmal
_____ 8. acerbic
_____ 9. acidulous
_____ 10. acephalous

a. disgusting (fits two words)
b. lowered (fits three words)
c. irritating
d. sarcastic, sharp, bitter in speech (fits two words)
e. run away in secret, especially to avoid capture
f. without a head or leader

GRISLY LIST 2

The divorce had been **acrimonious**, but Steve didn't expect this: There, before his very eyes, stood his ex. At least what looked like his ex or, perhaps, what faintly resembled his ex. In any case, what loomed in front of him was this **Amazonian** version of his ex, adorned in an **anachronistic** outfit more fitting an **agrestic** gladiator film than a doctor's office.

"What's she been taking?" he wondered. He tried to look **aloof** and **ambivalent**.

"Hi, Betty."

"Would she mention the money?" he asked himself. "She always was **acquisitive**. Those **acrid** memories of credit card disasters!"

"Hi Steve," came her throaty greeting. "I thought I'd stop by to settle the balance of what you owe me. You perform the surgery for free and I call off my lawyer."

"Now, that was an **affront**," he grumbled to himself. Well, she always was an **amoral** pain in the neck.

"But wait! The bloodwork will show her steroids. If I drop the dime on her, I'll get the kids and the alimony."

"No problem." Steve smiled with delight. "What day would you like to come in?"

1. **acquisitive hog** ə-kwiz'i-tiv Acquisitive means grasping and greedy. From Latin, *ad-* = to + *quaerere* = to seek.

> *When all sins are old in us and go upon crutches,*
> *(greed) does but then lie in her cradle.*
> —*Decker*

2. **acrid slanderer** ak'rid Anything acrid is sharp and bitter. From Latin, *acris* = sharp.

> *Their throats are open graves . . . .*
> *The poison of vipers is on their lips.*
> *Their mouths are full of cursing and bitterness.*
> —*Romans 3:13,14*

3. **acrimonious ex** ak-rə-mō'nē-əs An acrimonious person's speech is bitter and stinging. From Latin, *acer* = sharp.

> *It is much easier to be critical than to be correct.*
> —*Benjamin Disraeli*

4. **affrontive hatemonger** ə-frunt'iv An affront is an insult; hence, to be affrontive is to be openly insulting and purposely offensive. From Old French, *afronter* = to meet face to face.

> *A man who hates men is hated by them.*
> —*Ibn Gabirol*

5. **agrestic peasant** ə-grest'ik An agrestic person is rustic or crude and awkward. From Latin, *ager* = field.

> *A peasant between two lawyers is like a fish between two cats.*
> —*Spanish proverb*

6. **aloof stuffed shirt** ə-lōof' A person who is aloof is distant, indifferent, or disinterested. From Old English, *aloof* = toward the wind.

> *If a man makes me keep my distance, the comfort is,*
> *he keeps his at the same time.*
> —*Jonathan Swift*

7. **Amazonian man-eater** a-mə-zō'nē-ən Amazonian means a woman who is powerful and aggressive; warlike. The Amazons were a mythical group of women warriors in ancient Greece. It isn't an insult anymore, but Shakespeare used it as a slur. From Greek, *a* = without + *mazos* = breast.

> *A woman who tries to act like a man lacks ambition.*
> —*Graffito*

8. ***ambivalent* nit** am-biv′ə-lənt To be ambivalent is to have conflicting feelings: "I love him but I hate him." From Latin, *ambi* = on both sides + *valens* = being strong. Don't confuse ambivalent with ambiguous = having two or more meanings, or vague; as in, ". . . of ambiguous virtue." It is coupled with **nit** = the egg of an insect; a slang term for an idiot.

> *What man knows is everywhere at war with what he wants.*
> —*Joseph Wood Krutch*

9. ***amoral* psychopath** ə-môr′əl Anyone who is amoral is without morals or unable to tell the difference between right and wrong. From Latin, *a* = without + *moralis* = customs of behavior.

> *How oft the sight of means to do ill deeds, make deeds ill done!*
> —*Shakespeare*, King John

10. ***anachronistic* fogy** ə-nak-rə-nis′tik Anything or anyone out of its proper time is anachronistic. For example: a suit of armor in a modern war movie. From Greek, *anachronismos* = a wrong time reference.

> *You know you are getting old when you notice*
> *how young the derelicts are getting.*
> —*Jeanne Phillips*

QUIZ 2

Match the definitions with the words on the left.

_____ 1. acrid	a.	a powerful and aggressive woman
_____ 2. acrimonious	b.	insulting
_____ 3. acquisitive	c.	bitter and stinging in speech
_____ 4. affrontive		(fits two words)
_____ 5. agrestic	d.	greedy
_____ 6. aloof	e.	distant, indifferent
_____ 7. Amazonian	f.	having conflicting feelings
_____ 8. ambivalent	g.	out of its proper time
_____ 9. amoral	h.	rustic and crude
_____ 10. anachronistic	i.	without morals

GRISLY LIST 3

Alone, Sally sat with an **apathetic** gaze as her coffee grew colder and colder. Stood up again! She had an **antipathy** for blind dates but, then, no one else was asking her out. Well, not exactly no one: there were the **archaic** geezers who pinched her on the subway; the **arrogating** twerp that wanted her flat; and her boss, that **antediluvian** slob. Yuck!

But where were the men? Were her dreams of "true love" just an **antiquated** ideal? No knights in shining armor for her, just **arriviste** dogs with their fancy cars and seedy offers. Maybe she was too hasty with Brick, but he was so **arrogant,** and he didn't like her cat. The nerve! She pulled out her new pictures of Fluffy. Ah, Fluffy: the only one in her life that didn't seem to have some **anathematic** cloud over him.

"Can I warm up your coffee?" the waiter asked politely.

"I don't think that's possible," Sally sulked.

The waiter gently took one of the cutest shots of Fluffy, the one where she and Fluffy were cuddled together.

"He's beautiful."

"A man who likes cats? Are you for real?"

The waiter laughed, "I just miss my cat. She passed away a month ago. You know, animals help us look beyond. They keep us from being too **anthropocentric.**"

Sally didn't know what **anthropocentric** meant, but that didn't seem to matter. Her coffee was getting warmer.

1. ***anathematic* outcast** ə-nath-ə-mat'ik An anathema is anything accursed or damned, or anyone immensely detested. An anathematic person is disgusting, loathsome, hated, and/or hateful. From Greek, *anathema* = an accursed thing, something dedicated to evil.

> *I wish that for just one time you could stand inside my shoes;*
> *you'd know what a drag it is to see you.*
> —Bob Dylan

2. ***antediluvian* throwback** an-ti-də-lōō'vē-ən Antediluvian means "before the flood"; it is a reference to the flood in the Bible; hence, it means anyone (or anything) very old. From Latin, *ante* = before and *diluviam* = deluge.

> *Senescence begins*
> *And middle age ends*
> *The day your descendants*
> *Outnumber your friends.*
> —Ogden Nash

3. ***anthropocentric* pinhead** an-thrə-pə-sen'tric One who is anthropocentric views humans as the final aim of the universe or always interprets life in terms of human values. From Greek, *anthropos* = human being + *kentron* = center.

> *The noblest work of God? Man. Who found it out? Man.*
> —Mark Twain

4. ***antipathetic* drip** an-tip-ə-thet'ik To have antipathy is to have a strong dislike, aversion, or hate toward something. Hence, to be antipathetic is to be filled with aversion and repugnance or to cause that aversion in others. From Greek, *anti* = against + *pathos* = feeling.

> *They exchanged the quick, brilliant smile of women*
> *who dislike each other on sight.*
> —Marcus Pugh

5. ***antiquated* rustic** anʹti-kwāt-əd Anything antiquated is so old as to be obsolete or useless. From Latin, *antiquus* = ancient, old.

> *When I was young, the Dead Sea was still alive.*
> —George Burns

6. ***apathetic* robot** ap-ə-thetʹik An apathetic person is unconcerned, indifferent, and/or just plain not interested. From Greek, *a* = without + *pathos* = emotion.

> *Scientists announced today that they have discovered*
> *a cure for apathy. However, they claim no one has shown*
> *the slightest bit of interest in it.*
> —George Carlin

7. ***archaic* gaffer** är-kāʹik Anything or anyone who is archaic is either ancient or old-fashioned. From Greek, *archaikos* = old-fashioned.

> *My grandfather started walking five miles a day when he was sixty.*
> *He's ninety-seven now, and we don't know where the hell he is.*
> —Ellen DeGeneres

8. **shady *arriviste*** a-rē-vēstʹ An arriviste has newly acquired wealth by dubious methods. From French, *arriviste* = one who has just arrived.

> *Behind every great fortune there is a crime.*
> —Honoré de Balzac

9. ***arrogant* heartbreaker** ărʹə-gent One who is arrogant has an excessive amount of self-pride. From Latin, *arrogare* = to claim.

> *The infinitely little have a pride infinitely great.*
> —Voltaire

10. ***arrogating* squatter** arʹə-gā-ting To arrogate is to seize without right. From Latin, *arrogare* = to claim.

> *Thou shall not steal.*
> —Exodus 20:15

QUIZ 3

Match the definitions with the words on the left.

____ 1.	antiquated	a.	gained riches by corrupt methods
____ 2.	apathetic	b.	ancient or old-fashioned
____ 3.	archaic		(fits two words)
____ 4.	arriviste	c.	before the flood; old
____ 5.	arrogant	d.	excessively full of pride
____ 6.	arrogating	e.	cursed
____ 7.	antediluvian	f.	centered on humans
____ 8.	anathematic	g.	seizing without right
____ 9.	anthropocentric	h.	extremely disliked
____ 10.	antipathetic	i.	unconcerned, indifferent

GRISLY LIST 4

Maria tried to make her way among the **Augean** wreckage that cluttered her bedroom. Since her **asinine** sister had moved back in, this mess had become the norm. Her mother's **autocratic** voice thundered down the hall.

"Pick up your room or you're not going out tonight!"

Her mother ruled the roost with the **authoritarian** style of Attila the Hun. Maria looked at the huge pile of clothes that covered her sister's bed and then at the matches on the floor. An **audacious** smile crossed her face; she'd lost her room but not her **astigmatic** sense of humor.

"It's Nina's mess, not mine!" Maria shouted back.

"Don't make me get a switch!" Mother's **aspersive** threat answered. "Stop your **babbling**. You know your sister's at her cousin's. You're here; you clean."

Nina always told Mom she was at her cousin's when she was planning on going to some **bacchanalian** party. Maria stepped on her own wallet, lying amid the debris that littered the floor, and opened it. It was empty. That **avaricious** thief!

"Mom, Nina stole my money! She stole forty dollars!"

Maria's mother appeared to the door, switch in hand. Maria knew she was going to get it, but then a moan reverberated from under the clothes on Nina's bed and a hand gripping a Tequila bottle dropped to the side. Maria smiled.

1. *asinine* **annoyance** as'ə-nīn An asinine person behaves like an ass: silly, stupid, and obnoxious. From Latin, *asinus* = ass.

   > *No, Groucho is not my real name.*
   > *I'm breaking it in for a friend.*
   > —Groucho Marx

2. *aspersive* **piece of trash** ə-spûr'siv You may have heard the expression "to cast aspersions." To cast aspersions is to spread slander or lies about someone. But it works equally well as the adjective, aspersive. From Latin, *aspergere* = to sprinkle.

   > *Lie lustily, some filth will stick.*
   > —Thomas Hall

3. *astigmatic* **extremist** as-tig-mat'ik Anyone or anything that is astigmatic has an extremely skewed point of view: an astigmatism is a defect in vision. From Greek, *a* = without + *stigma* = a mark, puncture.

   > *Schizophrenia beats dining alone.*
   > —Unknown

4. *audacious* **bluffer** ô-dā'shəs Anyone audacious is extremely bold, recklessly brave, or boldly rude. From Latin, *audaci* = daring.

   > *My husband said he needed more space, so I locked him outside.*
   > —Roseanne Barr

5. ***Augean* pack rat** ô-jē'ən In Greek mythology, the Augean stables held 3,000 oxen and hadn't been cleaned for 30 years, until Hercules came along; hence, anything Augean is extremely filthy and degraded.

> *Dirt parts good company.*
> —*Scottish proverb*

6. ***authoritarian* tyrant** ə-thôr-i-târ'ē-ən Anyone authoritarian demands obedience. From Latin, *auctor* = writer.

> *He who strikes terror into others is himself in continual fear.*
> —*Claudian*

7. ***autocratic* monster** ô-tə-krat'ik An autocratic person is domineering and rules with absolute power. From Greek, *autokrates* = self-ruling, ruling alone < *auto* = self + *krate* = power.

> *A friend in power is a friend lost.*
> —*Henry Adams*

8. ***avaricious* gold digger** av-ə-rish'əs Avaricious people will do anything for money—all because of greed. From Latin, *avarus* = greedy.

> *I'm a very good housekeeper;*
> *whenever I leave a man,*
> *I keep his house.*
> —*Zsa Zsa Gabor*

9. ***babbling* brook** bab'ling Babbling means making incoherent sounds, talking foolishly or excessively. It also describes the sound a brook makes flowing over rocks. From Latin, *balbutire* = to stammer.

> *A chattering barber asked Archelaus how he would like his hair cut.*
> *He answered, "In silence."*
> —*Plutarch*

10. ***bacchanalian* frat rat** bak-ə-nāl'yən Bacchanalian, meaning drunken and festive, comes from Bacchanalia, a drunken, orgiastic festival of ancient Greece given in honor of Bacchus, the Greek god of wine.

> *Alcohol is like love: the first kiss is magic,*
> *the second is intimate, the third is routine.*
> *After that, you just take the girl's clothes off.*
> —*Raymond Chandler*

Match the definitions with the words on the left.

____ 1.	asinine	a.	spreading slander
____ 2.	aspersive	b.	ruling with absolute power
____ 3.	astigmatic	c.	drunken, orgiastic
____ 4.	audacious	d.	enforces obedience
____ 5.	Augean	e.	extremely filthy, degraded
____ 6.	authoritarian	f.	like an ass; silly, stupid
____ 7.	autocratic	g.	with an extremely skewed view
____ 8.	avaricious		of life
____ 9.	babbling	h.	recklessly brave; boldly rude
____ 10.	bacchanalian	i.	greedy
		j.	talking foolishly

GRISLY LIST 5

"So, is this a threesome? But I forgot my handcuffs." Mark always resorted to **bawdy** humor under stress, but the **beetling** looks on the robbers' faces and the sawed-off shotgun under his chin told him it might be time to get serious.

"I guess you want my wallet," he said, and **begrudgingly** handed it over. Up to this point it had been a perfectly **banal** day. He stepped into this building, a **bedraggled** mess, to shake off the rain, but then found himself facing two **baleful** thugs.

"There's a lot of cash in there; are you sure we can't go Dutch? It's my Mom," Mark said with **bathetic** irony. "She'll ground me if I show up broke. She'll **badger** me to death."

The **baneful** creep with the shotgun grabbed the wallet and threw it at his friend.

"Where are you going to spend it if you're dead?"

With his usual **Barmecidal** dryness, Mark countered, "Okay, I'll take thirty percent and I'll pick up the beer tab."

"Hey, homes!" the thug shouted. "This wallet has three hundred dollars in it."

The gunman took out a five and stuffed it in Mark's shirt. "I guess this is your lucky day," he sneered, and the two split out into the storm.

Mark pulled five more wallets out of his coat pockets and fingered the day's take, which was more than he expected. "Not bad for a pickpocket. Well, maybe it *is* my lucky day!"

1. ***badgering* bore** baj'ə-ring Badgering means nagging or bothering. From Medieval English, *bagge* = badge, because of the mark on the badger's face, but use of the word as a slur comes from the badger's feisty personality.

> *Lady Astor:*
> *Winston, if I were married to you, I'd put poison in your coffee.*
> *Sir Winston Churchill:*
> *Nancy, if you were my wife—I'd drink it!*

2. ***baleful* butcher** bāl'fəl Anything baleful could be harmful, threatening harm, deadly, or ominous. From Old English, *bealu* = calamity + *ful* = full.

> *A serpent will still bite, even though it's been kept*
> *and tended a long time.*
> *—Panchatantra*

3. ***banal* also-ran** bə-nal' To be banal is to be ordinary, common. From Old French, *banal* referred to objects belonging to feudal serfs; hence, common, ordinary.

> *Just remember, so long as you don't hurt anybody,*
> *or talk badly about them, or take advantage of them,*
> *you'll always be disappointingly dull.*
> *—Eric Idle*

4. ***baneful* backstabber** bān'fəl Beware! A baneful person is deadly. From Old English, *bana* = to strike, wound.

> *If called by a panther, don't anther.*
> *—Ogden Nash*

5. ***Barmecidal* host** bär-mi-sī'dəl Barmecidal applies to anyone who pretends hospitality or gives the illusion of having plenty. In *Arabian Nights*, Barmecide was a noble who gave a beggar a pretended feast with empty dishes.

> *With affection beaming in one eye, and calculation out of the other.*
> *—Charles Dickens*

6. ***bathetic* wise guy** bə-thet'ik Bathos is a false pathos, an abrupt change from the lofty to the trivial, the anticlimax. Hence, bathetic means insincerely sentimental. From Greek, *bathos* = depth.

> *The ring of the false coin is not more recognizable*
> *than that of a rhyme setting forth a false sorrow.*
> *—Thomas Bailey Aldrich*

7. ***bawdy* sleazebag** bô'dē One who is bawdy is humorously coarse and lewd. A bawd is a prostitute or a keeper of a house of prostitutes. There's also bawdry, which has the same gist as bawdy. From Middle English, *bawde* = a lewd person.

> *I used to be Snow White, but I drifted.*
> *—Mae West*

8. **bedraggled loon** bi-drag'əld A bedraggled one is wet, dirty, and disheveled. From Middle Low German, *be* = make + *draggen* = to dredge.

> *(W. H.) Auden's face looks like a wedding cake*
> *that was left out in the rain.*
> —Stephen Spender

9. **beetling bully** bēt'ling Besides the bugs known as beetles (which means 'the little biter'), another use of beetle comes from Middle English, *bitel*, which means projecting. Beetling means menacing because he/she hangs or towers over.

> *Gold rope wearer, neighborhood terror,*
> *can't hang around my mother*
> *'cause she says I scare her.*
> —Ice-T, "Rhyme Pays"

10. **begrudging giver** bi-gru'jing Begrudging means envying or resenting the good fortune of another or being reluctant to give. From Medieval English, be + *gruchen* = to grumble.

> *He gives only the worthless gold who gives from a sense of duty.*
> —James Russell Lowell

QUIZ 5

Match the definitions with the words on the left.

___ 1. badger	a.	nag
___ 2. baleful	b.	deadly (fits two words)
___ 3. banal	c.	to envy or resent, or to give but
___ 4. baneful		not want to give
___ 5. Barmecidal	d.	humorously coarse and lewd
___ 6. bathetic	e.	insincerely sentimental
___ 7. bawdy	f.	boring, dull, common, ordinary
___ 8. bedraggled	g.	menacing
___ 9. beetling	h.	pretending hospitality
___ 10. begrudge	i.	wet and dirty

MATCH EACH QUOTE WITH THE APPROPRIATE WORD.

1. The deadliest sin were the consciousness of no sin.
—Thomas Carlyle

2. By keeping men off you keep them on.
—John Gay

3. Off with her head!!
—the Red Queen, Lewis Carroll, Alice's Adventures in Wonderland

4. When the world has once begun to use us ill it afterwards continues the same treatment with less scruple or ceremony, as men do to a whore.
—Jonathan Swift

5. One may have good eyes and see nothing.
—Italian proverb

6. I don't care about Jesus. I don't care about Allah.
All I care about is the almighty dollah.
—D.J. Quik

7. He rolled the executions on his tongue like berries.
*—Osip Mandelstam,
speaking of Stalin*

8. A false friend and a shadow attend only while the sun shines.
—Benjamin Franklin

9. Rich gifts wax poor when givers prove unkind.
—Shakespeare

10. By ignorance is pride increased;
those most assume who know the least.
—John Gay

____ a. autocratic (two answers)
____ b. aloof
____ c. amoral
____ d. abject
____ e. begrudging
____ f. arrogant
____ g. bathetic
____ h. astigmatic
____ i. avaricious

Chapter 2

*Insults should be well avenged
or well endured.*
—Spanish proverb

ONE OF THE UNUSUAL ways in which this book approaches vocabulary is that it combines an adjective with a noun. Why is that important? If you study the word *antediluvian* by itself, you may or may not remember its meaning. But if you attach it to a noun, making it a slur, as in *antediluvian throwback,* you are more likely to remember the definition. Therefore, you will keep it in your long-term memory because it is an insult, not some random word.

As you look at the next list, once again pick out the words that are unfamiliar, but this time write down names: names of friends, enemies, politicians, or movie characters that fit the words. By doing this, you've combined the words with thoughts that are already in your long-term memory. Go ahead and doodle a caricature as well. Make a copy of each drawing with the word underneath and place one on your bathroom mirror. When you feel the word is fixed in your memory, replace it with another.

GRISLY LIST 6

It had seemed like such a good idea at the time, but now, with the one-way ticket to Mongolia in hand, Fred felt pretty dumb. Last night, with the **bibulous** influence of vodka and ice and his own **belligerent** mood, this seemed romantic, but now? True, the love of his life had left him; she'd ditched him for one of the worst **bellicose** idiots on the football team. True, said idiot was his **bête noire**, the one who had **belittled** him time and time again for being a nerd. True, he'd been a sap, a **biddable** sap at that, for the two months he and his ex-girlfriend had been together. So what had changed? "Why am I now **berating** myself for being a coward?" he wondered. "Why can't I just board the plane and leave this **benighted** life?"

Fred peered at his passport, and then eyed the **bestial** jocks that smirked as they walked past him. His ex and the **bilious** galoot also drifted by. It suddenly dawned on him: why go to Mongolia when 65 percent of the women in Brazil are single? "Rio," he mused, "Here I come."

1. ***belittling* scoffer** bi-lit′ling To belittle is to make something small, to insult, to put down. Thomas Jefferson invented this word in 1780.

> *He can see a louse as far away as China*
> *but is unconscious of an elephant on his nose.*
> *—Malay proverb*

2. **bellicose bouncer** bel'i-kōs If you're bellicose, you like to fight or argue. From Latin, *bellum* = war.

> *Those who in quarrels interpose,*
> *must often wipe a bloody nose.*
> —John Gay, Fables

3. **belligerent rival** bə-lij'ər-ənt A belligerent person is warlike, ready to fight, aggressively hostile. It's derived from Latin, *belliger* = waging war.

> *To fight is a radical instinct; if men have nothing else to fight over*
> *they will fight over words, fancies or women,*
> *or they will fight because they do not like each other's looks,*
> *or because they have met walking in opposite directions.*
> —George Santayana

4. **benighted hero-worshiper** bi-nī'tid A benighted person is surrounded by darkness, or is intellectually, culturally, or morally "in the dark." From Old English, *beon* = am + night from Gothic, *nahts* = night.

> *In the country of the blind the one-eyed man is king.*
> —Erasmus

5. **berating broad** bə-rā'ting To berate someone is to severely scold him or her. Be + Old French, *reter* = to blame, accuse.

> *Talking to pieces is the trade of those who cannot construct.*
> —Ralph Waldo Emerson

6. **bestial brawler** bes'chəl Anything bestial is like a beast: brutal, savage and vile. From Latin, *bestia* = beast.

> *At worst, is not this an unjust world,*
> *full of nothing but beasts of prey,*
> *four-footed or two-footed?*
> —Thomas Carlyle

7. **cruel bête noire** bet nwär' A bête noire is the person that you most hate or fear. In French, *bête noire* literally means black beast.

> *If a pit bull romances your leg, fake an orgasm.*
> —Hut Landon

8. **bibulous boozer** bib'yə-ləs One who is bibulous has a predilection to drink too much booze. From Latin, *bibere* = to drink. Akin to imbibe.

> *I was so drunk last night I fell down and missed the floor.*
> —Dean Martin

9. **biddable gofer** bid'ə-bəl A biddable person is willing to do whatever is asked of him or her. It's a combination of bid and -able. Bid comes from Old English, *biddan* = to beg, ask.

> *He who humbles himself too much gets trampled upon.*
> —Yugoslavian proverb

10. ***bilious* brute** bil'yəs To be bilious is to be cross and bad-tempered. The word is based on bile, which is secreted by the liver. Once it was believed that black bile caused depression and yellow bile caused one to be angry. From Latin, *bilis* = liquid gunk secreted by the liver.

> *When angry, count to four; when very angry, swear.*
> —*Mark Twain*

QUIZ 6

Match the definitions with the words on the left.

____ 1.	belittling		a.	to severely scold
____ 2.	bellicose		b.	drunken
____ 3.	belligerent		c.	intellectually backwards
____ 4.	benighted		d.	like a beast; brutal, savage
____ 5.	berate		e.	given to fighting (fits two words)
____ 6.	bestial		f.	willing to do what is asked
____ 7.	bête noire		g.	your most feared or hated enemy
____ 8.	bibulous		h.	to be cross, bad-tempered
____ 9.	biddable		i.	insulting
____ 10.	bilious			

GRISLY LIST 7

Bill Bullian **blustered** by the **blithering** beggars and **blowsy** tramps that littered this seedy side of town.

"Garbage! The whole lot is garbage," he **blatantly** bellowed, loud enough for the sad wastrels to hear a block away.

"Sir?" asked Charlie sheepishly as he followed his boss down the alley.

"**Boondoggling** bums!" Bill shouted with **bombastic** flair. "That's all they are! **Boondoggling Boeotian** bums. All of them should be shot!"

Bill **boorishly** shoved aside a beggar that stumbled in their way and then stopped in front of a rather **bland** building and looked up.

"Here it is. This is where I'll start my empire, just as soon as we can get the riffraff out. It's not my fault if they are so damn stupid. Survival of the fittest, they say. The more intelligent animal always supplants the dumb."

"But is it safe?" Charlie asked, rather **bootlessly**.

But his warning was unheeded. Bill bounded up the steps, only to have the floor buckle under him. He plummeted helplessly out of sight with the most surprised look on his face. Charlie peered over the edge.

"Yes, Mr. Bullian, survival of the fittest."

1. ***bland* hole-in-the-wall** blănd Bland means mild or dull, tasteless, and insipid. From Latin, *blandus* = mild.

> *Television: the bland leading the bland.*
> *—Unknown*

2. ***blatant* user** blāt'nt Anything blatant is either offensively noisy or excessively conspicuous. Coined by Sir Edmund Spenser in his play *The Blatant Beast*, meaning a bellowing beast, perhaps derived from Latin, *blatire* = to babble.

> *The nail that sticks up gets hammered down.*
> *—Japanese proverb*

3. ***blithering* idiot** blit͟H'ə-ring Anyone who blithers speaks nonsensically. From Old Norse, *blaor* = nonsense.

> *A fool is known by his babbling.*
> *—English proverb*

4. ***blowsy (blowzy)* bimbo** blou'zē A blowsy person is coarse and ruddy or untidy. The derivation is obscure but it might come from Medieval English, *blowze* = beggar, wench.

> *My girlfriend was fat. How fat was she? She sweats gravy.*
> *—Ben Creed*

5. ***blusterous* hothead** blus'tə-rəs A blusterous person is a blowhard, swaggering in like a storm off the coast of Florida. From Latin, *blustern* = to blow violently.

> *His rash fierce blaze of riot cannot last,*
> *for violent fires soon burn out themselves;*
> *small showers last long,*
> *but sudden storms are short.*
> *—Shakespeare, Richard II*

6. ***Boeotian* bum** bē-ō'shən Boeotian means stupid or dim-witted. In Athens, Greece, there was this hick town called Boeotia where the folk got a reputation for being kind of dull—they didn't have the cultural refinement like the city slickers down in Athens or up in Thebes. And to their credit—or to their discredit, as the case may be—we still use their name as a fancy way of insulting someone's intelligence.

> *Never attribute to malice what can be*
> *adequately explained by stupidity.*
> *—Nick Diamos*

7. ***bombastic* bigwig** bom-bas'tik Bombastic means to speak or write with pretentious but meaningless words. From Latin, *bambax* = cotton.

> *Every ass loves to hear himself bray.*
> *—English proverb*

8. **boondoggling slacker** boon'dôg-ling To boondoggle is to waste time doing pointless work like paper shuffling to avoid doing any real work. An American scoutmaster, R. H. Link, may have coined the term to describe the cord worn around a Boy Scout's neck (1929). It also may have been a slang word used by cowboys to describe work done on their saddle when their chores were done.

> *Some folks can look so busy doing nothin'*
> *that they seem indispensable.*
> —F. M. Hubbard

9. **boorish bruiser** boor'ish A boor is a rude, clownish peasant; hence, anyone boorish is extremely rude. From Dutch, *boer* = a farmer.

> *Rudeness is the weak man's imitation of strength.*
> —Eric Hoffer

10. **bootless schmo** boot'lis Anyone bootless is either useless or without success. From Old English, *bot* = advantage + -less. Here it is coupled with **schmo**, meaning a fool, from Yiddish.

> *Even the most useless person can serve as a bad example.*
> —Unknown

QUIZ 7

Match the definitions with the words on the left.

____ 1.	bland	a.	to brown-nose
____ 2.	blatant	b.	useless
____ 3.	blither	c.	do pointless work to avoid any
____ 4.	blowsy		real work
____ 5.	blusterous	d.	extremely rude
____ 6.	Boeotian	e.	fat and coarse-looking
____ 7.	boondoggle	f.	speak nonsensically
____ 8.	boorish	g.	blowing violently; swaggering
____ 9.	bootless	h.	stupid
____10.	bootlick	i.	dull, tasteless, and insipid
		j.	offensively noisy; conspicuous

GRISLY LIST 8

Susie tried to look smooth, but her **borborygmic** stomach gurgled loudly enough for other dancers to hear. Maybe she'd been **brash** to not eat before the audition. It didn't matter. Her competition, those **bourgeois** wannabes, didn't have a chance. "A bunch of **brazen** hussies," thought Susie. "I'll show those **bovine** amateurs." She leaned over to touch her toes, but found it difficult.

A rather **brackish** stage manager approached the dancers. "Girls, we'll go in the order that you signed the list. Susie? You're here?"

Confidently, Susie smiled back but said nothing. Even the stage manager knew her by name. She didn't need to **bootlick** like the **braggadocian** ballerinas that cluttered the backstage. She could hear them whispering; probably they were **brabbling** about her upping their chances. She heard her name called, and paraded out with such **bovaristic** self-assurance that even the queen of Egypt would have trembled. She curtseyed low and heard her back crack.

1. ***bootlicking* smoothie** boōt'lik To bootlick is to brown-nose, to flatter to gain advantage. This is an English colloquial expression and literally means to lick another's boot.

> *Just as foods produce disgust for the palate,*
> *so perfumed and gallant words make our ears belch.*
> — *Pietro Aretino*

2. ***borborygmic* bozo** bôr-bə-rig'mik One who is borborygmic is bothered by stomach rumblings. From Greek, *borborygmos* = stomach rumbling.

> *An empty stomach can't tolerate anything.*
> —*Yiddish proverb*

3. ***bourgeois* pen pusher** boōr-zhwä' The bourgeois is the middle class. In Marxist theory, anyone bourgeois is above the working class; hence, materialistic and in favor of the status quo. It can also be used to describe anyone conventional and unrefined. From Late Latin, *burgus* = castle.

> *The bourgeois prefers comfort to pleasure, convenience to liberty,*
> *and a pleasant temperature to that deathly inner consuming fire.*
> —*Hermann Hesse*

4. ***bovaristic* name-dropper** bō-və-ris'tik A bovarist sees himself/herself with a glamorized, exaggerated view. It is derived from Gustave Flaubert's novel, *Madame Bovary* [1856].

> *When they came to shoe the horses,*
> *the beetle stretched out his leg.*
> —*English proverb*

5. ***bovine* amateur** bō'vīn Anyone who is bovine looks, acts, or has a mind like a cow. From Latin, *bos* = ox.

> *A cow is of a bovine ilk*
> *One end is moo, the other, milk.*
> —*Ogden Nash*

6. ***brabbling* hardhead** brab'ling To brabble is to quarrel over nothing. From Dutch, *brabbelen* = to quarrel, jabber.

> *Quarreling is like cutting water with a sword.*
> —*Chinese proverb*

7. **brackish pirate** brak'ish Anything brackish is salty or distasteful. When salty is said of pirates, it's metaphorical. From Middle Dutch, *brak* = salty.

> Likely comment:
> *Shiver me timbers.*
> Your response:
> *I never shiver anyone else's timbers.*

8. **braggadocian loudmouth** brag-ə-dō'shən This is the adjective form of braggadocio. A braggadocio is either a braggart or someone who is overconfident. Edmund Spenser invented this word by combining brag with an Italian ending [1590].

> *Brag's a good dog but dares not bite.*
> —*English proverb*

9. **brash glory hog** brash To be brash is to be offensively or foolishly bold. It may be a blend of bold and rash, or possibly a blend of brassy and rash.

> *The rash call the brave cowards.*
> —*Professor Snurd*

10. **brazen hussy** brā'zən Shamelessly bold, and boldly shameless, someone who is brazen flaunts what others would hide. Brazen probably derives from brassy. From Old English, *braes* = brass.

> *Losing my virginity was a career move.*
> —*Madonna*

QUIZ 8

Match the definitions with the words on the left.

_____ 1. borborygmic   a. boldly shameless
_____ 2. bourgeois   b. braggart
_____ 3. bovarist   c. salty
_____ 4. bovine   d. to quarrel over nothing
_____ 5. brabble   e. an exaggerated view of self
_____ 6. brackish   f. like a cow
_____ 7. braggadocian   g. offensively bold
_____ 8. brash   h. with stomach rumblings
_____ 9. brazen   i. speak with high-sounding words
_____ 10. bombastic   j. middle class

GRISLY LIST 9

The **callow** trio, fresh from Kansas, made their way through the **Byzantine** alleys to the rave. Rounding a corner, they had to delicately step over several **cadaverous** partygoers who'd passed out in front of the entrance.

"Lucy, I don't think we're in Kansas anymore," Sally offered as the **cagey** three clutched one another more tightly.

At the entrance, the bouncer **brusquely** frisked each of them and then shooed them inside. For a minute they stood dumbfounded by the smoke, the noise, and the confusion.

"So where's your date?" Elise asked Lucy, but before she could answer, a reveler fell before them, **cachinnating** uncontrollably.

"Let's try the dance floor," Lucy replied.

It didn't take them long to find Paul, Lucy's date; he was writhing in the center of the dance floor with his hands firmly grabbing the **cacopygian** heinie of some tart with blue hair. When he saw Lucy, he **callously** shoved the tart aside, brushed his hair back with **bumptious** bravado, swaggered over to her, and squeezed her close to him.

"Hey baby, I've been waiting for you."

Remembering her kickboxing classes, Lucy found the appropriate place for her knee and let Paul crumple to the floor. She spun around with a **calculated** smile on her face.

"Okay, who wants ice cream?"

1. **brusque roughneck** brusk Anyone brusque is rough and abrupt. From Latin, *ruscum* = butcher's broom.

> O, to what purpose dost thou hoard thy words,
> that thou returnest no greeting to thy friends?
> —William Shakespeare,
> Richard II

2. **bumptious braggart** bump'shəs As if being conceited isn't enough, a bumptious person is disagreeably conceited. Bumptious is possibly a blend of bump and presumptuous.

> He was like a cock who thought the sun had risen to hear him crow.
> —George Eliot

3. **Byzantine trickster** biz'ən-tēn Anything Byzantine is like the Byzantine Empire, fraught with complexity, deviousness, and intrigue.

> Government is an association of men who do violence to the rest of us.
> —Leo Tolstoy

4. **cachinnating kook** kak'ə-nā-ting A cachinnating person laughs too loud and/or too much. From Latin, *cachinnatus* = laughed immoderately.

> No one is more profoundly sad than he who laughs too much.
> —Jean Paul Richter

5. ***cacopygian* eyesore** kak-ə-pig′ē-ən One who is cacopygian has an ugly butt. Callipygian, on the other hand, means one has a well-shaped or beautiful rear. From Greek, *kakos* = bad + *pyge* = rump.

> *I got hit by a Volkswagen*
> *and had to go to the hospital to have it removed.*
> —Pat McCormick

6. ***cadaverous* poseurs** kə-dav′ər-əs Anything cadaverous is like a cadaver, pale and ghastly. From Latin, *cadaveros* = like a corpse.

> *The worst evil of all*
> *is to leave the ranks of the living before one dies.*
> —Seneca

7. ***cagey* card shark** kā′jē To be cagey is to be sly and wary, careful not to get caught. The origin is uncertain but it's possibly from American English, cage + -y.

> *There is enough for the needy*
> *but not for the greedy.*
> —Mohandas Gandhi

8. ***calculating* crook** kal′kyə-lā-ting A calculating person is cunning in a selfish way, devising plots to further him/herself. From Latin, *calculus* = pebble, a small stone used in arithmetic.

> *It is the masterpiece of villainy*
> *to smooth the brow,*
> *and so outface suspicion.*
> —John Howard

9. ***callous* home wrecker** kal′əs To be callous is to be uncaring and unfeeling. From Latin, *callum* = hard skin.

> *It is nothing.*
> *They are only thrashing my husband.*
> —Portuguese proverb

10. ***callow* rookie** kal′ō Callow means to lack one's feathers; hence, to be immature. From Old English, *calu* = bare, bald.

> *When I grow up I want to be a little boy.*
> —Andy Warhol

Match the words with the definitions on the right.

____ 1.	brusque	a.	careful not to get caught
____ 2.	bumptious	b.	an ugly butt
____ 3.	Byzantine	c.	devising plots
____ 4.	cachinnate	d.	disagreeably conceited
____ 5.	cacopygian	e.	fraught with complexity, deviousness, and intrigue
____ 6.	cadaverous	f.	immature
____ 7.	cagey	g.	to laugh too loud or too much
____ 8.	calculating	h.	pale, like a dead body
____ 9.	callous	i.	rough and abrupt
____ 10.	callow	j.	uncaring and unfeeling

GRISLY LIST 10

"You're fired!" the **cantankerous** old man spewed.

Bobby had never been **cashiered** before. The shame! And to have it done so **capriciously**!!

"But you just hired me! I need money for the prom."

"Ah. The poor baby," came the **cantish** reply. "Stop your **carping** and take it like a man."

"But why?" the **carking** teenager wondered. He'd put up with this nut's **captious castigating** for two weeks, but this was too much.

"You've been making **carnal** passes at my daughter."

"She's forty-five!" Bobby squealed.

"So you don't deny it?"

"I do."

"Are you accusing me of **calumny**? Because if you are, I'll sue you for every penny you've got."

That was enough. Bobby had had it. No job was worth this. He grabbed his backpack and started out the door.

"Hey, come back here. I was just kidding."

Bobby didn't look back.

1. *calumnious* **pack of lies** kə-lōōm′nē-əs Calumny is a false, malicious insult that blackens someone's reputation. Thus, anyone calumnious is slanderous. From Latin, *calumnios* = full of tricks, deception.

> *At every word a reputation dies.*
> —Alexander Pope

2. ***cantankerous* old fart** kan-tang'kər-əs A cantankerous person is bad-tempered. From Medieval English, *contakour* = a troublemaker, or possibly a blend of contentious and rancorous.

TOMBSTONE EPITAPH
Finally, in his last hour
He had a real reason to be sour.

3. ***cantish* swindler** kan'tish To be cantish is to be insincerely sentimental, hypocritically conveying kindness, or have religious devotion. Cant can also refer to the special jargon of thieves, beggars, etc. From Latin, *cantus* = song.

An open foe may prove a curse,
But a pretended friend is worse.
—John Gay

4. ***capricious* social butterfly** kə-prē'shəs To be capricious is to be erratic and flighty. From Italian, *capriccio* = a shivering, a whim.

A woman talks to one man,
looks at a second,
and thinks of a third.
—Bhartrihari

5. ***captious* wench** kap'shəs A captious person is too quick to find fault, or is likely to try to ensnare or perplex others in an argument. From Latin, *captios* = sophistical.

Most women set out to try to change a man,
and when they have changed them
they do not like him.
—Marlene Dietrich

6. ***carking* whiner** kär'king To cark is to worry and fret. From Medieval English, *cark* = to be anxious.

Why torture yourself when life will do it for you?
—Laura Walker

7. ***carnal* Casanova** kär'nəl A carnal person is completely obsessed with flesh and sexual desire. From Latin, *caro* = flesh.

Beds are the poor man's opera.
—Italian proverb

8. ***carping* crab** kär'ping To carp is to complain or point out imperfections. From Latin, *carpere* = to pluck, harass.

It is the growling man who lives a dog's life.
—Francis Fenelon

9. **cashiering** taskmaster ka-shēr'ing To cashier is to dismiss in dishonor. From Middle French, *casser* = to break, discharge.

10. **castigating** screamer kas'ti-gā-ting To castigate is to punish or rebuke severely. From Latin, *castigare* = to purify, chastise.

I don't believe in nagging at a man.
You can accomplish so much more by hitting him with something.
—*N. Hoifjeld*

QUIZ 10

Match the words with the definitions on the right.

_____ 1. calumnious   a. anxious
_____ 2. cantankerous   b. bad-tempered
_____ 3. cantish   c. complaining
_____ 4. capricious   d. erratic and flighty
_____ 5. captious   e. fleshly and worldly desire
_____ 6. carking   f. insincerely sentimental
_____ 7. carnal   g. slanderous
_____ 8. carping   h. to dismiss in dishonor
_____ 9. cashier   i. to punish or rebuke severely
_____ 10. castigate   j. too quick to find fault

MATCH EACH QUOTE WITH THE APPROPRIATE WORD.

1. Every man has a wild animal inside him.
—*Frederick the Great*

2. Man is his own worst enemy.
—*Cicero*

3. A man's venom poisons himself more than his victim.
—*Charles Buxton*

4. He has the greatest blind side who thinks he has none.
—*Dutch proverb*

____ a. bête noire   ____ c. bestial
____ b. bilious   ____ d. benighted

5. I was shadow boxing the other day,
figured I was ready for Cassius Clay.
—*Bob Dylan*

6. A useless life is an early death.
—*Goethe*

7. Remember, you're fighting for this woman's honor,
which is probably more than she ever did.
—*Groucho Marx*

8. Some so speak in exaggerations and superlatives that we
need to make a large discount from their statements
before we can come at their real meaning.
—*Tyron Edwards*

____ e. bombastic   ____ g. bootless
____ f. carnal   ____ h. belligerent

9. Most quarrels amplify a misunderstanding.
—*André Gide*

10. I never wonder to see men wicked,
but I often wonder to see them not ashamed.
—*Jonathan Swift*

11. Man is worse than an animal when he is an animal.
—*Rabindranath Tagore*

12. Wind puffs up empty bladders; opinion, fools.
—*Socrates*

13. Just as you are pleased at finding faults,
you are displeased at finding perfections.
—*Lavater*

14. Violent delights have violent ends.
—*Shakespeare*

____ i. brazen
____ j. brabble
____ k. callous

____ l. bovarist
____ m. bellicose
____ n. carp

Chapter 3

*Words are, of course,
the most powerful drug
used by mankind.*
—Rudyard Kipling

BY NOW YOU MIGHT be saying, "Isn't this book too pessimistic?" Duh. So is one-third of the dictionary. I've actually received a great deal of flak for writing this book. What I don't see are people throwing away dictionaries because of those unpleasant words. I didn't invent them. In any event, any student will probably feel more positive about these words when he or she sees them on a test and is able to answer the question.

Now, as you go through this book, you're bound to come across words that fit a drawing you have already made. That's okay. Just add that word to the other word next to the picture, and presto! You have a more vicious slur, like "that belittling, acerbic pile of pus!" Get a dartboard. Take the picture and center it on the board. Toss darts at it. By the time the picture crumbles, the words will be permanently fixed inside your head.

GRISLY LIST 11

"So, I'm your number one?" a **chagrined** Burt asked.

"You're my number one," Kelly **cavalierly** quipped as she tossed some more lobster down her gullet.

"And Manuel and Henry?"

"Number two and number three. But you are **categorically** my number one. You should feel happy."

"I feel **castrated**."

"Oh, don't **cavil**. What do you want, some **censorious** wife jealously questioning your every move, or me? I thought last night was fun."

Last night had been fun, but now Burt felt like he'd been with a **changeling**, a **charlatan**.

Kelly joked with **casuistic** flair, "Burt, monogamy is so outdated, a relic of some puritanical, patriarchal nightmare. Our natural instinct is to explore. You're not going to get all gushy on me, are you?"

"Me? Gushy? Why, no. It's just that—how do I say this?—you're my number two."

"Number two?" Her voice turned **caustic**. "I'm your number two?"

Burt knew he'd be sleeping alone as he watched his number two attack her lobster like a vampire sticking its teeth into a baby's neck.

1. ***castrating* witch** kas'trā-ting To castrate is to remove someone's testicles. From Latin, *castratus* = gelded, emasculated.

> *Women just want men who'll share your hopes and dreams.*
> *If you don't, we'll bitch at you until you die.*
> —*Stephanie Hodge*

2. *casuistic* **evader** kazh-ōō-is'tik Casuistry is solving problems of right and wrong by using universal laws of ethics, but it also applies to using subtly false logic about moral issues. From Latin, *cadere* = to fall.

> Likely comment:
> *Now what if you had to have sex with a hundred gorgeous pinups just to*
> *save your wife's life. Would you do it then? Uh? Uh?*
> Your response:
> *Well, if you were my wife, it would be a tough decision.*

3. *categorical* **liar** kati-gôr'i-kəl Categorical means completely, without qualifications, absolute. Thus, a categorical liar is a complete liar. From Greek, *kategorein* = to accuse.

> *He occasionally stumbled over the truth,*
> *but hastily picked himself up and hurried on as if nothing had happened.*
> —Winston Churchill

4. *caustic* **scold** kô'stik A caustic person or thing is bitter, critical, sarcastic, corroding and/or acidic. From Greek, *kaustikos* = burning.

> EPITAPH:
> *This caustic scold*
> *got a little old.*

5. *cavalier* **player** kav-ə-lēr' A cavalier person is casually or arrogantly indifferent to important issues. From Late Latin, *caballarius* = horseman.

> *Nothing is more conducive to peace of mind*
> *than not having any opinion at all.*
> —G. C. Lightenberg

6. *caviling* **kvetch** kav'ə-ling A caviling person complains with little cause, or raises irritating objections. From Latin, *cavillari* = to jeer, scoff, quibble. It is coupled with **kvetch** = a chronic complainer, from Yiddish.

> *It is in disputes as in armies, where the weaker side sets up false lights, and*
> *makes a great noise, to make the enemy believe them*
> *more numerous and strong than they really are.*
> —Jonathan Swift

7. *censorious* **police state** sen-sôr'ē-əs A censorious person (or government) is severely critical and faultfinding. From Latin, *censere* = to tax, value, judge.

> *Whatever you condemn, you have done yourself.*
> —Georg Groddeck

8. *chagrined* **laughingstock** shə-grind' One who is chagrined is humiliated and embarrassed. The expression "much to his chagrin" depicts the irritation of being humiliated or disappointed. From French, *chagrin* = distressed.

> *George Bush will lead us out of this recovery.*
> —Dan Quayle

9. **filthy little *changeling*** chānj'ling Historically a changeling was an ugly, mischievous baby elf switched by elves for a real human baby. It now can mean an elf, a turncoat, or an idiot. From Latin, *cambire* = to trade + -ling, a suffix of nouns used usually pejoratively; e.g., underling.

> *All children are essentially criminal.*
> —Denis Diderot

10. **sly *charlatan*** shär'lə-tən A charlatan is a fake who pretends to be an expert. From Italian, *ciarlare* = to chatter + *(cerre)tano* = hawker, quack.

> *A thing worth having is a thing worth cheating for.*
> —W. C. Fields

QUIZ 11

Match the words with the definitions on the right.

_____ 1. castrate
_____ 2. casuistic
_____ 3. categorical
_____ 4. caustic
_____ 5. cavalier
_____ 6. caviling
_____ 7. censorious
_____ 8. chagrined
_____ 9. changeling
_____10. charlatan

a. an elf, a turncoat, or an idiot
b. bitter, critical, sarcastic, corroding, and/or acidic
c. casually indifferent
d. complaining with little cause
e. humiliated and embarrassed
f. someone who pretends to be an expert
g. critical and faultfinding
h. to remove the testicles
i. using subtle but misleading reasoning
j. absolute

GRISLY LIST 12

Shondra didn't feel she needed **chastising**, especially from her father, **chauvinist** pig that he was; she'd been **chary** with the funds for the women's group, some might even say **cheeseparing**, but Shondra felt that as long as she was treasurer, she would be (and had been) extra careful.

"I'm not trying to make you feel bad, honey, it's just that women don't have good heads for money."

This might have set another woman off on a tirade, but Shondra had grown up with this kind of sexist babbling. She smiled, donned her jacket, and waltzed out the door, leaving her father in the **Cimmerian** cloud he'd grown up in. Besides, she had other man problems; sometimes she felt like

Circe, only cursed, because every man she ever touched turned into a pig. These were her thoughts as she walked a **circuitous** two blocks to get to her car. That is why she didn't see the **churlish** stranger until it was too late.

"Hey baby, whatcha got in the bag?"

This wasn't the **chimerical** foe she feared and fought so many times in her dreams; this was very real. Before she could blink, the stranger had yanked away her purse and pushed her into an alley. She tried to get it back, but he slapped her hard, knocking her down.

"Don't get feisty, girl; let's see what you got and then we'll see what you got."

He opened the bag and let out a shout, "We're going to party all night."

There was a loud thud and the stranger fell. Shondra's father, bat in hand, took several more swings and then threw in a few kicks until the man lay still. She'd seen (and feared) her father's **choleric** mood before, but not like this. For the first time that she could ever remember, she ran and hugged him. He patted her on the back.

"Think you could let your old man escort you to your women's group tonight?"

"Yes, Dad, I think I will tonight."

1. **chary** money-grubber châr´ē Chary can either connote being careful or being stingy. From Old English, *cearu* = care.

    > *Money isn't everything: Usually it isn't even enough.*
    > —Anonymous

2. **chastising** moralizer chas´tī-zing To chastise is to punish with a stick, or scold severely. From Latin, *castigatas* = driven to be faultless.

    > *The man who acts the least, upbraids the most.*
    > —Homer

3. **chauvinist** pig shō´və-nist A chauvinist has a blind devotion to his cause, his race, or (more recently common) his gender. The word comes from Nicholas Chauvin, who was famous for his blind devotion to Napoleon Bonaparte. "Chauvinist pig" was coined by 1970s feminists to decry men who repress women or who resist change.

    > *The husband is the head, the wife is the neck;*
    > *she can turn him whichever way she wants.*
    > —Russian proverb

4. **cheeseparing** self-server chēz´pâr-ing Anything cheeseparing is as worthless as the rind pared from cheese, but it also describes one who is stingy, miserly. From Latin, *case* = cheese + *parare* = to prepare.

    > *A miser is like a pig, useful only when dead.*
    > —Czech proverb

5. *chimerical* **dreamer** kī-mer'i-kəl In Greek mythology, a chimera was a fire-breathing monster. Now, it's any amazing monster, or an unreal, imaginary creature or notion; hence, to be chimerical is to indulge in imaginary fancies or to be unrealistic. (Originally, it was a goat that had survived winter.)

> *The loss of our illusions is the only loss from which we never recover.*
> —Ouida

6. *choleric* **old coot** kol'ə-rik Choleric means bad-tempered. A long time ago, it was believed the body was made up of four humors. The yellow humor, choler, was the humor that caused anger and irritability. From Greek, *cholera* = a name of several intestinal diseases.

> *Anger begins in madness, and ends in regret.*
> —Hasdai

7. *churlish* **firebrand** chûr'lish One who is churlish is surly, stingy, and hard to manage. The word is derived from Old English, *ceorl* = a freeman of lowest rank.

> *We've upped our standards. Up yours.*
> —Pat Paulsen

8. *Cimmerian* **stooge** si-mîr'ē-ən Cimmerian means gloomy and engulfed in darkness. In Homer's *Odyssey*, the Cimmerians were a mythical people who lived in perpetual darkness.

> *Men loved darkness rather than light, because their deeds were evil.*
> —John 3:19

9. *Circean* **charmer** sûr'sē-ən Circean means any woman who is dangerously or fatally attractive. In Greek mythology, Circe was the enchantress who turned the companions of Odysseus into pigs by means of a magic potion. Of course, a lot of women believe you don't need a woman to turn men into pigs.

> *(God) gave women intuition and femininity. And, used properly,*
> *that combination easily jumbles the brain of any man I've ever met.*
> —Farrah Fawcett

10. *circuitous* **misleader** sər-kyōō'i-təs Anyone circuitous uses roundabout evasions to be untruthful. From Latin, *circuire* = to go around.

> *A lie can run around the world six times*
> *while the truth is still trying to put on its pants.*
> —Mark Twain

Match the words with the definitions on the right.

____ 1.	chary	a.	any woman who is fatally or dangerously attractive
____ 2.	chastising		
____ 3.	chauvinist	b.	bad-tempered
____ 4.	cheeseparing	c.	careful; stingy
____ 5.	chimerical	d.	indulging in imaginary fancies
____ 6.	choleric	e.	living in perpetual darkness
____ 7.	churlish	f.	punishing; severely scolding
____ 8.	Cimmerian	g.	blindly devoted to a cause; sexist
____ 9.	Circean	h.	stingy
____10.	circuitous	i.	surly, stingy, peasant-like
		j.	roundabout

GRISLY LIST 13

Hunter took one bite; a more **cloying** pile of crap she had never tasted. This aberration her prospective mother-in-law called pie somehow found new ways to **constrict** her nasal passages. Had it not been for her **concupiscent** interest in this woman's son, she would have puked and run out the door.

"It's wonderful," she heard herself say. "I can't find the words."

Was she being **condescending**? She hoped not. She tried to give her fiancé a **collusive** get-me-out-of-here look, but his **complacent** eyes were glued to the football game.

"Would you like more?" her host **coercively** asked.

"Oh, no. I've got to watch my figure."

Her soon-to-be mother-in-law frowned and, with **conniving** delight, pinched her son's cheek as if he were a **cockered** poodle.

"Oh, but my baby likes his women well-rounded. Doesn't he, dearest."

Not to be outdone in this catfight, Hunter **confabulated**. "I need to lose a few pounds to fit into my mother's wedding gown."

That wasn't exactly true, but hey, she could tell it stung like the dickens.

1. ***cloying* footlicker** kloi'ing Anything cloying causes disgust because it's excessive, be it food, sentimentality, or flattery. From Old French, *encloyer* = to drive a nail; hence, to stop up, to glut.

> *The best of things, beyond their measure, cloy.*
> —Homer

2. ***cockered* pet** kok'ərd Cocker means to protect too much or to pamper. From the Old English word *cocer*, meaning sheath.

> *He who spares the rod hates the child.*
> —*Proverbs 13:24*

3. ***coercive* gangster** kō-ûr'siv To coerce is to force someone to do something; hence, anyone who is coercive is forcing others to do something against their wills. From Latin, *coercere* = to surround, restrain.

> *Force is all conquering but its victories are short-lived.*
> —*Abraham Lincoln*

4. ***collusive* clique** kə-lōō'siv To be collusive is to connive with others, to plot schemes in secret, to agree to deceive. From Latin, *colludere* = to play.

> *There are some frauds so well conducted*
> *that it would be stupidity not to be deceived by them.*
> —*Charles Caleb Colton*

5. ***complacent* layabout** kəm-plā'sənt A complacent person is self-satisfied and smug. From Latin, *complacere* = to be very pleasing.

> *We cannot really learn anything*
> *until we rid ourselves of complacency.*
> —*Mao Tse-Tung*

6. ***concupiscent* skirt-chaser** kon-kyōō'pi-sənt Anyone who is concupiscent has an abnormal sexual desire. From Latin, *concupiscere* = to desire greatly.

> *I have an intense desire to return to the womb. Anybody's.*
> —*Woody Allen*

7. ***condescending* smarty-pants** kon-di-sen'ding To condescend is to stoop down to deal with others lower in status. From Late Latin, *condescendere* = to let oneself down.

> *The richer your friends, the more they will cost you.*
> —*Elizabeth Marbury*

8. ***confabulating* screwball** kən-fab'yə-lā-ting To confabulate is to chat, but the other connotation is to replace fact with fantasy in memory. From Latin, *confabulari* = to talk together.

> *People lie because they can't help making a story better*
> *than it was the way it happened.*
> — *Carl Sandburg*

9. ***conniving* con artist** kə-nī'ving To connive is to either feign ignorance of another's wrongdoing or cooperate secretly in an evil scheme. From Latin, *conivere* = to wink.

> *Who makes the fairest show means most deceit.*
> —*Shakespeare*

10. ***constricting* hard-nose** kən-strik'ting To constrict is to make something thinner, to squeeze something, to uncomfortably restrict a person's ability to move. From Latin, *constringere* = to draw together.

You cannot put the same shoe on every foot.
—Publilius Syrus

QUIZ 13

Match the words with the definitions on the right.

____ 1.	cloying	a.	causing disgust from excess
____ 2.	cocker	b.	to stoop from a high place to talk
____ 3.	coercive		with those lower in station
____ 4.	collusive	c.	forcefully compelling
____ 5.	complacent	d.	with an unusual sexual desire
____ 6.	concupiscent	e.	protect too much or pamper
____ 7.	condescend	f.	replace fact with fantasy
____ 8.	confabulate	g.	scheming in secret
____ 9.	conniving		(fits two words)
____10.	constrict	h.	self-satisfied and smug
		i.	squeeze, restrict

GRISLY LIST 14

Mike sat at the bar and tried to wash the memory of the cold-hearted **coquette** away. His greatest wish was to drink himself into **crapulous** oblivion and then start a fight with the first **contumacious** jerk that was willing to put up his dukes. The bartender, a jolly, **corpulent** fellow, poured him another.

"Women are by nature **contentious**. You can't do right by them."

Mike nodded. He didn't really agree, but in his present **crabbed** mood, anything negative about women sounded right. The bartender went on.

"You see, they will **cosset** you until you are no longer a man. Then they hate you because now you have become a **craven** dog, a **cowering** rabbit. They will take a man who is **crass** and unrefined and turn him into a gentleman, and then they'll dump him."

"That's the truth."

The front door swung open and two women waltzed in. As they sat down, one threw a flirty smile in Mike's direction. Mike, with just the right amount of liquid courage, straightened his tie and went for the bait. The bartender sighed and shook his head.

1. ***contentious* old-timer** kən ten′shəs Argue, fuss, and fight: that's all a contentious person wants to do. From Medieval English, *contenden* = to compete.

> *In quarreling the truth is always lost.*
> – Syrus

2. ***contumacious* nonconformist** kon-tə-mā′shəs Anyone who is contumacious obstinately resists authority. From Latin, *contumax* = haughty, stubborn.

> *There are three sides to every question:*
> *your side, his side, and to hell with it.*
> —Unknown

3. **cold-hearted *coquette*** kō-ket′ A coquette teases but doesn't please; she's a flirt. From French, *coqueter* = to flirt; literally, to strut like a rooster.

> *A coquette is woman*
> *without any heart,*
> *who makes a fool of a man*
> *that hasn't got any head.*
> —Madam Deluzy

4. ***corpulent* tank** kôr′pyə-lənt To be corpulent is to be fat. From Latin, *corpulentus* = well-bodied.

> *She was so big she could kick-start a 747.*
> —George "Goober" Lindsey

5. ***cosseted* mama's boy** kos′i-tid To cosset means to treat like a pet. From Old English, *cossetung* = kissing.

> *A real dog, pampered by his mistress, is a lamentable spectacle.*
> *He suffers from fatty degeneration of his moral being.*
> —Agnes Repplier

6. ***cowering* captive** kou′ə-ring To cower is to crouch or shrink from fear. From Swedish, *kura* = to squat.

> *Tell the truth and run.*
> —Serbian proverb

7. ***crabbed* complainer** krabd Anyone crabbed is always in a bad temper. From Medieval English, *crabbe* = crustacean.

> *Start every day off with a smile and get it over with.*
> —W. C. Fields

8. ***crapulous* lush** krap′yə-ləs A crapulous person lacks any moderation in food or booze. From Latin, *crapula* = drunkenness.

> EPITAPH:
> *Ashes to ashes,*
> *dust to dust*
> *If the women don't get you,*
> *then the whiskey must.*

9. **crass shock jock** kras One who is crass is crude, without sensitivity, and extremely gross. From Latin, *crasses* = thick, gross, fat.

Likely comment:
Hey buddy, so how's the bladder infection?!
Your response:
Check your soup.

10. **craven dog** krā′vən One who is craven is a coward through and through. From Latin, *crepare* = to crack, rattle.

It is better to be a coward for a minute,
than to be dead the rest of your life.
—Irish proverb

QUIZ 14

Match the words with the definitions on the right.

_____ 1. contentious	a. cowardly
_____ 2. contumacious	b. crude, without sensitivity
_____ 3. coquette	c. drunken
_____ 4. corpulent	d. fat
_____ 5. cosset	e. given to arguing
_____ 6. cower	f. in a bad temper
_____ 7. crabbed	g. obstinately resists authority
_____ 8. crapulous	h. a flirt
_____ 9. crass	i. to treat like a pet
_____ 10. craven	j. to crouch or shrink from fear

GRISLY LIST 15

"I'm too late?" the **credulous** tourist asked as he **cringed** outside the gate.

"What? Are you deaf, too?" sneered the **crotchety** old man from behind the counter.

"But the train's still here."

"I guess you're blind to boot," came the **crusty** reply. "All boarders must be through the gate by 10:31. It's 10:32. See the sign?"

Wilber looked everywhere but saw no sign. Others might have made a fuss, but Wilber was a **cultural marginal**; that is to say, his parents had shuffled him around from country to country until he had become completely psychologically lost, with little will of his own. Somehow he felt **culpable**. True, he had been there since 9:30 that morning, and this **cunctative** clerk had taken a long break before returning to the booth. Still, he figured it must be his own fault.

"When does the next train leave?"

The **curmudgeon** rasped, "Next week."

"Next week? But where will I stay?"

"The Hotel Ritz." The geezer offered with a **cupidinous** and **cunning** gleam. "Forty-five a night and breakfast is not included."

The sap lifted his briefcase onto the counter. "All right, but I'll need to refrigerate my botulism samples."

1. ***credulous* sucker** krej'ə-ləs This credulous one believes too easily, is too easily convinced. From Latin, *credere* = to believe.

> *I'm not saying this woman is stupid,*
> *but when the wind blows, her forehead buckles.*
> —Brett Butler

2. ***cringing* scaredy-cat** krin'jing To cringe is to shrink back in fear. From Old English, *cringean* = to yield or fall in battle.

> *Many would be cowards if they had courage enough.*
> —Thomas Fuller

3. ***crotchety* codger** kroch'i-tē A crotchet is an odd idea; hence, one who is crotchety is full of stubborn notions, twisted, and eccentric. From Medieval English, *crotchet* = hook. It is coupled with **codger** = an eccentric old man.

> *I wouldn't want to belong to any club*
> *that would have me as a member.*
> —Groucho Marx

4. ***crusty* crone** krus'tē Crusty is anything like crust, the hard shell surrounding bread; hence, a crusty person is harsh and rude. From Latin, *crusta* = shell, crust. It is coupled with **crone** = an ugly, withered old woman.

> *I am free of all prejudices. I hate everyone equally.*
> —W. C. Fields

5. ***culpable* suspect** kul'pə-bəl To be culpable is to be deserving of blame. From Latin, *culpa* = blame.

> EPITAPH:
> *Though he said it was a frame*
> *His alibi was lame.*

6. ***cultural marginal*** kul'chər-əl A cultural marginal is someone who is lost between two cultures.

> *Human life is reduced to real suffering, to hell,*
> *only when two ages, two cultures and religions overlap.*
> —Hermann Hesse, Steppenwolf

7. *cunctative* **daydreamer** kungk′tā-tiv Get used to waiting, since a cunctative person procrastinates. From Latin, *cunctari* = to linger, hesitate.

> *My mother said, "You won't amount to anything*
> *because you procrastinate." I said, "Just wait."*
> —Judy Tenuta

8. *cunning* **quack** kun′ing One who is cunning is clever or skillful in cheating. From Medieval English, *cunnen* = to know.

> *"Will you walk into my parlor?" said a spider to the fly;*
> *"Tis the prettiest little parlor that ever you did spy."*
> —Mary Howitt

9. *cupidinous* **gruntling** kyōo-pi′di-nəs A cupidinous person is a greedy, avaricious, and rapacious. From Latin, *cupidus* = eager, desirous. It is coupled with **gruntling** = slang, a small or baby pig.

> *The avaricious man is like the barren sandy ground of the desert*
> *which sucks in all the rain and dew with greediness,*
> *but yields no fruitful herbs or plants for the benefit of others.*
> —Zeno

10. **hypercritical** *curmudgeon* kər-muj′ən A curmudgeon is a surly, stubborn, and bad-tempered person. The origin is uncertain. Perhaps from Scottish, *curmurring* = a low rumbling in the stomach, or from French, *coeur mechant* = an irritable heart.

> *Success didn't spoil me. I've always been insufferable.*
> —Fran Lebowitz

QUIZ 15

Match the definitions with the words on the left.

_____ 1. credulous	a. greedy, avaricious, rapacious
_____ 2. cringe	b. believes too easily
_____ 3. crotchety	c. full of stubborn notions, twisted, and eccentric
_____ 4. crusty	
_____ 5. culpable	d. harsh and rude
_____ 6. cultural marginal	e. lost between two cultures
_____ 7. cunctative	f. one who is bad-tempered
_____ 8. cunning	g. procrastinating
_____ 9. cupidinous	h. skillful in deception
_____10. curmudgeon	i. to be deserving blame
	j. to shrink back in fear

REVIEW 3

MATCH EACH QUOTE WITH THE APPROPRIATE WORD.

1. Strong and bitter words indicate a weak cause.
—*Victor Hugo*

2. Quacks are gamesters and they play / With craft and skill to ruin and betray; / With monstrous promise they delude the mind, / And thrive on all that tortures humankind.
—*George Crabbe*

3. Golden dreams make men awake hungry.
—*English proverb*

4. When you get home, throw your mom a bone.
—*Dorothy Parker*

____ a. charlatan   ____ c. chimerical
____ b. calumnious   ____ d. caustic

5. A surfeit of the sweetest things the deepest loathing to the stomach brings.
—*Shakespeare*

6. Plots, true or false, are necessary things, To raise up commonwealths, and ruin kings.
—*John Dryden*

7. Who draws his sword against the prince must throw away the scabbard.
—*James Howell*

8. The most insignificant people are the most apt to sneer at others.
—*William Hazlit*

9. The fear of ill exceeds the ill we fear.
—*Madam Sevigne*

____ e. condescend   ____ h. cloy
____ f. cower   ____ i. collusive
____ g. contumacious

10. Many would be cowards, they had enough courage.
—*English proverb*

11. When once a man is determined to believe, the very absurdity of the doctrine confirms him in his faith.
—*Junius*

12. One of these days is none of these days.
—*H. G. Bohn*

13. Of all the bad things by which mankind is curst
their own bad tempers surely are the worst.
—*Cumberland*

____ j.　credulous　　　　　____ l.　curmudgeon
____ k.　craven　　　　　　____ m.　cunctative

Chapter 4

*The qualities necessary to
a demagogue are these:
to be foul-mouthed, base-born,
a low, mean fellow.*
—Aristophanes

AS YOU IMPROVE YOUR VOCABULARY, you'll hear others use words that you never heard before. News reporters, radio announcers—here and there, they will drop erudite little morsels into their banter. You never heard them previously because your brain tuned the word out and made sense of the word in the context of the sentence. So, it is important that you sound the word out. You might ask: Why?

If you want to remember someone's name, you practice it at every opportunity. If you want to learn a foreign language, you must speak it out loud. That holds true for vocabulary as well. Take time to look at the pronunciation at the end of each word and sound it out. But don't stop there. Look for every opportunity to use it throughout the day—within reason! Use discretion, but use the words.

GRISLY LIST 16

The **decrepit** beggar leaned against the building with his arm outstretched, hoping for a handout. He was a bit **daft** but he still remembered his years as a **decadent** executive, before his own **debauchery** and others' treachery had done him in. To think that he had once been feared by so many and now here he stood, a **debilitated** ghost, a mere shadow of what he once had been, **debased** by poverty and drunkenness.

"Hey, buddy, could you spare a dollar?"

"Get a job," a passerby answered **curtly**, without looking up.

This didn't anger him at all; that's what he used to do when a beggar had dared to bother him. He shrugged and looked to the next. That's when he saw him: the **dastard**, the **deceptive** weasel who had supplanted him. The fool was **dawdling** up ahead, his arm around his mistress. The beggar knew he wouldn't recognize him.

"Repent!" he howled as his enemy came closer. "Your doom is at hand. Repent!!"

His old foe laughed and kept walking. The beggar began to chase him down the street.

"Your wife, Katie, knows and she'll crush you completely."

The mention of his wife's name startled the old enemy; he pushed his mistress away and started to run.

"Blood! I see blood and doom. Behind your back they plot against you this very moment. Repent!"

The old man started to laugh as he watched his adversary run horrified down the street.

"Yep," he said out loud, "I've still got it in me."

1. **curt cold fish** kərt One who is curt is brief and to the point—to the point of rudeness, that is. From Latin, *curtus* = short.

> *Many a man's tongue broke his nose.*
> —Seamus MacManus

2. **daft ding-a-ling** daft Think of Daffy Duck; someone daft is silly, foolish, and/or crazy. From Medieval English, *dafte* = awkward.

> *One hundred thousand lemmings can't be wrong.*
> —Graffito

3. **dastardly turncoat** das'tərd-lē A dastard is a mean, cowardly, sneaky person; hence, dastardly should be used when someone is both vicious and cowardly. From Old Norwegian, *dasask* = to get tired.

> *Ever will a coward show no mercy.*
> —Thomas Mallory

4. **dawdling slowpoke** dôd'ling A dawdling person is a laggard, a sluggard who piddles about, finding little things to do to waste time. From Medieval English, *dadel* = chattering (of birds).

> *I've been on a calendar but never on time.*
> —Marilyn Monroe

5. **debased deadbeat** di-bāsd' To debase is to lower or cheapen the value or dignity of something. From Late Latin, *de* = down, utterly + *bassus* = low.

> *He that is down need fear no fall.*
> —John Bunyan

6. **debauched dataholic** di-bôchd' One who is debauched has succumbed to immoral living and excessive lusts. From Old French, *desbaucher* = to seduce, originally to separate the branches from the trunk.

> *Debauchery is perhaps an act of despair in the face of infinity.*
> —Edmond and Jules De Goncourt

7. **debilitated quitter** di-bil'i-tā-tid One who has been debilitated has been weakened, enfeebled. From French, *debiliter* = to render weak.

> *Show him death and he'll be content with fever.*
> —Persian proverb

8. **decadent deviant** dek'ə-dənt Anyone decadent is in a state of decline or decay. From Vulgar Latin, *decadere* = to fall away.

> *Man was not born wicked;*
> *he becomes so, as he becomes sick.*
> —Voltaire

9. **deceptive weasel** di-sep'tiv To be deceptive is to be deceitful and dishonest. From Latin, *decipere* = to ensnare.

> *O, what a tangled web we weave,*
> *when first we practice to deceive.*
> —Walter Scott

10. **decrepit duffer** di-krep'it Decrepit means either broken down or worn out by old age. From Latin, *decrepitus* = broken down.

> *It's hard to be nostalgic when you can't remember anything.*
> —Unknown

QUIZ 16

Match the definitions with the words on the right.

____ 1. curt	a. worn out by old age
____ 2. daft	b. deceitful and dishonest
____ 3. dastardly	c. given over to excessive lusts
____ 4. dawdle	d. in a state of decline or decay
____ 5. debased	e. lowered or cheapened
____ 6. debauched	f. rudely brief
____ 7. debilitated	g. silly, foolish, and/or crazy
____ 8. decadent	h. to waste time
____ 9. deceptive	i. vicious and cowardly
____ 10. decrepit	j. weakened or feeble

GRISLY LIST 17

How things had **degenerated** this far, Shelby wasn't sure, but she wasn't going to second-guess her actions now, so she continued to stuff the **defalcated** money into the trunk of her car. It had all started so innocently: get herself off drugs, go to church, get close to God, move to a commune in Brazil. And then things got weird.

First, there were the **demeaning** sermons about women being the devil. Next came that **defamatory** article about the government being the great Satan. After that they had to throw away their clothes and shave their heads. She felt **degraded**! Then all hell broke loose, with **defenestrating** henchmen tossing people out of buildings and so on. Finally, Pastor Elijah, that **demented demagogue**, went nuts, absolving all the marriages and requiring all the women to be his wives.

Even her **dejected** days on heroin had been better than this! Wasn't religion supposed to be good for you? It wasn't supposed to be this **deleterious** leech sucking the lifeblood out of you. She knew that if she didn't leave now, these nuts were prepared to send her home in a coffin. She slammed the trunk and hopped into her Impala. She cranked the engine and it was only then that she noticed the extra wires dangling from under the dashboard.

1. ***defalcating* employee** di-fal′kā-ting To defalcate is to steal funds entrusted to one's care, or embezzle. From Latin, *defalcare* = to cut off.

EPITAPH:
This priest fled to Vegas with embezzled funds
Unaware he was stealing from militant nuns

2. ***defamatory* dirtbag** di-fam′ə-tôr-ē Anyone who is defamatory is slanderous, likely to damage someone's reputation. From Latin, *diffamare* = take away another's reputation.

I hate the man who builds his name
on ruins of another's fame.
—John Gay

3. ***defenestrating* ruffian** di-fen′i-strā-ting To defenestrate means to throw out the window. From Latin, *fenestra* = window.

We're gonna make him an offer he can't refuse.
—Marlon Brando, The Godfather

4. ***degenerate* backslider** di-jen′ər-it As a noun, degenerate means a morally corrupt and depraved person. As a verb, degenerate means to sink to a worse condition. As an adjective, degenerate means being in a worse state than before. From Latin, *degenerare* = to become unlike one's race.

Whenever I'm caught between two evils,
I take the one I've never tried.
—Mae West

5. ***degraded* drudge** di-grā′dəd Anyone degraded is lowered, debased, or corrupted morally. From Latin, *de* = down + *gradus* = a step, degree. It is coupled with **drudge** = one who does menial, tedious labor.

By working faithfully eight hours a day, you may eventually
get to be a boss and work twelve hours a day.
—Robert Frost

6. ***dejected* mutt** di-jek′təd In low spirits, a dejected person is sad because of a setback. From Latin, *de* = down + *jacere* = to throw.

He's turned his life around. He used to be depressed and miserable.
Now he's miserable and depressed.
—David Frost

7. ***deleterious* litterbug** del-i-tîr′ē-əs Anything deleterious is harmful to your health. From Greek, *deleter* = a destroyer.

Diseases are the penalties we pay for over indulgence.
—Edward Bulwer

8. **black-hearted *demagogue*** dem'ə-gôg A demagogue is a leader who, to gain power, stirs up mobs by appealing to their prejudices. From Greek, *demos* = the people + *agogos* = leader.

> *The demagogue is one who preaches doctrines*
> *he knows to be untrue to men he knows to be idiots.*
> —H. L. Mencken

9. ***demeaning* mudslinger** di-mē'ning To demean another is to lower his/her dignity. The root word is *mean* = inferior, low in station.

> *Do not use a hatchet to remove a fly from your friend's forehead.*
> —Chinese proverb

10. ***demented* lunatic** di-men'təd Dementia is the gradual worsening of one's ability to think; hence, one who is demented has lost all mental functions. It can also be used to describe one who is insane, twisted, or just plain out of his gourd. From Latin, *demens* = mad, out of one's mind.

> EPITAPH:
> *We knew he was one crazy fella*
> *When he tried to get fresh with a gorilla*

QUIZ 17

Match the words with the definitions on the right.

____ 1. defalcate	a. a leader who stirs up mobs
____ 2. defamatory	b. harmful
____ 3. defenestrate	c. in low spirits
____ 4. degenerate	d. insane
____ 5. degraded	e. lowered (fits two words)
____ 6. dejected	f. morally corrupt and depraved
____ 7. deleterious	g. slanderous
____ 8. demagogue	h. steal funds entrusted to one's care
____ 9. demeaned	i. to throw out the window
____ 10. demented	

GRISLY LIST 18

Lucinda had had enough of Kari's **deprecating** suggestions. She'd put up with her **denigrating** comments to her coworkers for six months.

"Kari, now that I'm supervisor I think we should go over your work performance."

Kari gave a **dentigerous** smile. "Work performance?"

"I'm not sure if we can keep you here. We can't have any **derogatory** gossip poisoning the atmosphere."

"Gossip? I don't gossip."

"You told Sherry I was a **depraved** hag."

"What, me? No. You must be mistaken."

"I have Sherry's statement in writing here. It reads: 'Kari said you were a **deranged** nightmare. She also called Kurt a **depredatory** dog who pickpockets in the cafeteria.' You also said Bob was **derelict** in his duties as editor."

"I never said that."

"I have several other corroborating statements from other coworkers about your tendency to **deride** people's reputations. Shall I call them all in here to confront you?"

Kari looked uncertain.

"So am I fired?"

"No. We've all agreed to put you on the gossip column. We need someone with your **derisive** talent to help make this paper fly."

1. **denigrating** backbiter den'ə-grā-ting To denigrate is to belittle another's reputation by blackening it. From Latin, *denigrare* = to blacken.

> Slanderers are like flies,
> that pass all over a man's good parts
> to light only on his sores.
> —Rule of Life

2. **dentigerous** adversary den-tij'ər-əs Anyone dentigerous is bearing his teeth. From Latin, *dens* = tooth + -*gerous* = bearing.

> I loathe people who keep dogs. They are cowards
> who haven't got the guts to bite people themselves.
> —August Strindberg

3. **depraved** flesh-peddler di-prăvd' Anyone depraved is morally corrupted. From Latin, *depravare* = to make crooked.

> This is my last year to fool around.
> Then I'm going to settle down and marry a rock star.
> —from the movie Modern Girls

4. **deprecating** schmuck dep'ri-kā-ting To deprecate is to express disapproval, to belittle, or to argue against. From Latin, *deprecatus* = to ward off by prayer. It is coupled with **schmuck** = a despicable, foolish jerk.

> Evil report, like the Italian stiletto, is an assassin's weapon.
> —Madam de Maintenon

5. **depredatory** carjacker di-pred'ə-tôr-ē Someone who is depredatory will rob and strip you of your goods. From Late Latin, *depraedatus* = plundered.

> The rich rob the poor and the poor rob one another.
> —Sojourner Truth

6. ***deranged* dimwit** di-rānjd' To put it mildly, a deranged person is off-kilter, insane, loony, daffy, half-baked, etc. From Old French, *des-* = apart + *rengier* = to put in a row.

> *The madman thinks the rest of the world crazy.*
> —Publilius Syrus

7. **God-forsaken *derelict*** der'ə-likt Derelict has several meanings: as an adjective it can signify someone is neglectful, or that something is abandoned; as a noun it can signify an abandoned ship or a bum. From Latin, *derelictus* = abandoned.

> *We're all of us sentenced*
> *to solitary confinement*
> *inside our own skins,*
> *for life.*
> —Tennessee Williams

8. ***deriding* Momus** di-rī'ding To deride is to laugh with contempt or ridicule another. From Latin, *de-* = down + *ridere* = to laugh. It is coupled with **Momus** = the Greek god of blame and ridicule.

> *The more I see of men,*
> *the more I like my dogs.*
> —Madame de Staël

9. ***derisive* detractor** di-rī'siv Derisive means contemptuous or mocking. From Latin, *de-* = down + *ridere* = to laugh.

> *Why don't you put your face in dough and make jackass cookies?*
> —Soupy Sales

10. ***derogatory* scandalmonger** di-rog'ə-tôr-ē To be derogatory is to put others down, to speak slightingly of them. From Latin, *derogare* = detract from.

> *In judging others,*
> *folks will work overtime for no pay.*
> —Charles Carruthers

QUIZ 18

Match the words with the definitions on the right.

___ 1. denigrating	a.	bearing teeth
___ 2. dentigerous	b.	given to robbing
___ 3. depraved	c.	insane
___ 4. deprecate	d.	morally corrupted
___ 5. depredatory	e.	neglectful or abandoned
___ 6. deranged	f.	ridiculing (fits two words)
___ 7. derelict	g.	slandering (fits two words)
___ 8. deriding	h.	to express disapproval
___ 9. derisive		
___10. derogatory		

GRISLY LIST 19

Bari was **destitute**, so she had little choice but to listen to the **didactic** prattle of her new boss, a **dictatorial** fiend who could've given Hitler a run for his money.

"Now pay careful attention: when you serve drinks, lean forward, keeping your back arched like so, and set the drink down like so with a curtsy."

With these and countless other **desultory** instructions, she **despondently** trudged out to try her first waitress job wondering why, with a degree in anthropology, she had to wear a push-up bra.

It didn't help that her first customer was a rather twisted **deviate**, and a **diabolically** ugly one at that, but then this was the Wango Pango Bar and Grill. Could this get any more **despicable**? The lecher leered at her as she leaned forward.

"Oh, baby, I like the way you curtsy. Why don't you curtsy on my lap?" He wheezed as he pinched her butt.

Suddenly the thought of moving back home and going for her Ph.D. didn't sound so bad. She pinched the customer's cheek hard and smiled **deviously**.

"You cute little **despoiler**, you," Bari said.

"The spoil what?" he asked, but she was already gone.

1. **despicable** little devil di-spik'ə-bəl To be despicable is to be contemptible, deserving hate. From Latin, *despicari* = to despise.

> *No one can have a higher opinion of him than I have,*
> *and I think he's a dirty little beast.*
> —W. S. Gilbert

2. ruthless **despoiler** di-spoil'ûr To despoil is to rob, to plunder everything of value. From Latin, de- + *spoliare* = to spoil, rob.

> *Thieves respect property;*
> *they merely wish the property to become their property*
> *that they may more perfectly respect it.*
> —G. K. Chesterton

3. **despondent** hard-luck case di-spon'dənt One who is despondent has lost all courage and hope. From Latin, *despondere* = to lose courage.

> *You are free, and that is why you are lost.*
> —Franz Kafka

4. **destitute** washout des'ti-tōōt To be destitute is to lack even the bare necessities of life, to be poverty-stricken. From Latin, *destitutus* = put away, abandoned. It can be used as a noun or an adjective.

> *The destitute does not live, but dies by inches.*
> —Russian proverb

5. ***desultory* dweeb** des′əl-tôr-ē Anything desultory is disconnected, random, and aimless. From Latin, *desilire* = to leap down.

> *The less men think, the more they talk.*
> —Montesquieu

6. **twisted *deviate*** dē′vē-āt A deviate turns away from what is normal or right, or from what the majority feels is normal—especially if it involves anything sexual. As a verb, deviate means to turn aside from the path you're on. From Latin, *deviatus* = turned from the straight road.

> *I believe that sex is the most beautiful,*
> *natural, and wholesome thing*
> *that money can buy.*
> —Steve Martin

7. ***devious* double-crosser** dē′vē-əs Anyone or anything devious is winding or deceiving. From Latin, *devius* = off the road.

> *One may smile, and smile and be a villain.*
> —Shakespeare, Hamlet

8. ***diabolical* despot** dī-ə-bol′i-kəl To be diabolical is to have the attributes of the devil. From Greek, *diabolos* = devil.

> *No doubt Jack the Ripper excused himself*
> *on the grounds that it was his human nature.*
> —A. A. Milne

9. ***dictatorial* bigshot** dik-tə-tôr′ē-əl A dictatorial person is tyrannical, bossy, or domineering. From Latin, *dictator* = chief magistrate.

> *Dictators always look good until the last minutes.*
> —Thomas Masaryk

10. ***didactic* schoolteacher** dī-dak′tik Didactic means instructive or intended to give moral instruction. One who is didactic is too inclined to teach, excessively instructive, to the annoyance of others. From Greek, *didaktikos* = apt at teaching, instructive.

> *Education is a state-controlled manufactory of echoes.*
> —N. Douglas

Match the words with the definitions on the right.

___ 1.	despicable	a.	deserves to be despised
___ 2.	despoil	b.	having the traits of the devil
___ 3.	despondent	c.	instructive, too prone to teach
___ 4.	destitute	d.	random, disconnected, aimless
___ 5.	desultory	e.	lack even the bare necessities of
___ 6.	deviate		life
___ 7.	devious	f.	to rob
___ 8.	diabolical	g.	to turn aside from the path
___ 9.	dictatorial	h.	tyrannical, domineering
___ 10.	didactic	i.	winding or deceiving
		j.	without courage and hope

GRISLY LIST 20

The **diffident** chump couldn't seem to pluck up his courage to pop the question. Sitting next to her, he was always so **discombobulated**, and he'd **digressed** from whatever it was he had hoped to say. She was, after all, part of the upper crust and he was but a mere speck in the **disenfranchised** herd. But today would be different; with his rose clasped in his hands, this day would be different.

"My dear, my one and only. This moment has meant so much to me. I've longed to—"

"What's going on?" she looked **disdainfully** at him, then her gaze fell on someone outside the window.

Though he was perplexed by her **dilatory** interruption, he dutifully followed her eyes.

"It's a saleswoman. What I was trying to say was that I have longed to sit before you and beg—"

His **disingenuous** love waved him away, "What's she doing here?"

"She's selling flowers to the gentleman." Now, my **discursive** little one, I have longed to, to, to—"

"All of them?"

"What?"

Suddenly, his one and only squealed with delight. The gentleman stood before them, his arms full of roses. The chump took a **disconsolate** look at his one rose and, with a **disgruntled** sigh, tossed it onto the others.

"Hey Bud," he shouted, "Here's one more. You'll need it."

1. ***diffident* wallflower** dif'i-dənt One who is diffident lacks self-confidence. From Latin, *diffidens* = mistrust, despairing.

> *What is more mortifying than to feel*
> *that you have missed the plum*
> *for want of courage to shake the tree?*
> —Logan Pearsall Smith

2. ***digressive* yapper** dī-gres'iv A digressive person wanders from the main point. From Latin, *digressus* = having departed or gone aside.

> *He's a wonderful talker*
> *who has the art of telling you nothing*
> *in a great harangue.*
> —Molière

3. ***dilatory* goof-off** dil'ə-tôr-ē Anything dilatory tends to cause delay. From Latin, *dilator* = delay.

> *Saturday afternoon,*
> *although occurring at regular and well-foreseen intervals,*
> *always takes this railway by surprise.*
> —W. S. Gilbert

4. ***discombobulated* dumbbell** dis-kəm-bob'yə-lā-tid Anyone discombobulated is completely perplexed and/or frustrated. It's possibly an alteration of discomfit.

> *I'm in a phone booth at the corner of Walk and Don't Walk.*
> —Unknown

5. ***disconsolate* victim** dis-kon'sə-lit A disconsolate person is unhappy, dejected, beyond any comfort. From Latin, *dis* = cause to be the opposite + *com* = with + *solari* = to solace, comfort.

> EPITAPH:
> *Before we could tell him of the sweepstakes he'd won*
> *He solved all his woes with point of a gun.*

6. ***discursive* speechifier** dis-kər'siv A discursive person wanders from one topic to another. From Latin, *discurrere* = to run to and fro.

> *Wise men talk because they have something to say;*
> *fools talk because they have to say something.*
> —Plato

7. ***disdainful* highbrow** dis-dān'fəl To be disdainful is to look down on others with contempt. From Latin, *dedignari* = to think unworthy.

> *The higher the monkey climbs, the more you see of his ass.*
> —"Vinegar Joe" Stilwell

8. ***disenfranchised* herd** dis-en-fran′chīzd Anyone who has been disenfranchised has been deprived of the rights of citizenship or of the hope of those rights. From Old French, *dis* = not + *franc* = free.

> *I feel a lot better since I gave up hope.*
> —Unknown

9. ***disgruntled* hag** dis-grun′tld One who is disgruntled has been made unhappy and cross. From Latin, *dis* = apart + an obsolete, idiomatic English expression, *gruntle* = to cause to be more favorably inclined. Grunt comes from Latin, *grunnire* = to grunt.

> *I told my mother-in-law that my house was her house,*
> *and she said, "Get the hell off my property."*
> —Joan Rivers

10. ***disheveled* drifter** di-shev′əld Anyone disheveled is uncombed and untidy. From Old French, *descheveler* = to tousle < dis- + *chevel* = hair.

> *She was a large woman who seemed*
> *not so much dressed as upholstered.*
> —James Barrie

QUIZ 20

Match the words with the definitions on the right.

_____ 1. diffident
_____ 2. digressive
_____ 3. dilatory
_____ 4. discombobulated
_____ 5. disconsolate
_____ 6. discursive
_____ 7. disdainful
_____ 8. disenfranchised
_____ 9. disheveled
_____ 10. disgruntled

a. beyond any comfort
b. completely perplexed
c. deprived of the rights of citizenship
d. lacking self-confidence
e. look down on or scorn
f. unhappy or cross
g. to cause delay
h. uncombed and untidy
i. wander from the main point (fits two words)

REVIEW 4

MATCH EACH QUOTE WITH THE APPROPRIATE WORD.

1. A wise fellow who is worthless always charms the rabble.
—Euripides

2. Cutting honest throats by whispers.
—Sir Walter Scott

3. It is a bitter dose to be taught obedience after you have learned to rule.
—Publilius Syrus

4. We said nonsense, but it was important nonsense.
—Nora Astorga

_____ a. demagogue   _____ c. daft
_____ b. debased   _____ d. demean

5. War makes thieves; peace hangs them.
—George Herbert

6. The rich man may never get into heaven,
but the pauper is already serving his term in hell.
—Alexander Chase

7. A clean glove often hides a dirty hand.
—English proverb

8. Every dog is entitled to one bite.
—Anonymous

9. Ordinarily, he's insane, but he has lucid moments
when he's merely stupid.
—Heinrich Heine

_____ e. deranged   _____ h. destitute
_____ f. depredatory   _____ i. dentigerous
_____ g. devious

10. No sooner is a temple built to God,
but the devil builds a chapel hard by.
—George Herbert

11. It is the old practice of despots to use a part of the people
to keep the rest in order.
—Thomas Jefferson

12. Pedantry crams our heads with learned lumber,
and takes out our brains to make room for it.
—Charles Colton

13. If you are too hesitant to ask the way, you will be lost.
—Malay proverb

14. The lie indirect is often as bad, and always meaner and more cowardly than the lie direct.
—Hosea Ballou

____ j. deceptive
____ k. diffident
____ l. didactic

____ m. dictatorial
____ n. diabolical

Chapter 5

Words ought to be a little wild
for they are the assault of thoughts
on the unthinking.
—John Keynes

IF YOU'RE IN SCHOOL browsing through this book, you have probably made some friends and some enemies. Take a look around you, at your enemies, for example, and think of what you might say about them in your yearbook. On a separate paper, write down their names next to the words in this list. Perhaps Luis, the ruthless despoiler, might be voted most likely to end up at Folsom prison. Or, Betty, the destitute twit, is most likely to end up homeless. When you finish I suggest you toss the paper, or shred it, so it doesn't fall into the wrong hands. In the end, you'll remember the vocabulary whenever you see them.

GRISLY LIST 21

The **dispiteous** general had once looked so polished, but now you could hardly recognize him, **disheveled** and **dissipated** as he was. He poured himself another drink as the sound of gunshots echoed in the valley.

"We'll combine forces with the North and kick these peasants out to sea."

His lieutenant nodded with a sly, **dissembling** smile.

"The common people, they are too **disputatious**; democracy will never work here. And, they say I was too **disparaging** of the press. Me?"

The gunshots rang out, closer now.

"What this country needed was a strong leader."

The lieutenant handed his **dissolute** chief another drink.

"I gave them strength. I gave them peace."

The general watched as the mob rolled triumphant and vengeful down the street toward the capital. His brilliant coup was now a **dismal** failure.

"So what if I had to silence a few **dissidents**."

The lieutenant remembered his sister's face and sighed. No need to **dissimulate** any longer: he pulled out his revolver.

1. *disingenuous* **lover** dis-in-jen'yoo-əs Disingenuous means lacking candor or sincerity. From Latin, *dis* = to be the opposite of + *ingenuus* = native, inborn, freeborn, noble.

    A little truth helps the lie go down.
    —*Italian proverb*

2. *dismal* **failure** diz'məl Anything dismal is either very dreary or completely inept or boring. From Old French, *dis mal* = unlucky days.

    Great souls have wills; feeble ones have only wishes.
    —*Chinese proverb*

3. ***disparaging* accuser** di-spar'i-jing To disparage is to put someone down, to speak slightingly of others. From Old French, *desparagier* = to marry one of inferior rank.

> *There are different ways of assassinating a man:*
> *by pistol, sword, poison, or moral assassination.*
> *They are the same in their results*
> *except that the last is more cruel.*
> —Napoleon I

4. ***dispiteous* fascist** dis-pit'ē-əs One who is dispiteous is ruthless, cruel, and pitiless. From Latin, *despicere* = to look down on.

> *Any excuse will serve a tyrant.*
> —Aesop

5. ***disputatious* grump** dis-pyə-tā'shəs A disputatious person is always ready to argue. From Latin, *disputare* = to discuss; hence, to argue.

> *He that blows coals in quarrels he has nothing to do with*
> *has no right to complain if the sparks fly in his face.*
> —Benjamin Franklin

6. ***dissembling* deceiver** di-sem'bling To dissemble is to conceal something under a false appearance; to disguise. From Latin, *dissimulare* = to feign, altered by French *semble* = to appear.

> *To know how to dissemble is the knowledge of kings.*
> —Richelieu

7. ***dissident* hard-liner** dis'i-dənt To be dissident is to disagree. From Latin, *dissidere* = to disagree.

> *If, by ill luck, people understood each other, they would never agree.*
> —Baudelaire

8. ***dissimulating* impostor** di-sim'yə-lā-ting To dissimulate is to dissemble, to hide one's true feelings. From Latin, *dissimulare* = to feign.

> *The United States brags about its political system,*
> *but the president says one thing during the election,*
> *something else when he takes office,*
> *something else during midterm,*
> *and something else when he leaves.*
> —Deng Xiaoping

9. ***dissipated* drunk** dis'ə-pā-ting To be dissipated is to have wasted time with an excessive or intemperate devotion to pleasure. From Latin, *dissipare* = to scatter < *dis-* = apart + *supare* = to throw.

> *Drunkenness is voluntary madness.*
> —Seneca

10. ***dissolute* guzzler** dis′ə-lo͞ot A dissolute person is immoral and/or dissipated, having wasted away from excess and debauchery. From Latin, *dissolutus* = loosened, disconnected.

> *Everybody should believe in something;*
> *I believe I'll have another drink.*
> —*Unknown*

Match the words with the definitions on the right

____ 1. disingenuous
____ 2. dismal
____ 3. disparage
____ 4. dispiteous
____ 5. disputatious
____ 6. dissemble
____ 7. dissident
____ 8. dissimulate
____ 9. dissipated
____ 10. dissolute

a. conceal under a false appearance (fits two words)
b. gloomy; inept
c. wasted from immoral living (fits two words)
d. ready to argue
e. ruthless, cruel, pitiless
f. speak slightingly of others
g. to disagree
h. insincere

GRISLY LIST 22

With **dogged** determination, the old woman, **doddering** upon her cane, made her way into the church. Pastor Rick was busy with the bulletin and didn't notice the woman **dithering** outside his office until her **distraught** voice echoed against the walls.

"They took it all. Everything is gone." She whimpered **dolorously**, her eyes sad and empty.

"What's gone?

"The liturgy!" she shouted out.

"Sunday's second service has the traditional liturgy."

"This liturgy is **divisive**. That's what it is. Everything should stay the same."

"I see."

"And you don't baptize the proper way," the **doctrinaire** continued. "You just sprinkle. That's not right," she said **dogmatically**.

"We're Presbyterian. They dunk them across the street at First Baptist."

"Who are you?" she blurted out as she gazed about the room with **distrait** curiosity.

"I'm Pastor Rick. This is First Presbyterian."

The old woman nodded, and without another word, turned and **docilely** waddled out.

Rick picked up the phone and punched in a number.

"Cliff? Heads up. She's on her way."

1. ***distrait* screw-up** di-strā′ To be distrait is to be absent-minded or inattentive. From Latin, *distrahere* = to draw (or pull) apart.

   It's nice to be here in Iowa.
   —Gerald Ford in Ohio

2. ***distraught* loner** di-strôt′ Hand them a hanky. Anyone distraught could be anxious, upset, or even crazed. Distraught is a Middle English alteration of *distrait*. From Latin, *distractus* = pulled apart.

   Fate finds for every man his share of misery.
   —Euripides

3. ***dithering* ditz** diŧħ′ə-ring To dither is to tremble or bumble in a nervously excited, confused, or timid way. From Middle English, *didder* = tremble.

   Favorite drink:
   Double shot of espresso with a PCP twist.

4. ***divisive* agitator** di-vī′siv Anything divisive causes splits, factions, or disagreements. From Late Latin, *divisivus* = divisive < *dis-* = apart + *vidua* = widow.

   The quarrels of friends are the opportunities of foes.
   —Aesop

5. ***docile* dupe** dos′əl A docile person is easy to manipulate, control, and not likely to create problems. From *docilis* = easily taught.

   Mongo merely pawn in chess game of life.
   —Mel Brooks, Blazing Saddles

6. **stiff-necked *doctrinaire*** dok-trə-nâr′ Doctrinaire means holding to a belief system in an unyielding, dogmatic way. It can be used as an adjective or a noun. From Latin, *docere* = to teach.

   Stiff in opinion, always in the wrong.
   —John Dryden

7. ***doddering* dotard** dod′ə-ring To dodder is to tremble from old age, ready to fall down. From Old English, *dyderian* = to baffle, delude.

   Old age comes at a bad time.
   —Sue Banducci

8. ***dogged* diehard** dôg′id To be dogged is to be stubborn or determined, resolute. From Medieval English, *dogge* = dog.

   The foolish and the dead never change opinion.
   —James Russell Lowell

9. **dogmatic** jackass dôg-mat'ik A dogmatic person is arrogantly opinionated or pushes a specific dogma, or doctrine. From Greek, *dogma* = opinion, judgment.

> *His bedroom window is made out of bricks.*
> —Bob Dylan

10. **dolorous** nebbish dō'lər-əs Anything or anyone dolorous exhibits, brings about, or entails sorrow or pain. From Latin, *dolere* = to suffer. It is coupled with **nebbish** = from Yiddish, an inept, shy, dull person, usually ignored.

> *Even when the gates of Heaven*
> *are closed to prayer,*
> *they are open to tears.*
> —Talmud

QUIZ 22

Match the words with the definitions on the right.

____ 1. distrait	a.	absent-minded
____ 2. distraught	b.	arrogantly opinionated
____ 3. dithering		(fits two words)
____ 4. divisive	c.	causing factions or quarrels
____ 5. docile	d.	easy to manage
____ 6. doctrinaire	e.	nervously excited or confused
____ 7. doddering	f.	sad
____ 8. dogged	g.	stubborn
____ 9. dogmatic	h.	trembling from old age
____ 10. dolorous	i.	upset

GRISLY LIST 23

The **doughty** gaffer strode into the living room carrying a shovel.
"I've killed him. That'll teach him."

His **dour** and **dowdy** wife, her hair in a messy bun, was in an exceptionally **dyspeptic** mood and had no time for games.

"Get that shovel out of my house!"

"Done for," the old man **driveled**. "The **draconian** monster tried to creep back into France but I gave him the old one-two. He thought he could sneak up on us, the **duplicitous** coward!"

His wife threw a potato that hit the **doting** gaffer squarely on the nose.

"Ouch!"

"I said, get that shovel out of my house."

The old man's demeanor turned surprisingly **ductile**. He looked **dubiously** at the shovel and his surroundings, and then shuffled out.

1. ***doting* dummy** dō'ting One who is doting is either feeble-minded because of old age or foolishly and excessively expressing fondness for someone. From Middle Dutch *doten* = be silly.

   > *I did but see her passing by*
   > *And yet I love her till I die.*
   > —*Thomas Ford*

2. ***doughty* dummkopf** dou'tē Literally, doughty means brave, but it is now used humorously, often questioning the validity of the compliment. From Old English, *dohtig* = worthy.

   > *It is easy to be brave from a safe distance.*
   > —*Aesop*

3. ***dour* party pooper** dour A dour person is serious and gloomy. From Latin, *duras* = hard.

   > *We are growing serious, and, let me tell you,*
   > *that's the very next step to being dull.*
   > —*Joseph Addison*

4. ***dowdy* dame** dou'dē A dowdy person is distastefully ordinary or shabby. From Early Modern English, *dowd* = an ill-dressed or slovenly woman.

   > *She wears her clothes as if they were thrown on with a pitchfork.*
   > —*Jonathan Swift*

5. ***Draconian* overlord** drā-kō'nē-ən Anything Draconian is extremely harsh. Draco was a seventh-century Athenian statesman who set up a system of laws known for their extreme severity.

   > *Use an accordion. Go to jail! That's the law.*
   > —*Bumper sticker*

6. ***driveling* dingbat** driv'ə-ling To drivel is to let saliva drip from one's mouth or nose, to slaver, and to talk childishly or foolishly. From Old English, *dreflian* = to slobber.

   > *He mouths a sentence as curs mouth a bone.*
   > —*Charles Churchill*

7. ***dubious* intellectual** dōō'bē-əs If it's dubious it's doubtful, uncertain, or questionable. From Latin, *dubare* = to be of two minds.

   > *My father had silicone shots in his head to enlarge his brain.*
   > *It worked. Now he has to wear a bra to keep his eyes in.*
   > —*Jack Graiman*

8. ***ductile* yes man** duk'təl Like putty, a ductile person is easily molded or led. From Latin, *ductus* = a lead.

   > *Last week I told my wife a man is like wine;*
   > *he gets better with age. She locked me in the cellar.*
   > —*Rodney Dangerfield*

9. ***duplicitous* cad** dōō-plis′i-təs One who is duplicitous is hypocritically cunning, double-dealing, and deceitful. From Latin, *duplicare* = to double. It is coupled with **cad** = a man who acts disrespectfully to women.

> *For I have sworn thee fair, and thought thee bright,*
> *Who art as black as hell, as dark as night.*
> —*Shakespeare*

10. ***dyspeptic* buttinski** dis-pep′tik If you're dyspeptic, then you either have impaired digestion or you're grouchy. Or maybe you're grouchy because your digestion is impaired. From Greek, *dys* = bad + *pepsis* = digestion.

> *The next pleasantest feeling in the world*
> *to being perfectly happy is being perfectly cross.*
> —*Finley Peter Dunne*

QUIZ 23

Match the words with the definitions on the right.

____ 1. doting	a.	brave
____ 2. doughty	b.	doubtful
____ 3. dour	c.	easily molded or led
____ 4. dowdy	d.	extremely harsh
____ 5. Draconian	e.	feeble-minded from old age
____ 6. drivel	f.	having impaired digestion, or grouchy
____ 7. dubious	g.	hypocritically cunning, double-dealing
____ 8. ductile	h.	shabby, ill-dressed, or slovenly
____ 9. duplicitous	i.	serious or gloomy
____10. dyspeptic	j.	to slaver, to talk foolishly

GRISLY LIST 24

"Life is merely a **dystopian** nightmare," the **elitist** droned on as he sipped his wine.

His **emasculated** servant chimed in, "Oh, you are right, sir."

"It devours us like an **edacious** vulture and then spits us out."

"My wife might agree with you on that. With the cancer and all, she's become quite **emaciated**."

Too **egocentric** to listen, the young man went on. "Life isn't life; it's an **egregious** murderer. Like an **eldritch** banshee, it sucks us dry until all that's left of us is an **effete** bag of bones incapable of doing anything worthwhile."

"Shall I get you some dessert, sir?"

"No. Get my sleeping pills; I want to put an end to my misery."

This startled the usually timid servant but then, in a surprising moment of **effrontery**, he blurted out, "Before you do, sir, if you'd be so kind as to give me my check."

1. *dystopian* **nightmare** dis-tō′pē-ən Dystopia is a fictitious place where life is horrible, the opposite of Eutopia, where life is perfect, and in contrast to Utopia, a make-believe world where everyone enjoys (supposedly) the perfect community. Sir Thomas More wrote a book called *Utopia* in 1516. Utopia is from the Greek, *ou* = not + *topos* = a place (because there is no such place). J. S. Mill coined the nonce-word, *dystopia*, in 1868 combining from the Greek, *dys-* = bad and *topos* = a place.

   Maybe this world is another planet's hell.
   —Aldous Huxley

2. *edacious* **glutton** i-dā′shəs Anyone edacious is consuming and devouring. From Latin, *edacitas* = gluttonous.

   The lust of avarice has so totally seized upon mankind
   that their wealth seems rather to possess them
   than they possess their wealth.
   —Pliny

3. *effete* **snob** i-fēt′ It comes from the Latin word, *effetus*, which means worn out by childbearing; hence, its present definition is infertile or unable to produce. However, it has also taken on the meaning of weakness caused by self-indulgence and decadence.

   They remind me of a very tired rich man who said to his chauffeur,
   "Drive off that cliff, James, I want to commit suicide."
   —Adlai Stevenson

4. *effrontuous* **daredevil** i-frun′chōō-əs Effrontery is shameless boldness, impudence; hence, anyone effrontuous is boldly shameful or shamelessly bold. From Latin, *effrons* = barefaced.

   In skating over thin ice, our safety is in our speed.
   —Emerson

5. *egocentric* **preppy** ē-gō-sen′trik To be egocentric is to be self-centered, totally engrossed in oneself. From Latin, *ego* = I + -centric from *centrom*.

   That man that lives for self alone,
   lives for the meanest mortal known.
   —Joaquin Miller

6. *egregious* **profiteer** i-grē′jəs Egregious means extremely bad or shocking. From Latin, *egregius* = separated from the herd.

   Kill one and you are a murderer.
   Kill millions and you are a conqueror.
   Kill all and you are a God.
   —Jean Rostand

7. **eldritch** wacko el'drich Anything eldritch is weird and eerie. From Medieval English, *elve* = elf.

> *He who does not fill his world with phantoms remains alone.*
> —Antonio Porchia

8. **elitist** snob i lēt ist An elitist believes government should be controlled by the richest, smartest, or most powerful, or that people who are the richest, smartest, etc., are just better in every way. From Latin, *eligere* = to set apart.

> *Even on the highest throne, we are still sitting on our ass.*
> —Michel de Montaigne

9. **emaciated** stick i-mā'shē-ā-tid To be emaciated is to be abnormally lean. From Latin, *emaciare* = to make lean.

> *She was built like a boy arrow.*
> —E. M. Ashcraft III

10. **emasculated** runt i-mas'kyə-lā-tid To be emasculated is to have one's testes cut off, either physically or emotionally. From Latin, *e* = out + *masculus* = male.

> *Married men live longer than single men.*
> *But married men are a lot more willing to die.*
> —Johnny Carson

QUIZ 24

Match the definitions with the words on the left.

____ 1. dystopian
____ 2. edacious
____ 3. effete
____ 4. effrontery
____ 5. egocentric
____ 6. egregious
____ 7. eldritch
____ 8. elitist
____ 9. emaciated
____ 10. emasculated

a. abnormally lean
b. believes government should be controlled by the best, or that some people are just naturally better than others
c. castrated physically or emotionally
d. consuming and devouring
e. extremely bad or shocking
f. self-centered
g. shameless boldness
h. weakness caused by self-indulgence
i. weird and eerie
j. dreadful

GRISLY LIST 25

Tom lay on his back, completely **enervated** from his indulgent **epicurean** adventure the night before. What exactly had happened? **Enigmatic** memories of the party **erratically** came in and out of focus. All he knew for sure was that he started out in his letterman's jacket and ended up prancing about in some **epicene** tunic. That was when the police arrived.

"They said you **embezzled** the funds from the cookie drive," his father thundered.

"Well, no, not exactly," he **equivocated**. "I accidentally used the money. I thought it was mine."

It was hard to lie with a hangover. Last night's **ephemeral** pleasure had turned into a lasting nightmare.

"Don't get **eristic** with me, boy."

"To be honest, I can't remember."

"What were you thinking?" his dad screamed.

Tom knew the answer: the **ennui**—his boring day-to-day existence and the monotony of school. But he knew what he had to say.

"Dad, I think someone slipped something into my soda."

1. ***embezzling* fat cats** em-bez'ling To embezzle is to steal money entrusted to one's care. From Old French, *en* = into + *besillier* = to destroy.

> *Public money is like holy water: everyone helps himself to it.*
> —Italian proverb

2. ***enervated* dropout** en'ər-vā-tid Anyone enervated is without strength, or weakened. From Latin, *enervis* = nerveless, weak.

> *Nothing of worth or weight can be achieved with half a mind,*
> *with a faint heart, and with a lame endeavor.*
> —Isaac Barrow

3. ***enigmatic* nut** en-ig-mat'ik Anything enigmatic is filled with riddles or puzzles. From Greek, *ainissesthai* = to speak in riddles.

> *What does a woman want?*
> —Freud

4. **mind-numbing *ennui*** on-wē' Ennui is fatigue due to boredom or inactivity. However, if you truly want to sound erudite, use the adjective (which is French) ***ennoye*** for anyone male or ***ennoyée*** for anyone female. From Old French, *enui* = displeasure.

> *She, while her lover pants upon her breast,*
> *Can mark the carvings in an Indian chest.*
> —Alexander Pope

5. ***epicene* oddity** ep′i-sēn   Epicene means characterizing either sex. It has come to mean someone who is effeminate. From Greek, *epikoines* = common.

> *He is every woman's man and every man's woman.*
> *—Gaius Scribonius Curio on Julius Caesar*

6. ***ephemeral* fair-weather friend** i-fem′ər-əl   Anything ephemeral is fleeting, transitory, short-lived. From Greek *ephemeros* = short-lived.

> *Your love is like the morning mist*
> *that leaves quickly with the dawn.*
> *—Hosea 6:4*

7. ***epicurean* self-seeker** ep-i-kyoo̅′rē-ən   An epicurean is a seeker of sensuous pleasure and luxury. Epicurus was an Ancient Greek philosopher who believed that the objective of life is the pursuit of pleasure moderated by morals, self-control, and cultural edification. Epicurean is not necessarily pejorative, but it might be if you're a puritan.

> *Who loves not women, wine and song*
> *remains a fool his whole life long.*
> *—Martin Luther*

8. ***equivocal* wheeler-dealer** i-kwiv′ə-kəl   To be equivocal is to give purposely vague answers, or to give answers that can be interpreted in more than one way. From Late Latin, *aequivocus* = to have the same sound.

> *A sudden lie may sometimes be only manslaughter upon truth;*
> *but by a carefully constructed equivocation truth is always,*
> *with malice aforethought, deliberately murdered.*
> *—Shakespeare*

9. ***eristic* pain** i-ris′tik   An eristic person is argumentative, controversial, or given to specious reasoning. From Greek, *erizein* = to dispute.

> *In arguing of the shadow, we forgo the substance.*
> *—John Lyly*

10. ***erratic* weirdo** i-rat′ik   Anything erratic is irregular, inconsistent, or wandering. From Latin, *erraticus* = wandering.

> *He who begins many things finishes nothing.*
> *—C. Simmons*

QUIZ 25

Match the definitions with the words on the left.

_____ 1. embezzle

_____ 2. enervated

_____ 3. enigmatic

_____ 4. ennui

_____ 5. epicene

_____ 6. ephemeral

_____ 7. epicurean

_____ 8. equivocal

_____ 9. eristic

_____ 10. erratic

a. effeminate

b. argumentative, controversial, or given to specious reasoning

c. seeker of sensuous pleasure

d. fatigue due to boredom

e. filled with riddles

f. fleeting, short-lived

g. irregular and wandering

h. steal entrusted money

i. giving purposely vague answers

j. without strength; weakened

REVIEW 5

MATCH EACH QUOTE WITH THE APPROPRIATE WORD.

1. But then, that's what young men are there for.
—*Adolf Hitler, commenting on heavy casualties*

2. How strange it is to see with how much passion.
People see things only in their own fashion!
—*Molière*

3. Life is a sexually transmitted disease.
—*Anonymous*

4. We are so accustomed to disguise ourselves to others,
that in the end we become disguised to ourselves.
—*François de la Rochefoucauld*

____ a. doctrinaire   ____ c. draconian
____ b. dystopia   ____ d. dissemble

5. That wretched disease that rivets a man so firmly to his own belief
that he becomes incapable of conceiving
other men may believe otherwise
—*Michel de Montaigne*

6. A yawn is a silent shout.
—*G. K. Chesterton*

7. Severities should be dealt out all at once, that by their suddenness
they may give less offense; benefits should be handed out drop by drop,
that they may be relished the more.
—*Niccolò Machiavelli*

8. [Men] are all but stomachs and we all but food;
they eat us hungrily, and when they are full, they belch us.
—*Shakespeare*

____ e. dispiteous   ____ g. dogmatism
____ f. edacious   ____ h. ennui

9. Show me the man who would go to heaven alone, and I will show you
one who will never be admitted there.
—*Owen Feltham*

10. With pleasure drugged, he almost longed for woe.
—*George Gordon, Lord Byron*

11. Everything by starts, and nothing long.
—*John Dryden*

12. We'll show you too some elders of the town
whose only joy is to put joy down.
—*A. P. Herbert*

____ i.   erratic   ____ k.   dour
____ j.   egocentric   ____ l.   epicurean

Chapter 6

Fate never wounds more deeply the generous heart,
than when a blockhead's insult points the dart.
—Samuel Johnson

ALTHOUGH MANY OF THESE WORDS ARE DE-RIVED FROM LISTS OF VOCABULARY most likely to be on the SAT or GRE, I felt that it was important that this book be a bit more erudite, and I have searched the dictionary to find words that would appeal to you word sleuths out there. Hence, you'll come across words like *potvaliant, umbrageous and contumacious*. Once you know their meanings, it's fun to spice up a conversation with them. You may not see them on a test, but that doesn't mean they aren't good to know.

However, if your main interest in this book is to improve your SAT or GRE scores, take another look at the quizzes. During each quiz you've written the answers before each word. Don't stop there. When you need to review, go back to each quiz, cover the answers, and write the words this time.

GRISLY LIST 26

Her teacher, the **execrable** Mr. Hornsworth, sipped his coffee and then **eructated** loudly. From the scowl on his face, Marissa got the impression that handing in her paper had **exacerbated** her predicament. Mr. Hornsworth had always been so **exacting**; she had hoped this might boost her flagging grade. But now he tossed the paper to the side, grabbed a bagel, and took an **esurient** bite.

"Aren't you going to read it?"

Exasperated, he sighed and set the bagel down.

"By gods," he started with his usual **euphuistic** style, "it's not as if you're going to go to college. It will be but two years before you are barefoot and pregnant."

Mr. Hornsworth was famous for this kind of **ethnocentric** babble. This angered the other women in class, but it only made Marissa work harder. It was rumored that there were so many **execrative** reviews about his bigoted comments that his job was on the line. He gave her paper the once-over.

"This isn't a word, ex..."

"**Excrementitious**. It means 'like crap.' It's in the unabridged dictionary."

He nodded and proceeded to read with growing intensity. Marissa waited nervously. He picked up his pen, slashed a big fat A on the top, and handed it back to her.

"Best paper this year; it gave me the creeps."

1. ***eructating* Grobian** i-ruk-tā'ting To eructate is to burp, to belch. From Latin, *e* = out + *ructare* = to belch. It is coupled with **Grobian** = a fictional patron saint of idiots.

> EPITAPH:
> *He burped and belched like prodigious thunder*
> *Till an avalanche took him six feet under*

2. ***esurient* chowhound** i-sŏŏr'ē-ənt Someone who's esurient is hungry or greedy. From Latin, *esurire* = hungering.

> *Treat debtors like your family; exploit them!*
> —*Ferengi acquisition rule #111*
> Deep Space 9

3. ***ethnocentric* bumpkin** eth-nō-sen'trik An ethnocentric person is blind to the value of other cultures and insists that his/her own culture is superior. From Greek, *ethnos* = race, culture + -centric.

> *Few people can be happy*
> *unless they hate some other person, nation or creed.*
> —*Bertrand Russell*

4. ***euphuistic* blowhard** yōō-fyōō-is'tik Having an affected and bombastic style of writing or speaking popular in the 16th century. Anyone who is euphuistic blows like Mount St. Helens. From Greek, *euphues* = graceful, shapely.

> *God is silent; now if we could only get man to shut up.*
> —*Woody Allen*

5. ***exacerbating* nuisance** ig-zas'ər-bā-ting To exacerbate is to make worse, irritate, or annoy. From Latin, *exacerbare* = to make angry.

> *Too many creatures, both insects and humans,*
> *estimate their own value by the amount of minor irritation*
> *they are able to cause to greater personalities than themselves.*
> —*Don Marquis*

6. ***exacting* perfectionist** ig-zak'ting Anyone or anything exacting is demanding, entailing rigorous effort or attention to detail. From Latin, *exigere* = to drive out.

> *I don't want any yes-men around me.*
> *I want everybody to tell me the truth,*
> *even if it costs them their jobs.*
> —*Samuel Goldwyn*

7. ***exasperating* pest** ig-zas'pə-rā-ting To exasperate is to irritate, annoy, or make angry. From the Latin, *exasperare* = to roughen.

> *Jesus loves you, but everybody else thinks you're a jerk.*
> —*Anonymous*

8. ***excrementitious* slob** ek-skrə-men-tish'əs Excrementitious means "like crap"—
excrement or feces. From Latin, *excrementum* = that which is sifted out, refuse.

Always look out for Number One
and be careful not to step in Number Two.
—Rodney Dangerfield

9. ***execrable* louse** ek'sik-rə-bəl Anyone execrable is revolting, detestable, utterly hated.
From Latin, *ex(s)ecrabil* = accursed.

You're a good reason why some animals eat their young.
—Jim Samuels

10. ***execrative* scuzzbag** ek-sik'rə-tiv An execrative person is either denouncing, or detestable and loathsome. From Latin, *exsecrat* = accursed.

EPITAPH:
Opened his big mouth once too often
Now he wordlessly waits in a wooden coffin

QUIZ 26

Match the definitions with the words on the left.

____ 1.	eructate	a.	affected and bombastic
____ 2.	esurient	b.	belch
____ 3.	ethnocentric	c.	demanding
____ 4.	euphuistic	d.	detestable (fits two words)
____ 5.	exacerbate	e.	hungry and/or greedy
____ 6.	exacting	f.	of or like excrement, feces
____ 7.	exasperate	g.	to think one's culture is superior
____ 8.	excrementitious		to all others
____ 9.	execrable	h.	to irritate, annoy
____ 10.	execrative	i.	to make worse, to irritate

GRISLY LIST 27

To be sure, Ellen was a **farouche** hermit, and a **fainéant** one at that; she
was lazy. But now, kneeling before the **exigent** king, she was accused of
being a witch. He blamed her for the **factious** unrest that swept the land and
the most **facinorous** plague the kingdom had ever seen. She knew her very
life hung in the balance. So Ellen began to **fabricate** a tale that would hold the
king spellbound. Her mother had been the greatest **fabulist** in the country,
and Ellen called upon her mother's lessons to help her in her time of need.
She started out small—this was not the time for **extraneous** blather—and

slowly her tale became more **farcical**. Finally the king and his court were enmeshed in her **fallacious** web, entranced like zombies. She smiled and snapped her fingers. The windows flew open and the plague rushed in like a dark cloud and took them all.

1. ***exigent* kingpin** ek'sə-jənt If something is exigent it requires immediate action; it is urgent or demanding. It can also mean something (or someone) that requires more than is reasonable. From Latin, *exigere* = to drive out.

> *He who demands, does not command.*
> *—Italian proverb*

2. ***extraneous* blathermouth** ik-strā'nē-əs Anything extraneous is not essential or is irrelevant. From Latin, *extraneus* = external, foreign.

> *But far more numerous was the herd of such*
> *who talk too little and who talk too much.*
> *—John Dryden*

3. ***fabricating* fink** fab'ri-kā-ting To fabricate is to make up stories. From Latin, *fabricatus* = to construct, build.

> *A half-truth is a whole lie.*
> *—Swedish proverb*

4. **far-fetched *fabulist*** fab'yoo-list A fabulist can be a storyteller (one who tells fables) or one who tells tall tales: a liar. From Latin, *fabula* = a story.

> *It is always the best policy to tell the truth,*
> *unless, of course, you are an exceptionally good liar.*
> *—Jerome K. Jerome*

5. ***facinorous* ilk** fə-sin'ə-rəs Anyone facinorous is enormously wicked. From Latin, *facinoros* = criminal.

> *It is easier to denature plutonium*
> *than to denature the evil spirit of man.*
> *—Albert Einstein*

6. ***factious* rabble-rouser** fak'shes To be factious is to stir up strife between unsuspecting clans. It's related to the word *faction*, a group working in a common cause against other groups. Don't confuse this word with *factitious*, which means something is not genuine or that something is fake. From Latin, *factio* = action, or mode of making.

> *There are fearful excitements on any side. Any side can accuse*
> *the other and feel virtuous without the hardships of virtue.*
> *—Christopher Fry*

7. ***fainéant* good-for-nothing** fā-nā-än' A fainéant person is one more lazy good-for-nothing. From French, *fait* = *nient* does nothing.

> *I like work; it fascinates me. I can sit and look at it for hours.*
> *—Jerome K. Jerome*

8. **_fallacious_ rubbish** fə-lā'shəs If something is fallacious it contains an error, or is misleading and deceptive, or perhaps delusive. From Latin, _fallacia_ = deception, artifice.

Truth is the safest lie.
—_Unknown_

9. **_farcical_ fibber** far'si-kəl If something is farcical it's like a farce: it is absurd, ludicrous. From Latin, _farcire_ = to stuff.

Everybody lies, but it doesn't matter because nobody listens.
—_Nick Diamos_

10. **_farouche_ gangrel** fä-rōōsh' To be farouche is to be shy. It can also mean fierce. It's French and literally means "neglected child." It is coupled with **gangrel** = a lanky beggar.

Men are bears with furniture.
—_Elaine Boosler_

QUIZ 27

Match the definitions with the words on the left.

____ 1.	exigent	a.	absurd, ludicrous
____ 2.	extraneous	b.	extremely wicked
____ 3.	fabricate	c.	lazy
____ 4.	fabulist	d.	misleading and deceptive
____ 5.	facinorous	e.	inessential or irrelevant
____ 6.	factious	f.	one who tells tall tales
____ 7.	faineant	g.	to make up stories
____ 8.	fallacious	h.	to stir up strife
____ 9.	farcical	i.	urgent or demanding
____ 10.	farouche	j.	wild

GRISLY LIST 28

"May I have your autograph?" the **feral** beggar asked.

She looked at him with **fastuous** astonishment. Here they were, her husband, the beggar, and she, stuck in an elevator, and he had the gall to ask for her autograph. But then, what if she said no? What kind of **felonious** creature was she dealing with? She took the picture from his sweaty, **febrile** hands, signed it, and gave it back. She then **fastidiously** wiped her hands.

"Thank you so much! You're much more beautiful in person."

The **fawning** combined with his **feculent** odor made her want to puke. She looked to her husband for help, but he was **fecklessly** punching the elevator buttons hoping something would click. Quickly, he began to **hyper-ventilate** and collapsed on the floor.

"I can't breathe! I can't breathe!"

The beggar grinned a **fatuous** smile and pulled a crowbar out of his jacket. Horrified, the starlet stared at his **fell** eyes.

"No problem," he sneered.

He jammed the crowbar between the doors and pried them open. They were only a foot above the second floor. He popped out and waved the **signed** photo.

"I can't wait till my buddies see this."

1. ***fastidious* prude** fa-stid′ē-əs Not easy to please and too refined, the fastidious person is easily disgusted. From Latin, *fastus* = disdain, contempt.

> *People who get shocked easily*
> *should be shocked a little more often.*
> —Mae West

2. ***fastuous* snoot** fas′chōō-əs To be fastuous is to look down on everyone with a haughty, scornful contempt. From Latin, *fastus* = scornful contempt.

> *With their snoots in the air, they would sniff and they'd snort,*
> *"We'll have nothing to do with the Plain-Belly sort!"*
> —Dr. Seuss, The Sneetches

3. ***fatuous* fool** fach′ōō-əs A fatuous person is not only stupid and oblivious, but also happy and contented to stay stupid. It comes from the Latin word, *fatuus* = foolish, silly (from which we also derive the word infatuation. Scary!).

> *Nothing in the world is more dangerous*
> *than sincere ignorance and conscientious stupidity.*
> —Martin Luther King, Jr.

4. ***fawning* social climber** fô′ning To fawn is to slavishly flatter. From Medieval English, *fawnen* = to rejoice; and later, to welcome, flatter.

> *A flatterer is a friend who is your inferior, or pretends to be so.*
> —Aristotle

5. ***febrile* fanatic** feb′rəl One who is febrile is feverish. From Latin, *febris* = fever.

> *Fanatic: the false fire of an overheated mind.*
> —William Cowper

6. ***feckless* weakling** fek′lis A feckless person is either too ineffective or negligent to succeed. From Medieval English, Scottish, *fek* = effect + -less.

> *He that is good for making excuses,*
> *is seldom good for anything else.*
> —Benjamin Franklin

7. ***feculent* spectacle** fek′yə-lənt Gross! Anything feculent is filthy, foul, and has the nature of feces. From Latin, *faex* = dregs, lees.

> *There is no odor so bad as that which arises from goodness tainted.*
> —Henry David Thoreau

8. ***fell* miscreation** fel Anyone who is fell is cruel and horrifying, with an ominous potential for killing and destruction. From Old French, *felon* = wicked.

> *There was a laughing devil in his sneer*
> *which raised emotions both of rage and fear;*
> *and where his frown of hatred darkly fell,*
> *hope withering fled, and mercy sighted farewell.*
> —George Gordon, Lord Byron

9. ***felonious* prowler** fə-lō′nē-əs One who is felonious is wicked and criminal. From Latin, *fello* = treacherous.

> *Fear the boisterous savage of passion less*
> *than the sedately grinning villain.*
> —John Casper Lavater

10. ***feral* feline** fer′əl To be feral is to be wild. If you like your cats wild, you can't get any wilder. From Latin, *fera* = wild beast.

> *When a woman really loves a man,*
> *he can make her do anything she wants to.*
> —Anonymous

QUIZ 28

Match the definitions with the words on the left.

____ 1.	fastidious	a.	cruel and horrifying
____ 2.	fastuous	b.	contented to stay stupid
____ 3.	fatuous	c.	feverish
____ 4.	fawn	d.	scornfully contemptuous
____ 5.	febrile	e.	having the nature of feces
____ 6.	feckless	f.	ineffective and irresponsible
____ 7.	feculent	g.	hard to please; refined
____ 8.	fell	h.	to slavishly flatter
____ 9.	felonious	i.	wicked and criminal
____ 10.	feral	j.	wild

GRISLY LIST 29

Something had to give. The tension had begun to **fester** between Betty and her roommate from day one. First, the room had a **fetid** smell that permeated everything. Second, her roommate would **flaunt** her silicone anytime Betty brought a man over and then **fleer** at Betty when the guys would gawk. Furthermore, though Angelica denied it, Betty was certain she was **filching** from her purse.

"She is such a **flagrant** liar." Betty thought. And last but not least, Angelica's **fistic** boyfriend was so **flatulent** that you could hook him to the gas line and solve the energy crisis.

"What **flagitious** thing can I cook up?" Betty pondered. It was then that Betty saw the letter, lost and forgotten in the middle of the garbage on the floor. With a **fey** gleam in her eyes, she opened her roommate's mail.

"A warrant? My poor, poor roommate."

1. ***festering* rot** fes′tə-ring Anything festering is filled with pus or bitterness. From Latin, *festula* = ulcer.

> *The best things, corrupted, become the worst.*
> —*Latin proverb*

2. ***fetid* pile of dung** fet′id Anyone or anything fetid smells rank from decay. From Latin, *foetere* = to stink.

> *Every man loves the smell of his own farts.*
> —*Graffiti on a cave wall in Ancient Greece*

3. ***fey* aberration** fā One in a fey mood is extremely excited and perhaps unusually or neurotically so. It was once thought extreme excitement might foreshadow impending death and fey meant doomed or fated to die. From Icelandic, *feigr* = doomed.

> *How oft when men are at the point of death have they been merry,*
> *which their keepers call a lightening before death.*
> —*Shakespeare*

4. ***filching* scavenger** fil′ching To filch is to steal; hence, a filching person is given to stealing. From Medieval English, *filchen* = to attack, take as plunder.

> *Every rascal is not a thief, but every thief is a rascal.*
> —*Aristotle*

5. ***fistic* slugger** fis′tik One who is fistic likes to box and/or fight. From Old High German, *fust* = fist + -ic.

> *I was shadow boxing the other day,*
> *figured I was ready for Cassius Clay.*
> —*Bob Dylan*

6. *flagitious* **felon** flə-jish'əs A flagitious person is shamefully wicked. From Latin, *flagiti* = shame, scandal.

> His lack of education is more than compensated for
> by his keenly developed moral bankruptcy.
> —Woody Allen

7. *flagrant* **faker** flā'grənt Anything flagrant is glaringly obvious or inexcusably bad. From Latin, *flagrans* = burning.

> The nail that sticks up gets hammered down.
> —Japanese proverb

8. *flatulent* **spastic** flach'ə-lənt One who is flatulent farts. You can also use flatulent to describe one who is full of self-importance. From Latin, *flare* = to blow.

> EPITAPH:
> He finally met his doom
> When his last fart went boom

9. *flaunty* **flirt** flôn'tē One who is flaunty is showy, vain, gaudy. From Norwegian, *flanta* = to gad about.

> She wore a low but futile décolletage.
> —Dorothy Parker

10. *fleering* **glitterati** flî ring To fleer is to laugh or smile contemptuously. From Norwegian, *flire* = to snicker, laugh.

> Men more gladly recall what they deride than what they esteem.
> —Horace

QUIZ 29

Match the definitions with the words on the left.

____ 1. festering	a. extremely excited
____ 2. fetid	b. farting
____ 3. fey	c. filled with pus or bitterness
____ 4. filch	d. glaringly obvious; inexcusably bad
____ 5. fistic	e. laugh derisively
____ 6. flagitious	f. likes to box and/or fight
____ 7. flagrant	g. shamefully wicked
____ 8. flatulent	h. showy, vain, gaudy, or flashy
____ 9. flaunty	i. steal
____ 10. fleer	j. stinking

GRISLY LIST 30

"You don't have to be so **flippant** about it," Dorothy said as she put her lipstick on. "If you want to go out with my ex, go out with my ex."

"I wasn't being flippant. I just thought you should know," Kimberly **flippantly** said as she **flounced** her hair.

"Whatever. He was too **fractious** for me. I had to kick him out."

"That's not how he tells it. He said you were constantly **fobbing** people's stuff and **fomenting** trouble with his family. He said he couldn't be a cop and stay with someone who **flouted** all the traffic laws."

"He would say that. Has he tried his fixation with you yet?"

"What?"

"It's really **foul.** I wanted to puke. That's what really ended it."

"What are you talking about?"

"You'll find out." Dorothy shook her head as she strutted out the door.

Kimberly looked **flummoxed** as she **floundered frenetically** through her purse.

"Where are my keys?"

1. *flippant* **old biddy** flip'ənt To be flippant is to talk inappropriately, with a lack of seriousness about a serious topic. From Icelandic, *fleipa* = to babble.

> *When the snake is old, the frog will tease him.*
> —Persian proverb

2. *flouncing* **fop** floun'sing To flounce is to move the body with quick, flinging motions in anger or impatience. From Scandinavian, *flunsa* = to hurry. It is coupled with **fop** = a vain, affected male who pays a lot of attention to his clothes, appearance, and so on.

> *A tart temper never mellows with age.*
> —Washington Irving

3. *floundering* **butterfingers** floun'də-ring To flounder is to move, speak, or act in an awkward and confused way. The origin of this word is unknown. It may be a blend of flounce and founder.

> *A drowning man takes hold of his own hair.*
> —Greek proverb

4. *flouting* **trespasser** flou'ting To flout is to mock, jeer, and show contempt. From Medieval English, *flouten* = to play the flute; hence, to whistle at.

> *When the mouse laughs at the cat, there is a hole nearby.*
> —Nigerian proverb

5. *flummoxed* **space cadet** flum'əkst A flummoxed person is bewildered and confused. The origin of this word is unknown.

> *I had a terrible education.*
> *I attended a school for emotionally disturbed teachers.*
> —Woody Allen

6. **fobbing thief** fob'ing A fobbing person steals something and replaces it with an inferior item. From Medieval English, *fobben* = to cheat.

> *The faults of a burglar are the qualities of a financier.*
> —George Bernard Shaw

7. **fomenting hell-raiser** fō-men'ting To foment is to stir up trouble. From Latin, *fomentum* = a warm application.

> *Thinkers prepare for revolution; bandits carry it out.*
> —Mariano Azuela, The Flies

8. **foul piece of filth** foul A foul person or thing is offensive to your senses—dirty, ugly, smelly—or to your morals: mean, obscene, and/or dishonorable. Foul can also refer to wet and stormy weather. From Greek, *faul* = rotten, lazy.

> *You are not worth the dust, which the rude wind blows in your face.*
> —Shakespeare, King Lear

9. **fractious activist** frak'shas To be fractious is to be rebellious or difficult to control. This word shares the same etymology as fraction. From Latin, *frangere* = to break.

> *No one can go on being a rebel too long*
> *without turning into an autocrat.*
> —Lawrence Durrell

10. **frenetic alarmist** frə-net'ik To be frenetic is to be frantic, feverishly moving about. From Greek, *phrenitis* = a brain disease.

> *The bow too tensely strung is easily broken.*
> —Publilius Syrus

QUIZ 30

Match the definitions with the words on the left.

_____ 1. flippant
_____ 2. flounce
_____ 3. flounder
_____ 4. flout
_____ 5. flummoxed
_____ 6. fob
_____ 7. foment
_____ 8. foul
_____ 9. fractious
_____ 10. frenetic

a. confused and bewildered
b. difficult to control
c. disrespectful or inappropriate in speech
d. frantic, moving excitedly
e. mock, jeer, show contempt
f. move the body with quick flinging motions in anger
g. offensive, mean, and obscene
h. replace an inferior item for what one steals
i. stir up trouble
j. to move, speak, or act in a awkward and confused way

REVIEW 6

MATCH EACH QUOTE WITH THE APPROPRIATE WORD.

1. You gotta say this for the white race: its self-confidence knows no bounds. Who else could go to a small island in the south Pacific where there's no poverty, no crime, no unemployment, no war and no worry, and call it a "primitive society"?
—*Dick Gregory*

2. Where speech is corrupted, the mind is also.
—*Seneca*

3. When the state is weak, the army rules.
—*Napoleon Bonaparte*

4. White lies are but the ushers to black ones.
—*Frederick Marryat*

____ a. fabulist   ____ c. execrative
____ b. ethnocentric   ____ d. fractious

5. Put a knife to thy throat if thou be a man given to appetite.
—*Proverbs 23:2*

6. The most contemptible are the most contemptuous.
—*Henry Fielding*

7. Flatterers are the worst kind of enemy.
—*Tacitus*

8. Affectation is a greater enemy to the face than the smallpox.
—*St. Evermond*

9. A fool takes a bath and forgets to wash his face.
—*Yiddish proverb*

____ e. foppish   ____ h. fastuous
____ f. fawn   ____ i. fatuous
____ g. esurient

10. Why babble about brutality and be indignant about tortures? The masses want that. They need something that will give them a thrill of horror.
—*Adolf Hitler*

11. With all his tumid boasts, he's like the swordfish, who only wears his weapon in his mouth.
—*Samuel Madden*

12. What luck for rulers that men do not think.
—*Adolf Hitler*

13. A cat pent up becomes a lion.
—*Italian proverb*

14. When women kiss, it always reminds one of prizefighters shaking hands.
—*H. L. Mencken*

____ j. fistic

____ k. euphuistic

____ l. biddable

____ m. flagitious

____ n. feral

Chapter 7

*The tongue is but three inches long,
yet it can kill a man six feet high.*
—Japanese proverb

I COULD HAVE USED A QUOTE FOR EVERY WORD IN THE BOOK, but I felt it was important that you also imagine what some characters might say. So I've included the "Likely comment" and "Your response" occasionally throughout the book. I wouldn't dismiss these too quickly. If you can picture what a person might say, you'll get a stronger image of them in your mind. If there is a word that you continually miss, even if I haven't mentioned what the "Likely comment" might be, try to imagine your own.

Consider what the person you're thinking about might say, or do, or eat. What might we say about them on their tombstone? If you're having trouble remembering some of the words, take the time to write down what you think their profession might be, or their favorite sandwich. It is just one more creative way to remember vocabulary words by putting them to use.

GRISLY LIST 31

José **fretfully** wrung his hands and looked around at the long line that circled the building, only to see the **frowzy** woman behind him glare back at him. Behind her it seemed as if every applicant's eyes bore into his with **froward** hatred. He gave a weak smile and then a **furtive** glance at the **frothy** babe powdering her nose in the line next to him. She didn't notice. The **funereal functionary** who sat in his chair before José ruffled the papers on his desk and bellowed in a **fustian** manner:

"I hope you are cognizant of the import of filling out these documents with the appropriate data in keeping with the specified directives we have furnished you with in the pamphlet. Any variation will be seen as perjury in which case you will be **fustigated** to the full extent of the law."

José paused, and then sheepishly replied, "No hablo inglés."

1. *fretful* **worrywart** fret'fəl A fretful person worries too much. From Old English, *fretan* = to eat up, consume.

   > How much pain has cost us the evils, which have never happened.
   > —*Thomas Jefferson*

2. *frothy* **Pollyanna** frô'thē Frothy literally means foamy, light, or worthless. From Indo-European, *preuth* = slavering, snorting.

   > Errors, like straws, upon the surface flow,
   > He who would search for pearls must dive below.
   > —*John Dryden*

3. *froward* **femme fatale** frō′wərd Anyone froward is not easily controlled. From Old Norse, *fram* = forward. It is coupled with **femme fatale** = an irresistibly attractive woman who leads men into dangerous situations.

Favorite motto:
Men are just desserts.

4. *frowzy* **heifer** frou′zē Anyone who is frowzy is shabby, knee-deep in stink and dirt. From Early Modern English, around 1500, *frowy* = rank-smelling.

She had a wart on the left side of her chin,
with one long black hair growing out of it.
When she sneezed, it cracked like a whip;
and if she caught cold, she flogged her cheek raw.
—*Pinky Thompson*

5. *fulsome* **drama queen** fŏŏl′səm Anything fulsome is disgustingly excessive. From Medieval English, *fulsom* = disgustingly excessive. This word may be a blend of meaning of full and foul + -some.

In everything the middle course is best; all things in excess bring trouble.
—*Plautus*

6. **brain-dead** *functionary* fungk′shə-ner-ē A functionary is one more cog in the wheel, a bureaucrat; this stagnating official knows the tyranny of red tape. From Latin, *functio* = to perform.

The only thing that saves us from the bureaucracy is its inefficiency.
— *Eugene McCarthy*

7. *funereal* **spoilsport** fyŏŏ-nîr′ē-əl Always dark and gloomy, a funereal person is like a funeral. From Latin, *funus* = a funeral.

I was going to buy a copy of The Power of Positive Thinking,
and then I thought: What the hell good would that do?
—*Ronnie Shakes*

8. *furtive* **culprit** fûr′tiv A furtive person is secretive and goes about in a sneaky, sly way. From Latin, *frutum* = theft.

Let wickedness escape as it may at the bar,
it never fails of doing justice upon itself;
for every guilty person is his own hangman.
—*Seneca*

9. *fustian* **fuddy-duddy** fus′chən Fustian is a stout cotton fabric, but it may also be one who is bombastic and pompous. This bore hasn't realized he only has an audience of one—himself. No one else is listening.

When there's a wind, garbage flies high.
—*Jewish proverb*

10. **fustigating hellcat** fus'ti-gā-ting To fustigate is to punish, beat, or criticize severely. From Latin, *fustigatus* = to cudgel to death (a cudgel is a short, thick stick used as a weapon).

> *I've got a good mind to join a club and beat you over the head with it.*
> —Groucho Marx

QUIZ 31

Match the definitions with the words on the left.

____ 1.	fretful	a.	a bureaucrat, a cog in the wheel
____ 2.	frothy	b.	bombastic and pompous
____ 3.	froward	c.	dark and gloomy
____ 4.	frowzy	d.	disgustingly excessive
____ 5.	fulsome	e.	foamy, light, or worthless
____ 6.	functionary	f.	not easily controlled
____ 7.	funereal	g.	done in a sneaky, sly way
____ 8.	furtive	h.	stinky and dirty
____ 9.	fustian	i.	beat severely; criticize harshly
____ 10.	fustigate	j.	worried

GRISLY LIST 32

"Check it out! Check it out!" the **garish** woman held out her left hand with **gasconading** pride as the **garrulous gadabouts** surrounded her with squeals of excitement at the size of the stone on her finger.

"Oh my God! You could park a tank on it," one giggled.

"Well, what's he like?" another asked with jealous curiosity.

"Well, he's not my usual type," The **gaudy** woman complained, "He's kind of **fusty** and **gangly** and he **garbles** his sentences so I can barely understand him. And his snore is so **galling** it could wake the dead."

Her friends' **gabbling** suddenly came to a halt until their partner in crime shrieked:

"But get this: he's eighty-nine!!"

1. **fusty gammer** fus'tē Anyone fusty is stale and/or old-fashioned. From Old French, *fust* = a wine cask > Early Modern English, *fust* = a musty smell.

> *If you want to avoid old age, hang yourself in youth.*
> —Yiddish proverb

2. **gabbling goon** gab'ling To gabble is to speak rapidly and meaninglessly. The root, gab, means to chatter. From Medieval English, *gabbe*.

> *Much chatter, little wit.*
> —Portuguese proverb

3. **restless *gadabout*** gad'ə-bout To gad is to move aimlessly and restlessly about, especially looking for gossip; hence, the noun gadabout came from the verb phrase *gad about* and describes one who flits about looking for pleasure or gossip. From Late Middle English, *gad* = to hurry.

> *Whomever gossips to you will gossip about you.*
> *—Spanish proverb*

4. ***galling* paparazzi** gô'ling Gall means something is bitter or severe, bitter in spirit, or rudely bold. One could say "The unmitigated gall of that gasconading goofball." Galling, however, primarily means something is irritating or exasperating. From Old English, *gealle* = a blister.

> *I like long walks,*
> *especially when they are taken by people who annoy me.*
> *—Fred Allen*

5. ***gangly* scrounger** gang'glē Anyone who is gangly is thin, tall, and awkward. This word is a possible derivation of *gangrel* = a lanky beggar.

> *We tolerate shapes in human beings*
> *that would horrify us if we saw them on a horse.*
> *—W. R. Inge*

6. ***garbling* wino** gär'bling To garble is to distort, confuse, or mix up part of a story . From Italian, *garbellare* = to sift.

> *Unintelligible language is a lantern without a light.*
> *—Samuel Johnson*

7. ***garish* goofball** gâr'ish Anyone garish is showy and/or wears bright makeup and attention-grabbing clothes. From Medieval English, *gauren* = to stare.

> *All human beings have gray little souls,*
> *and they all want to rouge them up.*
> *—Maxim Gorky*

8. ***garrulous* mall rat** gar'ə-ləs Anyone who is garrulous is excessively talkative about insignificant matters. From Latin, *garrire* = to chatter.

> *A gossip tells everybody not to tell anybody.*
> *—Unknown*

9. ***gasconading* bag of hot air** gas'kə-nā-ding To gasconade is to brag in a blustering manner. The blokes of Gascony, France, were reputed to be boastful and blustering, hence the origin of the word.

> *Little dogs make the most noise.*
> *—Maori proverb*

10. ***gaudy* spinster** gô'dē To be gaudy is to lack good taste. Gaudy comes from an obsolete English word, *gaud*, which was a cheap, showy trinket.

> *You'd be surprised how much it costs to look this cheap.*
> *— Dolly Parton*

Match the definitions with the words on the left.

___ 1.	fusty	a.	bitter or severe; rude boldness
___ 2.	gabbling	b.	excessively talkative about
___ 3.	gadabout		unimportant matters
___ 4.	gall	c.	one looking for gossip
___ 5.	gangly	d.	stale and/or old-fashioned
___ 6.	garble	e.	thin, tall, and awkward
___ 7.	garish	f.	to brag in a blustering manner
___ 8.	garrulous	g.	to chatter meaninglessly
___ 9.	gasconade	h.	to distort part of a story
___ 10.	gaudy	i.	showy (fits two words)

GRISLY LIST 33

The leader raised his arms above his head with **grandiose** flair.
"My people: What you give is what you get."
His **gormless** followers cheered. They loved this kind of **gibberish**.
He dropped his hands and **glowered** at their **gawking** faces.
"And when you give little, you get little."
A **gnathonic** worshiper, his **gaunt** face pleading, fell prostrate before him.
"And when you give nothing, you get nothing." The leader **grizzled** as the convention grew quiet, but then he began to jump up and down, his big belly bouncing with him and revealing his **gluttonous** nature. He shook his hand and **grandiloquently** shouted:
"But when you give plenty, you get plenty."
The crowd went wild. The higher the leader jumped, the wilder the crowd wailed until, quite by accident, the leader jumped off the stage.
And when he fell, he fell hard.

1. **gaunt** waif gônt A gaunt person is thin and bony. From Latin, *galbinus* = greenish-yellow.

> He looked like Death taken seasick.
> —Algernon Swinburne

2. **gawkish** peabrain gôk'ish To gawk is to stare with your eyes bugged out in an idiotic way. From a dialect of English, *gowk* = an idiot.

> When a finger points at the moon,
> the imbecile looks at the finger.
> —Chinese proverb

3. **_gibbering_ knucklehead** jib'ə-ring To gibber is to chatter, to speak a nonsensical language. The noun derivative is gibberish. The origin is uncertain but the word is imitative of nonsense.

While swimming he yelled, "Help!"
But we thought he said, "Kelp!"

4. **_glowering_ intimidator** glou'ə-ring To glower is to stare sullenly, scowl, or glare menacingly. From Middle Low German, *gluren* = to leer.

His eye, once so kindly, could have been grafted on
to the head of a man-eating shark and no questions asked.
—*P. G. Wodehouse*

5. **_gluttonous_ blob** glut'n-əs To be gluttonous is to eat to excessive proportions. From Latin, *gluttire* = to devour.

The glutton digs his grave with his teeth.
—*English proverb*

6. **_gnathonic_ underling** nā-thon'ik A gnathonic person is fawning and flattering. The word is taken from the character Gnatho in Terence's play *Eunuchus* (159 B.C.) who was notorious for being a sycophant.

An underling all of his life
Croaked when he saw
His boss with his wife

7. **_gormless_ zombie** gôrm'lis Also spelled *gaumless*. Anyone gormless is slow-witted and senseless. From Gothic, *gaumjan* = to heed, to notice + -less.

Puppets, who, though on idiotism's dark brink,
because they've heads, dare fancy they can think?
—*John Wolcott*

8. **_grandiloquent_ sweet talker** gran-dil'ə-kwənt A grandiloquent person is pompous and bombastic. From Latin, *grandis* = great + *loqui* = to speak.

He can compress the most words
into the smallest idea of any man I ever met.
—*Abraham Lincoln*

9. **_grandiose_ grandstander** gran'dē-ōs Anyone grandiose is either impressive or tries to seem impressive. From Latin, *grandis* = great.

My right elbow has a fascination that few can resist.
—*W. S. Gilbert*, The Mikado

10. **grizzling galoot** griz'ling To grizzle is to complain, grumble, or mutter. Chiefly British, the word is derived from Middle High German, *grisgramen* = to gnash one's teeth.

The dogs bark but the caravan moves on.
—*Arabic proverb*

QUIZ 33

Match the definitions with the words on the left.

_____ 1. gaunt   a. complaining, grumbling
_____ 2. gawk   b. eating excessively
_____ 3. gibber   c. fawning and flattering
_____ 4. glower   d. impressive
_____ 5. gluttonous   e. pompous and bombastic
_____ 6. gnathonic   f. scowl
_____ 7. gormless   g. slow-witted and senseless
_____ 8. grandiloquent   h. speak nonsensically
_____ 9. grandiose   i. stare with the mouth open
_____ 10. grizzling   j. thin and bony

GRISLY LIST 34

"What to do? What to do?" Willard **groused** as he plummeted through the air, feeling like a **hapless** nincompoop. "It's not every day you pull your ripcord only to watch your laundry disappear above you," he mused.

He'd been so **gullible** taking the parachute from his wife! That **gulositous**, **guileful** wench! He'd been **gruff** with her because she didn't **grovel**, but this? How could she? Soon, he'd be food for the **grubs**, a **grotesque** mess that others would have to pick up with a shovel. Should he try to leave a note? He could see the **hackneyed** phrase scrawled illegibly on some paper, "My wife did it!" Would anyone find it? Not likely. Suddenly the answer dawned on him. He had his cell phone!

1. **grotesque mess** grō-tesk' Grotesque describes anything bizarre, ludicrously absurd, or ugly. The word literally means a picture in a cave (grotto) and is taken from the Roman cave paintings, in which people and animals were bizarrely depicted with plant life.

Beauty is only skin deep, but ugly goes clear to the bone.
—*Unknown*

2. **grousing yahoo** grou'zing Grousing means nagging or complaining. From Middle French, *groucier* = to growl.

Had we not faults of our own,
we should take less pleasure in complaining of others.
—*Francis Fenelon*

3. **groveling** bootlicker gruv′ə-ling To grovel is to cower in a prostrate position. From Middle English, *grufelinge* = on one's face, prone.

> *Those who are surly and imperious to their inferiors*
> *are generally humble, flattering, and cringing to their superiors.*
> —*Thomas Fuller*

4. **grubby** little stinker grub′bē Anything (or anyone) grubby is infested with grubs (small larvae of an insect), or dirty, or simply inferior. From Medieval English, *grubben* = to dig.

> *You look like the second week of the garbage strike.*
> —*Neil Simon*

5. **gruff** old bag of bones gruf To be gruff is to speak or act roughly. From German, *grob* = rough, uncouth.

> EPITAPH:
> *If you can read this, you're too close;*
> *get off my grave, idiot!*
> —*Glen Super*

6. **guileful** hustler gīl′fəl To be guileful is to be clever at deceit and full of trickery. From Old English, *wigle* – witchcraft.

> *It is morally wrong to allow suckers to keep their money.*
> —*"Canada Bill" Jones*

7. **gullible** greenhorn gul′ə-bəl A gullible person is easily cheated—too trusting or naïve. From Middle English, *golle* = silly fellow, literally, an unfledged bird + -able.

> *The more crap you believe, the better off you are.*
> —*Charles Bukowski*

8. **gulositous** gobbler gyoo-lō′si-təs A greedy glutton, this is someone who wants and wants! From Late Latin, *gulosus* = gluttonous > *gula* = throat.

> *For their love lies in their purses,*
> *and whoso empties them by so much*
> *fills their hearts with deadly hate.*
> —*William Shakespeare*, Richard II

9. **hackneyed** writer hak′nēd A hackney is a horse used for ordinary travel, or the carriage for such travel; in other words, a drudge. That's where we get the word hack, a literary drudge. Anything hackneyed is so trite, so clichéd, that it is annoying. From Middle English, *hakene* < Hackney = an English village.

> *When in doubt, have two guys come through the door with guns.*
> —*Raymond Chandler*

10. **hapless** nincompoop hap′lis Anyone hapless is without luck. From Old English, *haeppen* = to go by chance + -less.

> *My father gave me a bat for Christmas.*
> *The first time I tried to play with it, it flew away.*
> —*Rodney Dangerfield*

Match the definitions with the words on the left.

____ 1. grotesque		a.	bizarre, ludicrously absurd
____ 2. grouse		b.	clichéd
____ 3. grovel		c.	cower in a prostrate position
____ 4. grubby		d.	full of trickery
____ 5. gruff		e.	greedy, gluttonous
____ 6. guileful		f.	infested with grubs; dirty
____ 7. gullible		g.	nag, complain
____ 8. gulositous		h.	rough in manner and/or speech
____ 9. hackneyed		i.	too trusting or naïve
____ 10. hapless		j.	without luck

GRISLY LIST 35

"One more **hebetating** day at work," Josie grumbled as she plopped herself at her desk. She hated work, hated it with such a passion, but she kept her cool.

Her supervisor sauntered by with his usual **hircine** banter. "How's it hanging?"

She pretended to laugh. "I'm just one little part of the **hoi polloi** that keeps this village running."

"Hey, no using **highfalutin** words I don't know."

"That could be difficult. Get a dictionary."

Josie's **iconoclastic** worldview was that women should live on Venus and men shouldn't live anywhere.

Like clockwork came his habitual **hubristic** remark. "I would have aimed better. Want me to teach you how?"

"Who in their right mind would want such a **horripilating** experience with someone so **ignoble** as you?"

"There you go with the big words again. How about you and me paint the town red tonight?"

"I go for the **homicidal** type. You're just too nice for me."

"Suit yourself," he fumed, waving his arms with **histrionic** bluster, "but I just might have to get myself another secretary."

"Will she be able to type?"

He shrugged and wandered off.

Josie opened her desk to check the tape recorder. "It's working," she mused. "A few more days of this and my lawyer will buy me an island."

1. **hebetating hick** heb'i-tā-ting One who is hebetating is becoming more stupid or dull by the minute. From Latin, *hebeture* = to make dull.

   Likely comment:
   What Einstein meant to say was, uh, what he meant to, uh, I forgot what I was, uh, me forget, duh, oof. Arf! Arf! (a little over the top)
   Your response:
   Here boy, fetch the stick.

2. **highfalutin garbage** hī-fə-loōt'n Highfalutin comes from an altered form of "high-floating" and is a humorous way to say something is pompous or pretentious.

   I read what the gossip columnists are saying
   about me and I think: This is a
   lot more interesting than my life.
   —Bono, lead singer of U2

3. **hircine gigolo** hûr'sīn One who is hircine behaves like a goat; thus, it can be interpreted as lustful (horny). From Latin, *hircus* = goat.

   Men are creatures with two legs and eight hands.
   —Jayne Mansfield

4. **histrionic ham** his-trē-on'ik A histrionic person overacts with buffoonish hilarity, using gesticulating gyrations. From Latin, *histro* = actor.

   One more drink and I'll be under the host.
   —Dorothy Parker

5. **hopeless *hoi polloi*** hoi pə-loi' Hoi polloi in Greek means "the many." It has become a term of contempt synonymous with the masses, the lower class, the common ruck, the great unwashed, etc.

   The nose of the mob is its imagination.
   By this, at any time, it can be quietly led.
   —Edgar Allan Poe

6. **homicidal maniac** hom-i-sīd'l Murder, anyone? A homicidal person wants to kill someone. From Latin, *homo* = man + *caedere* = to cut, kill.

   If once a man indulges himself in murder,
   very soon he comes to think little of robbing;
   and from robbing he comes next to drinking and Sabbath-breaking,
   and from that to incivility and procrastination.
   —Thomas De Quincey

7. **horripilating creature** hô-rip'ə-lā-ting Anything horripilating makes your hairs stand up from fear or disgust. From Latin, *horripilare* = to bristle with hairs.

   There is no terror in the bang, only in the anticipation of it.
   —Alfred Hitchcock

8. **hubristic egotist** hyōō-bris'tik Hubris is excessive pride. The ancient Greeks felt this was a great character flaw that would ultimately lead to one's downfall. The adjective, hubristic, can be used to characterize anyone filled with excessive pride.

> *Egotism is the anesthetic that dulls the pain of stupidity.*
> —*Frank Leahy*

9. **iconoclastic radical** ī-kon-ə-klas'tik Anyone iconoclastic attacks traditional beliefs and values. In the eighth-century Greek Orthodox Church, an iconoclast was a member of a faction that believed in the elimination of icons. From Late Greek, *eikon* = an image + *klaein* = to break.

> *Every revolution evaporates*
> *and leaves behind only the slime of a new bureaucracy.*
> —*Franz Kafka*

10. **ignoble rat fink** ig-nō'bəl The formal definition of ignoble is anything not belonging to nobility, but in contemporary usage it denotes one who has no honor. From Latin, *ignobilis* = not noble.

> *He has every attribute of a dog except loyalty.*
> —*Thomas P. Gore*

QUIZ 35

Match the definitions with the words on the left.

____ 1. hebetate	a.	attacking traditional beliefs
____ 2. highfalutin	b.	become more stupid or dull
____ 3. hircine	c.	filled with excessive pride
____ 4. histrionic	d.	like a goat; horny
____ 5. hoi polloi	e.	making your hairs stand up from fear or disgust
____ 6. homicidal	f.	murderous
____ 7. horripilating	g.	pompous, bombastic
____ 8. hubristic	h.	the masses, the lower class
____ 9. iconoclastic	i.	using gesticulating gyrations
____ 10. ignoble	j.	without honor

REVIEW 7

MATCH EACH QUOTE WITH THE APPROPRIATE WORD.

1. Uneasy lies the head that wears the crown.
  —*Shakespeare*

2. Only the shallow know themselves.
  —*Oscar Wilde*

3. Poor fellow, he suffers from files.
  —*Aneurin Bevan*

4. They never taste who always drink
They always talk who never think.
  —*Matthew Prior*

____ a. functionary   ____ c. garrulous
____ b. frothy   ____ d. fretful

5. Their kitchen is their shrine, the cook their priest, the table their altar, and their belly their God.
  —Charles Buck

6. The surest way of making a dupe is to let your victim think you are his.
  —Edward Bulwer

7. One is easily fooled by that which one loves.
  —Molière, *Tartuffe*

8. Men are women's playthings.
  —Victor Hugo

____ e. guileful   ____ g. gullible
____ f. gluttonous   ____ h. femme fatale

9. If an unlucky man were to sell shrouds, people would stop dying.
  —*Arab proverb*

10. Papa loved Mamma
Mamma loved men
Mamma's in the graveyard
Papa's in the pen.
  —*Carl Sandburg*

11. It is hard to fight against impulsive desire; whatever it wants it will buy at the cost of the soul.
—*Heraclitus*

12. I've got to take under my wing, tra la
A most unattractive thing, tra la
With a caricature of a face.
—*W. S. Gilbert*

____ i. grotesque   ____ k. homicidal
____ j. hapless   ____ l. gulositous

Chapter 8

Words are like money;
there is nothing so useless,
unless when in actual use.
—*Samuel Butler*

HAVE YOU EVER THOUGHT ABOUT WHEN YOU
STUDY? Most people see studying as some kind of intellectual
marathon, but very little learning takes place when you are spending
hours and hours of time poring over a book. It's much more important
to spend fifteen minutes studying and then take a break. Fifteen minutes here, another fifteen there—it all adds up. And, in the end, you'll
retain more of the information.

Furthermore, *where* you study may be just as important as *when* you
study. If you have a book in your hand, why lock yourself up in a library? You can take a book with you anywhere: a park, the beach, or the
mountains. Make your study time part of your recreation and your
recreation part of your study time.

GRISLY LIST 36

"Blow them all to hell," David **imperiously** shouted. The **imbruted** chess
club president scowled when he saw the two cheerleaders in the room. His
teammate Gilbert snorted.

"But we were planning on using this room to practice," Shannon ob-
jected.

"A little **impetuous** of you to plan on using this room when others had already signed up for it, isn't it?" the **impenitent** president answered as he
practiced his golf swing.

"But there's only two of you and you're not even playing chess!"

"That hardly matters, my little **ignoramus**. Our names are on the sign-up
sheet and yours are not. I'm afraid you've been **ignominiously** beaten. Now
get thee to a nunnery, take your pompoms with you, and never darken my
door again," David **imperialistically** blustered.

Shannon stood in the doorway and stared at the names on the chess club
roster. To the side was a poster with David and Gilbert's picture on it that
read: "Join the chess club. We are too **impecunious** to require dues. Only
geeks need apply."

Shannon quickly scribbled the names of her cheerleaders on the roster
and then slammed it down **impertinently** in front of the president.

"Checkmate."

1. ***ignominious* disgrace** ig-nə-min′ē-əs Shame! Anything ignominious implies an utter
loss of self-respect rendering someone a complete disgrace. From Latin, *ignominia* =
without a name.

> *Under this flabby exterior is an enormous lack of character.*
> —Oscar Levant

2. **clumsy *ignoramus*** ig-nə-rā′məs Ignoramus is a fancy way to call someone stupid. From New Latin, ignoramus means "we take no notice" and was used in the 1500s when a grand jury felt that there was insufficient evidence to proceed. In 1615, George Ruggle's play *Ignoramus* lampooned a lawyer by that name and gave the word the connotation of being stupid.

> *To be ignorant of one's ignorance is the malady of ignorance.*
> —*A. B. Alcott*

3. ***imbruted* beast** im-brōō′tid An imbruted lout is one who has sunk to the level of a brute, a beast. From Latin, *im* = into + *brutus* = stupid.

> *I never met a man I didn't want to fight.*
> —*Lyle Alzado*

4. ***impish* little cootie** imp′ish An imp is a young demon or a mischievous child not un-like a scampish squirt or a puckish pain in the neck. From Greek, *empyta* = offspring, a shoot of a plant.

> *Favorite motto:*
> *Have joy buzzer—will travel.*

5. ***impecunious* beggar** im-pi-kyōō′nē-əs Anyone impecunious is without money. From French, *impecunieux* = without wealth.

> *If a poor man asks for alms and you have nothing to give,*
> *console him with words, for it is forbidden to chastise a poor man,*
> *or raise your voice against him, since his heart is broken.*
> —*Maimonides*

6. ***impenitent* scofflaw** im-pen′i-tənt Anyone impenitent is without shame, regret, or remorse. From Latin, *impaenitens* = not repentant. It is coupled with **scofflaw** = a ha-bitual offender of the law.

> *Since I wronged you, I have never liked you.*
> —*Spanish proverb*

7. ***imperialistic* hawk** im-pîr-ē-ə-lis′tik An imperialist government is prone to dominate the political and/or economic affairs of weaker governments. From Latin, *imperare* = to command.

> *In the eyes of empire-builders men are not men, but instruments.*
> —*Napoleon I*

8. ***imperious* backbreaker** im-pîr′ē-əs One who is imperious is too bossy. From Latin, *imperios* = commanding, tyrannical.

> *I hold it better for the ruler to be feared than to be loved.*
> —*Niccolò Machiavelli*

9. ***impertinent* spitfire** im-pûr′tn-ənt Saucy and rude, an impertinent person never shows proper respect. From Late Latin, *impertinens* = not belonging.

> *Women complain about premenstrual syndrome,*
> *but I think of it as the only time of the month that I can be myself.*
> —*Roseanne Barr*

10. ***impetuous* whelp** im-pech′ōō-əs An impetuous person is rash, always jumping in before thinking of the consequences. From Latin, *impertere* = to rush upon.

Hasty climbers have sudden falls.
—*English proverb*

QUIZ 36

Match the definitions with the words on the left.

_____ 1. ignominious
_____ 2. ignoramus
_____ 3. imbruted
_____ 4. imp
_____ 5. impecunious
_____ 6. impenitent
_____ 7. imperialistic
_____ 8. imperious
_____ 9. impertinent
_____ 10. impetuous

a. a stupid person
b. a young demon or a mischievous child
c. completely disgraceful
d. like a brute
e. prone to dominate the affairs of weaker governments
f. rash
g. saucy and rude
h. too bossy, commanding, tyrannical
i. without money
j. lacking shame, regret

GRISLY LIST 37

"Could you repeat that?" Todd had had some **incoherent** customers before, but this took the cake. Everything had been going just fine until this **inane** creep came in with his **importunate** demands. He wanted to kick this guy's butt, but his boss had drilled it into his head: No matter how **impudent** the customer gets, the customer is always right.

"I thwed: Gwive mwe wour mwonwey or wour wife."

Todd was at a complete loss and felt completely **impotent** trying to discern the meaning of this **inarticulate** request. He tried to think of his grandfather's advice: the **impolitic** person opens his mouth; the wise man opens his ears.

"What was that again?"

This only seemed to have an **incendiary** effect on the **impoverished** wreck and he began to pound the counter.

"Gwive mwe wour mwonwey or wour wife!"

"My wife? I don't have a wife."

The gangrel pulled a knife out of his pocket. Suddenly everything became perfectly clear, and though it was **imprudent** to get sassy, he couldn't help it. "This job is not worth five bucks an hour."

1. ***impolitic* speculator** im-pol'i-tik One who is impolitic is unwise, impractical, lacking shrewdness. *Im-* is a variation of Latin *in-* = not + from Greek, *politicos* = of a citizen.

   > *Before you beat the dog,*
   > *learn the name of its master.*
   > —*Chinese proverb*

2. ***importunate* moocher** im-pôr'chə-nit Importunate means shamelessly insistent, sometimes annoyingly so. From Latin, *importunus* = unsuitable, troublesome.

   > *If a beggar be placed*
   > *in the midst of a grove of pear trees,*
   > *even there he will beg.*
   > —*Indian proverb*

3. ***impotent* dud** im'pə-tənt Literally, impotent means ineffective and powerless, but it also denotes male sexual dysfunction. From Latin, *in-* = not + *potis* = able.

   > *Powerlessness frustrates;*
   > *absolute powerlessness frustrates absolutely.*
   > —*Russell Baker*

4. ***impoverished* wreck** im-pov'ər-isht An impoverished person has been deprived of the ability to make a living and is thus reduced to poverty. From Latin, *pauper* = poor.

   > *O God! that bread should be so dear,*
   > *and flesh and blood so cheap!*
   > —*Thomas Hood*

5. ***imprudent* gambler** im-proōd'nt Without any thought of the consequences, an imprudent person is rash and indiscreet. From Latin, *in-* = not + *providens* = foreseeing.

   > *Fools rush in where angels fear to tread.*
   > —*Alexander Pope*

6. ***impudent* bit of fluff** im'pyə-dənt One who is impudent is saucy, impertinent, and shameless. From Latin, *impudens* = not modest.

   > *If you spit in a harlot's face she says it's raining.*
   > —*Yiddish proverb*

7. ***inane* flake** in-ān' Anyone inane is empty-headed and foolish. From Latin, *inanis* = empty.

   > *A fool in a hurry drinks tea with a fork.*
   > —*Chinese proverb*

8. *inarticulate* **twerp** in-är-tik′yə-lit One who is inarticulate can't speak coherently, but mumbles, sputters, and falters in speech. From Latin, *in-* = not + *articulatus* = to separate into joints.

> *Birds are entangled by their feet*
> *and men by their tongues.*
> —Thomas Fuller

9. *incendiary* **lout** in-sen′dē-er-ē An incendiary person or thing is inflammatory; it stirs up strife. From Latin, *incendi* = fire.

> *He who incites to strife is worse than he who takes part in it.*
> —Aesop

10. *incoherent* **imbecile** in-kō-hîr′ənt When something is incoherent it's not sticking together; if a person is incoherent, he or she is rambling and/or unintelligible because the words don't "stick together." From Latin, *in-* = not + *co-* = together + *haerere* = to stick.

> *Many a man's tongue shakes out his master's undoing.*
> —Shakespeare

QUIZ 37

Match the definitions with the words on the left.

____ 1. impolitic	a.	empty-headed; foolish
____ 2. importune	b.	ineffective and powerless
____ 3. impotent	c.	in poverty
____ 4. impoverished	d.	impertinent and shameless
____ 5. imprudent	e.	annoy with insistent requests
____ 6. impudent	f.	unintelligible (fits two words)
____ 7. inane	g.	unwise (fits two words)
____ 8. inarticulate	h.	willfully stirring up strife
____ 9. incendiary		
____ 10. incoherent		

GRISLY LIST 38

"You're too **inebriated** to drive." Juan tried to grab the keys, but his **incorrigible** employer would have none of it.

"What?"

"You're too drunk, smashed, intoxicated, hammered, loaded, blitzed!" Juan hoped the **inculcation** would register in Bert's **indocile** brain.

"And you're **incompetent!**" Bert replied **indignantly.** "And the ugliest, most **indolent** employee I've ever had! And tomorrow you'll still be ugly and I'll still be, I'll be the . . . "

Juan didn't like the **indecorous** comments, but knew he'd be out of a job with an **indigent** family to feed if he didn't find a way to get those keys away from his boozy boss.

"All right, but at least have another drink with me," Juan quipped. "Let's see who can finish the bottle first."

Bert took the bait and **indolently** guzzled the vodka down to the last drop, turned, and with an **indurate** smile, took three steps to his car. He never made it. Juan heaved his boss into the back seat and sighed.

"If it worked with Mom, it'll work with anyone."

1. *incompetent* **ne'er-do-well** in-kom′pi-tənt Inept. An incompetent person isn't capable of doing a task right. From Latin, *in-* = not + *competere* = be qualified.

> *A girl who can't dance says the band can't play.*
> —*Yiddish proverb*

2. *incorrigible* **offender** in-kôr′i-jə-bəl Habitually bad. One who is incorrigible cannot be reformed. From Latin, *in-* = not + *corrigere* = to correct.

> *Ill habits gather by unseen degrees,*
> *As brooks make rivers, rivers run to seas.*
> —*Ovid,* Metamorphoses

3. *inculcating* **schoolmaster** in′kul-kā-ting To inculcate is to teach with boring and forceful repetition. From Latin, *inculcatus* = to tread upon.

> *The average schoolmaster is and always must be essentially an ass,*
> *for how can one imagine an intelligent man*
> *engaging in so puerile an avocation?*
> —*H. L. Mencken*

4. *indecorous* **comment** in-dek′ə-rəs To be decorous is to conform to what is proper in decent society. Hence, an indecorous comment is indecent, improper, and tasteless. From Latin, *in-* = not + *decorus* = seemly, in good taste.

> *A man's venom poisons himself more than his victim.*
> —*Charles Buxton*

5. *indigent* **down-and-outer** in′di-jent Lacking the basic necessities of life, an indigent person needs a handout. From Latin, *indigere* = to be in need.

> *A fool and his money are soon parted.*
> —*English proverb*

6. *indignant* **hairsplitter** in-dig′nənt If you are indignant, you are angry or scornful. From Latin, *in-* = not + *dignari* = to deem worthy.

> *Moral indignation is jealousy with a halo.*
> —*H. G. Wells*

7. **indocile delinquent** in-dos'əl One who is indocile is not easy to teach or discipline. From Latin, *in-* = not + *docilis* = easily taught.

> *Never try to teach a pig to sing;*
> *you'll waste your time and you'll annoy the pig.*
> —*Unknown*

8. **indolent sloth** in'də-lənt Anyone indolent is sluggish, lazy, disinterested. In medicine, *indolent* denotes an injury that is slow to heal or a disease that doesn't cause any pain. From Latin, *in-* = not + *dolere* = to feel pain.

> *Hard work never killed anybody, but why take a chance?*
> —*Charlie McCarthy (Edgar Bergen's dummy)*

9. **indurate mule** in'dyə-rāt Indurate can mean hardened, callous, or stubborn. From Latin, *indurare* = to make hard.

> *Worse than a bloody hand is a hard heart.*
> —*Percy Bysshe Shelley*

10. **inebriated barfly** in-ē'brē-ā-tid To call someone inebriated is a fancy way of saying someone is drunk. From Latin, *inebriare* = to intoxicate.

> *Someone took the cork out of my lunch.*
> —*W. C. Fields*

QUIZ 38

Match the definitions with the words on the left.

_____ 1. incompetent   a. angry or scornful
_____ 2. incorrigible   b. drunk
_____ 3. inculcate   c. habitually bad
_____ 4. indecorous   d. hardened, callous, or stubborn
_____ 5. indigent   e. indecent, improper
_____ 6. indignant   f. lacking ability or skill
_____ 7. indocile   g. not easy to teach or discipline
_____ 8. indolent   h. lazy
_____ 9. indurate   i. lacking the basic necessities
_____ 10. inebriated   j. to teach by endless repetition

GRISLY LIST 39

"He's an **infamous** lady-killer, an **infernal** rat!" said Sarah.
"Really? He seems so **inhibited**. I can hardly get him to talk," Jade said.

Sarah's **inexorable** warning continued, "That's his trick. He acts all **inept** and shy, and then goes for the kill. You're just **infatuated**; that's why you can't see it."

Jade looked over at Simon as he worked at his desk and wondered. Her **inefficacious** attempts to meet the new hire had fallen short. Unexpectedly, he looked up from his desk and smiled at her.

Jade turned back to her confidante. "Are we talking about the same person?"

"He's an **ingrate**. Trust me. Men and women are **inimical**. You can't put the two together."

"So that's it." Jade thought, "That's why Sarah's been **ingratiating** herself to me!"

1. *inefficacious* **no-account** in-ef-i-kā'shəs Anything inefficacious is ineffective. From Latin, *in-* = not + *efficax* = effectual.

> We are all of us failures—at least, the best of us are.
> —James M. Barrie

2. *inept* **bungler** in-ept' One who is inept is unfit, awkward, and inefficient. From Latin, *ineptus* > *in* = not + *aptus* = suitable.

> The ass knows seven ways to swim;
> when he falls into the water, he forgets them all.
> —Armenian proverb

3. *inexorable* **obstructionist** in-ek'sər-ə-bəl An inexorable person or thing is unyielding and cannot be moved. From Latin, *in-* = not + *exorare* = to move by urgent requests. It is coupled with **obstructionist** = one who obstructs progress.

> He's a fool that will not yield.
> —Shakespeare

4. *infamous* **outlaw** in'fə-məs Anyone infamous is bad, *really* bad, and famous for being bad. From Latin, *infamis* = disgraced.

> Likely comment:
> This town ain't big enough for the both of us.
> Your response:
> Okay. We'll start expanding. Bring in new businesses, attract the tourists,
> lay down a ground plan, build more suburbs, parks, restaurants,
> maybe a movie theme park.

5. *infatuated* **dope** in-fach'ōō-ā-tid To infatuate is to cause someone to lose common sense or arouse another to be foolishly in love. To be infatuated is to be stupidly in love. From Latin, *infatuare* = to be made a fool < *fatuus* = foolish.

> Love is being stupid together.
> —Paul Valéry

6. *infernal* **rat** in-fûr′nəl One who is infernal is cooking up some hellish plot, is troublesome, or deserves to go to hell. From Latin, *infernus* = underground, lower.

She's gone to meet her maker
Since heaven wouldn't take her

7. **selfish** *ingrate* in′grāt An ingrate is one who is ungrateful. From Latin, *in-* = not + *gratus* = grateful.

I gave him a staff for his support
and he uses it to break my head.
—Indian proverb

8. *ingratiating* **suck-up** in-grā′shē-ā-ting To ingratiate is to try to gain another's favor by deliberate effort to achieve an advantage. From a Latin phrase, *in gratiam* = for the favor.

Charm is a way of getting the answer yes
without asking a clear question.
—Albert Camus

9. *inhibited* **pup** in-hib′it To be inhibited is to hold back. It is synonymous with shy or timid. From Latin, *inhibitus* = to hold in.

Of all base passions, fear is the most accursed.
—Shakespeare, Henry VI

10. *inimical* **cutthroat** in-im′i-kəl Anyone or anything inimical is like an enemy, hostile and unfriendly. From Latin, *inimicus* = hostile.

God, save me from my friends,
I can protect myself from my enemies.
—Marshal de Villars

QUIZ 39

Match the definitions with the words on the left.

____ 1. inefficacious	a. famous for being bad
____ 2. inept	b. fiendish
____ 3. inexorable	c. ineffective
____ 4. infamous	d. like an enemy, hostile
____ 5. infatuated	e. shy
____ 6. infernal	f. stupidly in love
____ 7. ingrate	g. to bring oneself into another's favor by conscious effort
____ 8. ingratiate	
____ 9. inhibited	h. unfit, awkward, and inefficient
____10. inimical	i. an ungrateful person
	j. unyielding

GRISLY LIST 40

"I'm completely **insolvent**. I don't have a penny to my name!" Adrian shouted.

He slammed the door shut on the small, **innocuous** girl selling cookies, but as soon as he sat down, there was another knock. When he opened the door, a religious recruiter shoved a pamphlet into his gut that read: "The **iniquitous** will burn in hell."

"I think you know where to take this **insipid** pamphlet," Adrian said.

He slammed the door in the man's **insensate** face and sat down to drink his coffee when the phone rang.

"If this is another one of those **insipient** phone sales pitches, get lost."

He slammed the phone down, but it immediately rang again. This time he let the caller get a few words in.

"Honey, it's your wife! Remember me?"

"I don't love you anymore," Adrian said. "I want a divorce." Snarling **insolently**, he hung up the phone. Then he began to chuckle at what he had just **instigated**. He looked about the house with an **insatiable** lust, not wanting to leave one stone unturned. He was careful to wipe anything he might have touched. Then, with an **insidious** grin, he looked at the stash in his bag: jewels, cash, and credit cards.

"This guy won't know what hit him."

1. ***iniquitous* scum** i-nik′wi-təs Iniquity means a lack of righteousness; wickedness; injustice; hence, one who is iniquitous is wicked. From Latin, *iniquus* = not equal.

> *A wicked man is his own hell.*
> —*Thomas Fuller*

2. ***innocuous* lamebrain** i-nok′yōō-əs Innocuous either means harmless or so irritatingly dull as to be annoying. From Latin, *in-* = not + *nocere* = to hurt.

> *After making love I said to my girl, "Was it good for you, too?"*
> *And she said, "I don't think this was good for anybody."*
> —*Garry Shandling*

3. ***insatiable* addict** in-sā′shə-bəl Anyone who is insatiable can't be satisfied. From Latin, *in-* = not + *satiare* = to fill, to provide with enough.

> *To a drunkard, no liquor is bad;*
> *to a merchant, no money is tainted;*
> *to a lecher, no woman is ugly.*
> —*Talmud*

4. ***insensate* bonehead** in-sen′sət To be insensate is to have no sensations, no feelings, no sensitivity, no sense, and no intelligence. From Late Latin, *insensatus* = irrational < *in-* = without + *sensatus* = gifted with sense.

> *When you use your brain it's a violation of the child-labor law.*
> —*Joe E. Lewis*

5. ***insidious* cheat** in-sid'ē-əs Anyone insidious is crafty, sly, and more dangerous than seems apparent. From *insidiae* = an ambush.

> *First secure an independent income, then practice virtue.*
> —Greek proverb

6. ***insipid* priss** in-sip'id Dull and tasteless, anyone who is insipid is boring. From Latin, *in-* = not + *sapidus* = savory.

> *A bore is someone who, when you ask him how he is, tells you.*
> —Unknown

7. ***insipient* sitting duck** in-sip'ē-ənt This is just another erudite way to call someone stupid. Don't confuse insipient with its homonym, incipient, which means "in the first stage of existence," as in an incipient illness. If you do you'll end up being called an incipient, insipient dope. From Latin, *insipiens* = unwise, foolish.

> *The Lord made Adam. The Lord made Eve*
> *He made them both a little naïve.*
> —E. Y. Harburg

8. ***insolent* skank** in'sə-lənt One who is insolent is boldly rude, disrespectful. From Latin, *in-* = not + *solere* = to be accustomed.

> *I told my girlfriend that unless she expressed her feelings*
> *and told me what she liked I wouldn't be able to please her,*
> *so she said, "Get off me."*
> —Garry Shandling

9. ***insolvent* burnout** in-sol'vənt One who is insolvent is unable to pay his/her debts. From Latin, *in-* = not + *solvere* = to loosen.

> *Owe no man anything.*
> —Romans 12:8

10. ***instigating* irritant** in'sti-gā-ting To instigate is to urge, incite, or provoke, often to some evil purpose. From Latin, *instigatus* = goaded on.

> *Anarchy is the stepping stone to absolute power.*
> —Napoleon Bonaparte, I

Match the definitions with the words on the left.

____ 1. iniquitous   a. boldly disrespectful

____ 2. innocuous   b. can't be satisfied

____ 3. insatiable   c. dangerously crafty

____ 4. insensate   d. dull (fits two words)

____ 5. insidious   e. stupid

____ 6. insipid   f. urge on to some evil purpose

____ 7. insipient   g. unable to pay debts

____ 8. insolent   h. unrighteous; wicked

____ 9. insolvent   i. no sensations or intelligence

____ 10. instigate

REVIEW 8

MATCH EACH QUOTE WITH THE APPROPRIATE WORD.

1. Marriage is the only war in which you sleep with the enemy.
—Unknown

2. More are drowned in drink than in water.
—Scottish proverb

3. Shall we go on conferring our civilization upon the peoples that sit in darkness, or shall we give those poor things a rest?
—Mark Twain

4. Shame is an ornament to the young; a disgrace to the old.
—Aristotle

5. With endless pain this man pursues
What, if he gain'd, he could not use;
And t'other fondly hopes to see
What never was, no e'er shall be.
—Matthew Prior

____ a. imperialist	____ d. inebriated
____ b. ignominious	____ e. inimical
____ c. impolitic	

6. A kick in the ass is a step forward.
—Unknown

7. Most of the time, he sounds like he has a mouth full of wet toilet paper.
—Rex Reed (about Marlon Brando)

8. A fool who wants to hang himself grabs a knife.
—Yiddish proverb

____ f. insipient	____ h. inarticulate
____ g. instigate	

9. One ungrateful man does an injury to all who stand in need of aid.
—Publilius Syrus

10. Some act first, think afterward, and then repent forever.
—C. Simmons

11. The contagion of crime is like that of the plague. Criminals collected together corrupt each other. They are worse than ever when, at the end of their punishment, they return to society.
—*Napoleon Bonaparte, I*

12. They can gas me, but I am famous. I have achieved in one day what it took Robert Kennedy all his life to do.
—*Sirhan Sirhan, the murderer of Robert Kennedy*

____ i.   imprudent   ____ k.   incorrigible
____ j.   infamous   __ __ l.   ingrate

Chapter 9

Words,
with their weight,
fall upon the picture
like birds of prey.
—Jules Renard

IF YOU'VE FOLLOWED MY ADVICE THUS FAR, you've probably noticed a side benefit to knowing these words: people actually think you're smart. It never fails. All you have to do is drop one measly little word that no one else but you knows into a conversation and everyone thinks you're Einstein. Now you can be ethical and tell them, "No, no, I'm not really smart. I just read this great book, *Vicious Vocabulary . . . ,*" but I don't expect that. What I expect is that you'll smile smugly and let them wallow in their ignorance, since that's exactly what I would do.

Savor these words and use them at the most opportune moments— those times when the world waits with bated breath for that magical utterance. Then, and only then, drop the insult with the thud of Thor's hammer.

GRISLY LIST 41

"Why go on?" Santa mused as he watched the snow falling outside. "Another **insufferable** winter."

Of course, he knew it wasn't just the winter: It was the tedium of flying **interminably** around the world every year delivering presents; it was the **insubordinate** little ingrates who rarely if ever left any cookies or milk out; it was the **internecine** battles between the **intransigent** elf and reindeer unions; and since he left his wife, the **intrusive** addition of paparazzi constantly following him around. All of this **intolerable** mess had become an **inveterate** part of Christmas. Ho, ho, ho. Add all that to Dancer's **intemperance** hangup and Santa was ready to throw in the towel.

"I should move to Florida, get a tan, and forget about this," thought Santa as he sat **intractably** in his chair and stared out the window. As night fell, a nurse sidled up to him.

"George, it's time to take your medicine."

Santa frowned as he swallowed the pills and wondered, "Why does she always call me George?"

1. ***insubordinate* hireling** in-sə-bôr′dn-it Anyone insubordinate is disobedient and insolent. From Latin, *in-* = not + *sub-* = under + *ordinare* = to order.

> *Boldness, without rules of property, becomes insubordination.*
> —*Confucius*

2. ***insufferable* headache** in-suf'ər-ə-bəl An insufferable person is so bothersome that he's intolerable. From Latin, *in-* = not + *sufferre* = endure.

> *We trifle with, make sport of, and despise*
> *those who are attached to us, and follow those that fly from us.*
> —*William Hazlit*

3. ***intemperate* juicehead** in-tem'pər-it One who is intemperate lacks restraint or self-control, especially with alcohol. From Latin, *in-* = not + *temperare* = to keep correct degree, regulate.

> *My uncle was the town drunk and we lived in Chicago.*
> —*George Gobel*

4. ***interminable* ink-slinger** in-tûr'mə-nə-bəl Anything interminable is so lengthy, dull, or exasperating that it seems without an end. From Latin, *in-* = without + *terminare* = to end.

> *Imbeciles are writing the lives of other imbeciles every day.*
> —*Agatha Christie*

5. ***internecine* traitor** in-tər-nes'ən Anything internecine refers to conflict or struggle within a group and it can mean that something is destructive to both sides in a conflict. From Latin, *inter-* = between + *necare* = to kill.

> *For every back there is a knife.*
> —*Corporate proverb*

6. ***intolerable* contrarian** in-tol'ər-ə-bəl Someone or something intolerable is too painful to be endured! From Latin, *intolerabilis*. It is coupled with **contrarian** = one who always disagrees.

> *I'm going to memorize your name and throw my head away.*
> —*Oscar Levant*

7. ***intractable* stickler** in-trak'tə-bəl To be intractable is to be unruly, hard to manage, hard to move and, consequently, hard to get along with. From Latin, *in-* = not + *tractare* = to haul.

> *An obstinate man does not hold opinions, but they hold him.*
> —*Alexander Pope*

8. ***intransigent* hardcase** in-tran'sə-jənt One who is intransigent is unbending and stubborn. From Latin, *in-* = not + *transigere* = to come to a settlement.

> *Like all weak men, he laid an exaggerated stress*
> *on not changing one's mind.*
> —*W. Somerset Maugham,*
> Of Human Bondage

9. ***intrusive* gatecrasher** in-trōō'siv Anyone intrusive is intruding, pushy, invasive. From Latin, *intrusus* = pushed in.

> EPITAPH:
> *He asked for directions*
> *At the house of corrections*

10. **_inveterate_ criminal** in-vet′ər-it Inveterate means anything that has been so firmly established over a long period of time it is now habitual and deep-rooted. From Latin, *inveterare* = to make or become old.

> *Habit, if not resisted, soon becomes necessity.*
> —*St. Augustine*

QUIZ 41

Match the definitions with the words on the left.

_____ 1. insubordinate
_____ 2. insufferable
_____ 3. intemperate
_____ 4. interminable
_____ 5. internecine
_____ 6. intolerable
_____ 7. intractable
_____ 8. intransigent
_____ 9. intrusive
_____ 10. inveterate

a. going on without end
b. habitual and deep-rooted
c. hard to manage, hard to move
d. causing conflict within a group
e. inflexible, refuses to agree
f. insolent and disobedient
g. intruding, pushy
h. lacks restraint
i. unbearable and too painful to be
   endured (fits two words)

GRISLY LIST 42

Veronica was **irate**, which was surprising since she wasn't the **irascible** type. Across the room stood the **ithyphallic** idiot who had spread **invidious** gossip about her around the office. This might not be such a big deal if it were true, but no. She'd simply turned him down and this is what she gets: this **irksome**, **Janus-faced** Don Juan **jabbering** untruths about her begging him for more.

"Ha! That's a laugh," she fumed. "Me, begging for this **jaded** has-been? But how can I exact revenge? That's the question."

She glanced at the steak knife on her desk left over from lunch. "No," she cautioned herself. "No use getting **irrational** about this."

Then it dawned on her, a diabolical epiphany. She jotted down an address, sauntered over to her **jackleg** coworker, slipped it in his pocket, and whispered coquettishly:

"Eight o'clock. Don't be late."

1. **_invidious_ gossip** in-vid′ē-əs To be invidious is to deliberately stir up ill will or resentment. From Latin, *invidios* = envious.

> *He that cannot possibly mend his own case*
> *will do what he can to impair another's.*
> —*Francis Bacon*

2. *irascible* **controversialist** i-ras′ə-bəl Easily angered, an irascible person looks for things to get in a huff about. From Latin, *irasci* = to be angry.

> *An angry man opens his mouth and shuts his eyes.*
> —Marcus Parcius Cato

3. *irate* **loose cannon** ī-rāt One who is irate is furious, incensed, fuming. From Latin, *ira* = anger.

> *Anger would inflict punishment on another;*
> *meanwhile, it tortures itself.*
> —Publilius Syrus

4. *irksome* **jinx** ûrk′səm Anything irksome is irritating, tiresome, and annoying. From Medieval English, *irken* = to loathe, to be weary of.

> *I don't pay any attention to him. I don't even ignore him.*
> —Samuel Goldwyn

5. *irrational* **crackpot** i-rash′ə-nəl An irrational person lacks reason and doesn't have a lick of sense. From Latin, *in-* = not + *ratio* = a consideration, reason, strategy.

> *There is a mutiny in 's mind.*
> —William Shakespeare,
> King Henry VIII

6. *ithyphallic* **Don Juan** ith-ə-fal′ik Ithyphallic describes any lustful, obscene person. Originally, ithyphallic referred to the erect phallus carried in the festival of Bacchus. From Latin, *ithys* = straight + *phallus* = a likeness of the penis venerated as a symbol of procreation.

> *When the prick stands, the brains get buried in the ground.*
> —Yiddish proverb

7. *jabbering* **monkey** jab′ə-ring To jabber is to talk fast and nonsensically. From Late Middle English, it is probably imitative of nonsensical speech.

> *They talk most that have the least to say.*
> —Matthew Prior

8. *jackleg* **fumbler** jak′leg Jackleg is an alteration of the British word blackleg, a name for one who replaces a worker on strike. Hence, a jackleg laborer is unskilled or un-trained and possibly unscrupulous.

> *What he lacks in intelligence he more than makes up for in stupidity.*
> —Anonymous

9. *jaded* **junkie** jā′did A jaded person is either worn out or dulled from overindulgence. A jade is either a worn-out horse or a disreputable woman. From Old Norse, *jalda* = a mare.

> *One vice worn out makes us wiser than fifty tutors.*
> —Edward Bulwer

10. **Janus-faced two-timer** jā′nəs-fāst To be Janus-faced is to be deceitful or two-faced. In Roman mythology, Janus is a god with two faces.

> Who dares think one thing and another tell,
> my heart detests him as the gates of hell.
> —Homer

QUIZ 42

Match the definitions with the words on the left.

____ 1.	invidious	a. angry
____ 2.	irascible	b. deceitful
____ 3.	irate	c. easily angered
____ 4.	irksome	d. incompetent; makeshift
____ 5.	irrational	e. lacking reason
____ 6.	ithyphallic	f. lustful, obscene
____ 7.	jabbering	g. stirs up resentment, ill will
____ 8.	jackleg	h. talking fast and nonsensically
____ 9.	jaded	i. tiresome and annoying
____ 10.	Janus-faced	j. worn out from overindulgence

GRISLY LIST 43

The judge peered at the **jingoistic** mob with a **jaundiced** eye and then again at the accused who groveled before him, her **lachrymose** excuses wailing above the tumult. It had been years since the revolution, and the existing **kakistocracy** was hardly an improvement on the one it had replaced. The cultural cleansing had started as an effort to rid the government of any leftover corruption, but it had quickly become a witch hunt, a **juggernaut** that crushed any chance of progress.

"But what can I do?" he thought as he stared at the **jeering** and **jejune** faces of the crowd. "They want blood. If I let her go, it will be my neck against the **jugulating** knife." There was only one way to play this.

"Take her to jail; we will execute her on Sunday before the games."

The mob was disappointed, but this was protocol, and the judge watched them as they slowly moved on. "Later," he thought, "I'll pay some **lackadaisical** guard, some **laggard** to let her out. No one will miss her when they start the executions. There are so many."

1. ***jaundiced* character** jôn′dist Jaundice is a liver disease that causes the face and eyes to turn yellow, but jaundiced also means when one's view has been "colored"—that is, altered or distorted, especially by prejudice. From Latin, *galbinus* = yellowish.

> *Prejudice is the child of ignorance.*
> —William Hazlitt

2. ***jeering* lackey** jî ring To jeer is to make fun of or laugh in a rude manner. The origin of jeer is unknown.

> *How are you holding up during the lithium shortage?*
> —David Letterman

3. ***jejune* airhead** jə-jōōn′ Anything or anyone jejune is barren or dull. From Latin, *jenunus* = empty, dry, barren.

> *She was blonde, she was tan, and now she's gone.*
> —quote from a "friend" of Nicole Simpson

4. **bloodsucking *jingo*** jing′go A jingo is overly patriotic and too eager to go to war. The word was derived in 1878 from an English song that went, "We don't want to fight but my jingo if we do, we've got the ships; we've got the men; we've got the money too." Jingo may have initially been a euphemism for Jesus or Jinko, a Basque word for God. You can use the adjective and call someone a jingoistic bloodsucker.

> *Patriotism is the willingness to kill and be killed for trivial reasons.*
> —Bertrand Russell

5. **overpowering *juggernaut*** jug′ər-nôt A juggernaut is anything or anyone that demands blind devotion or terrible sacrifice, or any destructive, irresistible force. Juggernaut comes from the Sanskrit, meaning "lord of the world." It is the incarnation of Vishnu, the Hindu god, whose idol, when carried on a cart during religious rites, so excited worshipers that they hurled themselves under the wheels and were crushed.

> *Men are idolaters, and want something to look at and kiss and hug,*
> *or throw themselves down before; they always did, they always will;*
> *and if you don't make it of wood, you must make it of words.*
> —Oliver Wendell Holmes, Sr.

6. ***jugulating* killer** jug′yə-lā-ting To jugulate is to cut a throat, probably a jugular vein. From Latin, *jugulare* = to cut the throat of.

> *I have the perfect cure for a sore throat: cut it.*
> —Alfred Hitchcock

7. **horrific *kakistocracy*** kak-i-stok′rə-sē A kakistocracy is a government run by the worst elements of society. From Greek, *kakos* = bad + *cracy* = government < from Greek, *kratos* = power.

> *A slave begins by demanding justice*
> *And ends by wanting to wear a crown.*
> —Albert Camus

8. **lachrymose loser** lak′rə-mōs Poor, tearful little thing; one who is lachrymose cries too easily and too often. From Latin, *lacrima* = tear.

> *Tears are the silent language of grief.*
> —*Voltaire*

9. **lackadaisical slouch** lak-ə-dā′zi-kəl One who is lackadaisical is lethargic, listless, or lazy. From an archaic expression, *lackadaisy*, which is a variation of Old English *lackaday*, an alteration of *alack a day* = an expression of dismay.

> *Never put off until tomorrow*
> *what you can do the day after tomorrow.*
> —*Mark Twain*

10. **laid-back *laggard*** lag′ərd A laggard is either always falling behind or just plain late. From Norwegian, *lagga* = to go slowly.

> *If a thing's worth doing, it's worth doing late.*
> —*Frederick Oliver*

QUIZ 43

Match the definitions with the words on the left.

____ 1.	jaundiced	a.	barren, dull
____ 2.	jeer	b.	demands blind devotion
____ 3.	jejune	c.	is always falling behind
____ 4.	jingoistic	d.	too eager to go to war
____ 5.	juggernaut	e.	prejudiced
____ 6.	jugulate	f.	showing a lack of interest
____ 7.	lachrymose	g.	tearful
____ 8.	lackadaisical	h.	regime by society's worst
____ 9.	laggard	i.	to cut a throat
____ 10.	kakistocracy	j.	to make fun of in a rude way

GRISLY LIST 44

Maxine was feeling a bit frisky, even **lascivious**, some might say, but where did this come from? Her normal routine after breakfast was to **lethargically** stretch out on the couch and take a nap. She was the **leery** type, avoiding strangers, hardly a **libertine**.

But something inside her woke last night; she heard the music. It echoed throughout the vicinity until folks were literally opening their windows to **lapidate** the poor boys who were just singing their song.

"Imagine that," she thought, "all that ruckus happening in this neighborhood. You'd think they were some **larcenous** thugs sneaking into people's windows."

Anyway, something inside her was aroused; all night she had the **lewdest** dreams and, in spite of her roommate's **lambasting**, she snuck out as quickly as she could.

She threw herself on the grass feeling the warmth of the hot sun upon her face and grinned at the boys' **lecherous** smiles as they crept out of the shadows. Her **languid** world had been turned upside down. Coquettishly, she licked her paw.

1. **lambasting lug** lam-bās'ting Lambasting means beating or scolding severely. From Old Norse, *lam* = to make lame + *beysta* = to beat; to attack with words.

> EPITAPH:
> *Our lives were spared by this lambasting lug*
> *When he tried to lambaste a Mafia thug*

2. **languid couch potato** lang'gwid To be languid is to be weak, with no interest and little animation. Don't confuse this with *languorous*, which has the connotation of listlessness from laziness, bad weather, or daydreaming. From Latin, *languidus* = faint.

> *They laboriously do nothing.*
> —*Seneca*

3. **lapidating witch hunters** lap'i-dā-ting A lapidating person likes to stone people to death. From Latin, *lapidarius* = of stone.

> *It is often pleasant to stone a martyr,*
> *no matter how much we admire him.*
> —*John Barth*

4. **larcenous swine** lär'sə-nəs Anyone larcenous is prone to steal. From Latin, *latrocinari* < *latro* = mercenary soldier.

> *Thieves for their robbery have authority when judges steal themselves.*
> —*Shakespeare*, Measure for Measure

5. **lascivious harlot** lə-siv'ē-əs Lascivious is lustful, with a shameless interest in sex. From Latin, *lascivas* = wanton, sportive.

> *My sister claimed sexual harassment on the job,*
> *which was a little surprising, since she's a hooker.*
> —*George Miller*

6. **lecherous old goat** lech'ər-əs Anyone who is lecherous is excessively, offensively lustful. A lecher is an excessively lustful man. From Old French, *lechier* = to live a debauched life; literally, to lick.

> *At age 82, I sometimes feel like a 20-year-old,*
> *but there is seldom one around.*
> —*Milton Berle*

7. **_leery_ fence-sitter** lîr′ē A leery person looks on another with suspicion, distrust. From Middle English, _lore_ < _lere_ = knowing. It is possibly also influenced by the English word, _leer_ = to look over one's cheek.

> Trust in God but tie your camel.
> —Persian proverb

8. **_lethargic_ sluggard** lə-thär′jik A lethargic person is slow and dull from illness, fatigue, or drugs. From Greek, _lethe_ = forgetfulness + _argos_ = idle.

> EPITAPH:
> Back in five minutes.

9. **_lewd_ scumbag** lōōd Anyone lewd is inordinately lustful or indecent. From Medieval English, _lewede_ = vile < ignorant.

> Flies spread disease—keep yours zipped.
> —Unknown

10. **_libertine_ primitive** lib′ər-tēn A libertine is one without moral or sexual restraint. From Latin, _libertinus_ = of a freedman.

> EPITAPH:
> He lusted for sin
> But disease did him in

QUIZ 44

Match the definitions with the words on the left.

____ 1. languid	a.	to beat or scold severely
____ 2. lapidate	b.	overly lustful (fits three words)
____ 3. larcenous	c.	one with no moral restraint
____ 4. lascivious	d.	with little interest or animation
____ 5. leery	e.	thieving, given to stealing
____ 6. lecherous	f.	to stone people to death
____ 7. lambaste	g.	suspicious
____ 8. lethargic	h.	lazy or dull from illness
____ 9. lewd		
____ 10. libertine		

GRISLY LIST 45

You could almost see the **limacine** trail that oozed from the **lothario** as he sauntered into the bar. He found a perch in the corner from which to launch his **libidinous** hunt as the ladies strolled in. Others might try banging at the keys on the computer to catch a babe, but not this Don Juan; he was a bit of a **Luddite** and knew the only way for a real man to be out on the prowl was face-to-face.

As each woman shimmied in he tossed a **licentious** come-on, but the only responses he could generate were **listless** stares from vacant eyes.

"May I buy you a drink?" he offered to a rather **loquacious** doll sitting to his right.

"That depends. Do you want a restraining order filed against you?"

This took him by surprise; usually the **litigious** side of a girl didn't come out until after he dumped her, but not to worry. He moved on. There were lots of good fish in the sea. In fact, the odds were good. There was not a single man in the house. But when the music fired up and the **lubricious** girls began dancing with each other, the **lothario,** though he towered above the crowd, felt small, even **Lilliputian,** and only wished he could slip out unnoticed.

1. ***libidinous* floozy** li-bid'n-əs To be libidinous is to be hot to trot, lustful, lewd, etc. The word is based on libido, meaning sexual desire. From Latin, *libet* = it pleases.

    > *In breeding cattle you need one bull for every twenty-five cows,*
    > *unless the cows are known sluts.*
    > —*Johnny Carson*

2. ***licentious* lecher** lī-sen'shəs To be licentious is to be sexually and/or morally unrestrained. From Latin, *licere* = to be allowed.

    > *Men are always ready to respect anything that bores them.*
    > —*Marilyn Monroe*

3. ***Lilliputian* bureaucrat** lil-ə-pyoo'shən Anything Lilliputian is extremely small, but it can also imply pettiness. In Jonathan Swift's *Gulliver's Travels*, the inhabitants of Lilliput were pint-sized people whose small-minded attitudes matched their height. Use this aspersion when confronting dolts who bicker over petty details.

    > *Small and creeping things are the products of petty souls.*
    > —*Thomas Browne*

4. ***limacine* slimeball** lim'ə-sēn Anyone limacine resembles a slug. From Latin, *limax* = a slug.

    > *I got some new underwear the other day.*
    > *Well, new to me.*
    > —*Emo Philips*

5. ***listless* slugabed** list'ləs Anyone listless shows a lack of interest and spirit. From Old English, *lust* = desire, pleasure + *les* = without.

    > *To try may be to die, but not to care is never to be born.*
    > —*William Redfield*

6. **litigious shyster** li-tij'əs The plague of modern man: ready to sue at the drop of a hat, a litigious person licks his chops at every accident. From Latin, *litigium* = strife < *litigare* = to discuss; hence, to argue.

> *For certain people, after fifty,*
> *litigation takes the place of sex.*
> —Gore Vidal

7. **loquacious gabbler** lō-kwā'shəs This one likes to talk, perhaps too much. From Latin, *loqui* = to speak.

> *Where there is a surfeit of words,*
> *there is a famine of intelligence.*
> —Indian proverb

8. **loose *lothario*** lō-thâr'ē-ō A lothario is a seducer of women. Lothario was a character in Nicholas Rave's play *The Fair Penitent* (1703).

> *A lewd bachelor makes a jealous husband.*
> —English proverb

9. **lubricious Peeping Tom** loō-brish'əs Lubricious can mean slippery, shifty, or lewd. From Latin, *lubricus* = slippery.

> *Women should be obscene and not heard.*
> —Groucho Marx

10. **stubborn *Luddite*** lud'īt A Luddite is anyone who resists technical modernization. Ned Ludd, an 18th-century English worker, argued that machines were taking jobs away from workers. Luddites were workers who destroyed machines that were taking away their jobs.

> *If there is technological advance without social advance, there is,*
> *almost automatically, an increase in human misery.*
> —Michael Harrington

QUIZ 45

Match the definitions with the words on the left.

____ 1. libidinous	a.	a seducer of women
____ 2. licentious	b.	lacking interest and spirit
____ 3. Lilliputian	c.	like a slug
____ 4. limacine	d.	lustful, lewd (fits two words)
____ 5. listless	e.	ready to sue
____ 6. litigious	f.	slippery, shifty, or lewd
____ 7. loquacious	g.	small-minded, petty
____ 8. lothario	h.	resists technical modernization
____ 9. lubricious	i.	talking too much
____ 10. Luddite		

REVIEW 9

MATCH EACH QUOTE WITH THE APPROPRIATE WORD.

1. War is, at first, the hope that one will be better off;
next, the expectation that the other fellow will be worse off;
then, the satisfaction that he isn't any better off; and ,
finally, the surprise at everyone's being worse off.
—*Karl Kraus*

2. Men often make up in wrath what they want in reason.
—*Horatio Alger*

3. Most men are within a finger's breadth of being mad.
—*Diogenes*

4. She's the original good time had by all.
—*Bette Davis*

____ a. libertine   ____ c. irate
____ b. irrational   ____ d. internecine

5. I started out on burgundy but soon hit the harder stuff.
—*Bob Dylan*

6. Love grows, lust wastes.
—*William Penn*

7. Patriotism is a pernicious, psychopathic form of idiocy
—*George Bernard Shaw*

8. The fire you kindle for your enemy
often burns yourself more than him.
—*Chinese proverb*

9. The first external revelation of the dry rot in men is a tendency
to lurk and lounge.
—*Charles Dickens*

____ e. irascible   ____ h. listless
____ f. jingo   ____ i. intemperate
____ g. lascivious

10. Give a man a free hand and he'll run it all over you.
—*Mae West*

11. God hath given you one face and you make yourselves another.
—*Shakespeare, Hamlet*

12. Our wrangling lawyers are so litigious and busy here on earth,
that I think they will plead their clients' causes hereafter,
some of them in hell.
—*Robert Burton*

13. Some men study so much, they don't have time to know.
—*Talmud*

14. The followers of a great man often put their eyes out, so that they
may be the better able to sing his praise.
—*Friedrich Nietzsche*

____ j. inculcate
____ k. juggernaut
____ l. libidinous

____ m. litigious
____ n. Janus-faced

Chapter 10

Words have users,
but as well, users have words.
And it is the users that establish
the world's realities.
—LeRoi Jones

I ONCE WAS STUCK LISTENING TO A LAWYER BABBLE ON ABOUT HIS TENACITY IN BUSINESS.

He didn't have much respect for me until I said, "You know what they say, 'For every back there is a knife.'" A wide grin of admiration spread across his face. The rest of the conversation went much better.

My point is this: This is a vocabulary book, but it is also a quote book. If you want to improve your writing, you'll study the quotes as you do the vocabulary. You'll surprise yourself with the wisdom you'll gain. We don't value wisdom much anymore. Being shrewd and conniving is more popular—and rewarding. However, wisdom comes with its own gifts. If you peruse these pearls of wisdom, you'll find that it can come in handy at the most opportune moments.

Let me take this one step further. Why don't you write your own quotes? You can take a quote like: Inside every fat person is a thin person waiting to get out. And then switch it around: Inside every thin person is a fat person, etc. Or, inside every Frenchman is a Napoleon waiting to bust out. Or whatever. In the process of doing this you'll be working on something that will help you in your speech and in your writing.

GRISLY LIST 46

You could've laughed, either because it was so **ludicrous** or because it was so **lugubriously** pathetic. Here stood two **malevolent** generals hunched over a bomb, trying to think of how to deactivate it.

"Blackhurst, you're the bomb expert, you diffuse it."

"I'm an expert at dropping bombs; I don't know what makes them tick. You're in charge of the bomb squad."

"Admit it, Blackhurst," Thornhill said with a **lupine** grin, "this is one of your **Machiavellian** plots. You're quite the **malefactor**."

"What are you insinuating? That I locked myself in with you with a bomb? You must be mad."

"Yes, It was your **maleficent** plan to disappear before I had discovered it," Thornhill accused him with **magniloquent** flair. "And now you're stuck here with only seconds remaining. You might as well admit to it. After all, we are both going to die!"

Blackhurst's **maladroit** fingers began to fumble with the wires: red, green, yellow. The timer had twenty seconds to go.

"Yes! Since we're both going to die, I will tell you. I had to seize power before you had a chance. And now what does it matter? We are both going to die."

"You were right." Thornhill grinned **maliciously** as he pulled out a revolver. "I am in charge of the bomb squad."

The timer hit five seconds when Thornhill pulled the red wire, but the timer kept ticking.

"Whoops."

1. *ludicrous* **buffoon** lōō'di-krəs Anything ludicrous is laughable because it's so obviously absurd. From Latin, *ludus* = a play, game.

> *It is only one step from the sublime to the ridiculous.*
> —*Napoleon Bonaparte*

2. *lugubrious* **sad sack** lōō-gōō'brē-əs Anyone or anything lugubrious is sad or so unbelievably sad that it's laughable and ludicrous. From Latin, *lugere* = to mourn.

> *My mother didn't breast-feed me. She said she liked me as a friend.*
> —*Rodney Dangerfield*

3. *lupine* **lounge lizard** lōō'pīn Lupine means wolflike or violently hungry or avaricious. From Latin, *lupus* = wolf.

> *A gentleman is a patient wolf.*
> —*Henrietta Tiarks*

4. *Machiavellian* **schemer** mak-ē-ə-vel'ē-ən Anyone Machiavellian is characterized by unscrupulous cunning, full of plots and intrigue. In Niccolò Machiavelli's *The Prince*, political necessity is placed above morality, and the ruler uses deceit as the means to maintain power.

> *The greatest cunning is to have none at all.*
> —*Carl Sandburg*

5. *magniloquent* **boaster** mag-nil'ə-kwənt This pompous, boastful one talks big, but it's only so much hot air. From Latin, *magniloquus* = speaking in a lofty style.

> *He that speaks lavishly shall hear as knavishly.*
> —*English proverb*

6. *maladroit* **klutz** mal-ə-droit' Anyone maladroit is clumsy. From French, *mal* = bad + *droit* = right.

> *Men lose more conquests by their own awkwardness*
> *than by any virtue in the woman.*
> —*Ninon De Enclos*

7. **horrendous** *malefactor* mal'ə-fak-tər A malefactor is a doer of evil or crime. From Latin, *malefacere* = to do wrong.

> *He who greatly excels in beauty, strength, birth, or wealth,*
> *and he, on the other hand, who is very weak, or very disgraced,*
> *find it difficult to follow rational principles.*
> *The one sort grows into violent and great criminals,*
> *the other into rogues and petty rascals.*
> —*Aristotle*

8. **maleficent terror** mə-lef'ə-sənt Likely to cast an evil spell, a maleficent person is harmful and wicked. From Latin, *male* = evil + *facere* = to do.

> *Political power grows out of the barrel of a gun.*
> —Mao Tse-tung

9. **malevolent henchman** mə-lev'ə-lənt To be malevolent is to be malicious, to wish harm on others. From Latin, *male* = ill + *volens* = wishing.

> *The tyranny of the multitude is a multiplied tyranny.*
> —Edmund Burke

10. **malicious warlord** mə-lish'əs Anyone malicious has an active desire to do harm to others or to see them suffer. From Latin, *malus* = bad.

> *A tyrant's breath is another's death.*
> —English proverb

QUIZ 46

Match the definitions with the words on the left.

____ 1. ludicrous
____ 2. lugubrious
____ 3. lupine
____ 4. Machiavellian
____ 5. magniloquent
____ 6. maladroit
____ 7. malefactor
____ 8. maleficent
____ 9. malevolent
____ 10. malicious

a. a doer of evil
b. clumsy
c. laughable, absurd
d. pompous, boastful
e. acting so unbelievably sad it's laughable and ludicrous
f. unscrupulously cunning, filled with plots and intrigue
g. with evil intent (fits three words)
h. wolflike

GRISLY LIST 47

Heinrich cut into the tumor, fat and bulbous, and then threw it on the floor. At least it wasn't **malignant**. The **malodorous** fumes filled the makeshift surgery room. He gazed at his patient. Finally, the fugitive had passed out. That was so much better than listening to his **maudlin maundering**. They had nothing but whisky and rum for anesthetic.

"Hey, Sawbones!" the **martinet** called out. "Are you done? Don't forget—he dies; you die. No more **malingering**. Get to work."

It was in this **maligning** environment that Heinrich had to perform the surgery. He sewed up the **malleable** skin, trying to keep everything as clean as possible.

"He'll live," he said to his **martial** guest.

The henchman looked satisfied at his brother's surgery and then cocked his gun.

"Aren't you forgetting something?" the doctor asked. "I've sewed something inside your brother's stomach that only I will know how to find."

"Take it out!" the brother threatened.

"What am I? A **masochist**? You were going to kill me anyway. If you want your brother to live, you have to let me live."

As the doctor left his captor, he sighed. "Thank God I've got a good poker face."

1. *malignant* **mutant** mə-lig′nənt Like cancer, a malignant person has an evil or harmful influence. From Latin, *malignare* = to act maliciously.

> *The entire economy of the Western world*
> *is built on things that cause cancer.*
> —line from the movie Bliss

2. *maligning* **opponent** mə-līn′ing To malign is to slander or say something destructive. From Latin, *malignus* = wicked, malicious.

> *Even doubtful accusations leave a stain behind them.*
> —Thomas Fuller

3. *malingering* **loafer** mə-ling′gə-ring To malinger is to fake being ill to get out of work. From French, *malingre* = sickly, infirm.

> *It is better to have loafed and lost than never to have loafed at all.*
> —James Thurber

4. *malleable* **minion** mal′ē-ə-bəl To be malleable is to be easily shaped or molded. From Latin, *malleare* = to beat with a hammer.

> *As long as men worship the Caesars and Napoleons,*
> *the Caesars and Napoleons will duly rise and make them miserable.*
> —Aldous Huxley

5. *malodorous* **stinkpot** mal-ō′dər-əs One who is malodorous reeks, smells offensively bad. From Latin, *malus* = bad + *odor* = a smell.

> *Every stink that fights the ventilator thinks it's Don Quixote.*
> —Stanislaw J. Lec

6. *martial* **barbarian** mär′shəl Anyone martial is eager to fight or go to war. From Latin, *Martialis* = of Mars (the god of war).

> *When you're wounded and left on Afghanistan's plains*
> *And the women come out to cut up what remains*
> *Just roll to your rifle and blow out your brains*
> *An' go to your Gawd like a soldier.*
> —Rudyard Kipling

7. **overbearing *martinet*** mär-tn-et′ A martinet is a strict disciplinarian. The word comes from General Jean Martinet, a French 17th-century drillmaster.

> *Each man is a tyrant in tendency,*
> *because he would impose his idea on others.*
> —*Ralph Waldo Emerson*

8. ***masochistic* martyr** mas-ə-kis′tik A masochist is someone who needs to be abused or hurt to be sexually satisfied. Derived from a 19th-century Austrian writer, Leopold von Sacher-Masoch, who detailed the lifestyle.

> *Masochist: Someone who is only happy when miserable.*
> —*Anonymous*

9. ***maudlin* weeper** môd′lin Anyone maudlin is idiotically sentimental, perhaps from too much liquor. From Old French, Madeleine is the French spelling of the biblical Magdalene, who was often represented with eyes red from weeping.

> *Women's weapons, water-drops.*
> —*William Shakespeare*

10. ***maundering* moron** môn′də-ring To maunder is to move or act in a dreamy, vague way, or to speak meaninglessly or incoherently; to ramble carelessly. From Latin, *mendicare* = to beg.

> *He that knows little often repeats it.*
> —*Thomas Fuller*

QUIZ 47

Match the definitions with the words on the left.

_____ 1. malignant	a.	one who is bossy
_____ 2. malign	b.	derives pleasure from pain
_____ 3. malinger	c.	eager to fight
_____ 4. malleable	d.	fake being ill to avoid work
_____ 5. malodorous	e.	foolishly sentimental
_____ 6. martial	f.	slander
_____ 7. martinet	g.	stinks
_____ 8. masochistic	h.	to be easily shaped or molded
_____ 9. maudlin	i.	to move in a dreamy way or to speak meaninglessly
_____ 10. maundering	j.	with an evil influence

GRISLY LIST 48

"I'm God." The **megalomaniac** asserted.

"It's so nice to meet you. Since you're God, do you have other names that you go by, something that I can put in my report?" Gabriella tried to sound sincere, tried to not sound **mawkish**. This was a new patient and it was important to establish trust. They had found "God," a homeless **mendicant**, passing out stolen food to other homeless souls in the red-light district.

"While I'm on earth I go by Kathy Anders," Kathy said with a **melancholy** sigh.

Kathy had the **meretricious** allure of a streetwalker, and Gabriella thought it would be wise to note that. But the **mephitic** stink didn't quite fit. In any case, things were going well. She had a name, at least.

"So Kathy, if you are God, why are you here?"

Her mood did an about-face and she smiled, "I'm here to overthrow the government!"

Gabriella jotted down a note: "**Mercurial**."

"Oh? Why would you want to do that?"

"Can I trust you?" Kathy leaned forward and whispered, "It's become a **mendacious** band of **mercenaries**, a hardened **meritocracy** that ignores the poor."

"I see your point. But Kathy, I've never met God before; could you do something for me to prove that you really are God?"

"That's against the rules. And it's against the rules for you to ask. So I have to leave now."

Gabriella thought she would have to call security, but before she had a chance, "Kathy" began to fade until there was barely a ghost of her left. In that final eerie moment, before Kathy was altogether gone, she whispered:

"That's against the rules."

1. **mawkish softy** mô′kish One who is mawkish shows sentiment, tenderness, or understanding in false, feeble, or repulsive ways. From Medieval English, *mawke* = maggot. Originally, mawkish meant "repulsive" but, over time, came to mean "revoltingly sentimental."

> *The sentimental people fiddle harmonics on the string of sensualism.*
> *—George Meredith*

2. **crackbrained *megalomaniac*** meg-ə-lō-mā′nē-ak A megalomaniac is one deluded with grandeur and power. From Greek, *megalo* = large + *mania* = madness.

> Likely comment:
> *I am the reincarnation of Napoleon, Julius Caesar, and Cleopatra.*
> Your response:
> *Well, then you get the check.*

3. *melancholy* **baby** mel'ən-kol-ē In medieval times it was believed that black bile (one of the four humors of the body) caused gloominess and depression; hence, anyone who is melancholy (or **melancholic**) is depressed. From Greek, *melancholia* = black bile.

> *Melancholy is the pleasure of being sad.*
> —Victor Hugo

4. *mendacious* **mongrel** men-dā'shəs Anyone mendacious lies and has told lies in the past. From Late Latin, *mendaci* = given to lying.

> *Satisfy a dog with a bone and a woman with a lie.*
> —Basque proverb

5. **homeless** *mendicant* men'di-kənt A mendicant is a beggar (sometimes of a religious order) who depends on charity. From Latin, *mendicus* = having physical defects; hence, poor, a beggar.

> *It wasn't hard to tell we were poor*
> *when you saw the toilet paper dryin' on the clothesline.*
> —George "Goober" Lindsey

6. *mephitic* **skunk** mə-fit'ik Anyone or anything that is mephitic stinks. Mephitis is a bad or poisonous odor coming out of the ground from decomposing matter. From Latin, *mephitis* = vapor exhalation < from the Oscan mythology of Southern Italy.

> *A corpse and an uninvited guest stink after a couple of days.*
> —Mexican proverb

7. **bloodthirsty** *mercenary* mûr'sə-ner-ē A mercenary is influenced by a desire for monetary gain. The word can be used as an adjective as in, "His interest in church is completely mercenary," or as a noun, especially when referring to one who has been hired to fight for money, as in, "The mercenaries sacked the defenseless town." From Latin, *merces* = pay, wages.

> *I would wish you good luck, but for all I know you're trying to kill me.*
> —Jackie Mason

8. *mercurial* **minx** mər-kyŏŏr'ē-əl This mercurial person is apt to change moods with little cause. From Latin, *mercurialis* = of the god Mercury. It is coupled with **minx** = an impudent, flirtatious, or promiscuous girl.

> *I am a feather for each wind that blows.*
> —Shakespeare

9. *meretricious* **tart** mer-i-trish'əs One who is meretricious is seemingly attractive in a shallow or vulgar way but without truly having any real beauty. From Latin, *meretrix* = a prostitute. It is coupled with **tart** = a loose woman.

> *Many a man has fallen in love with a girl in a light so dim*
> *he would not have chosen a suit by it.*
> —Maurice Chevalier

10. **fancy schmancy *meritocracy*** mer-i-tok′rə-sē A meritocracy is a system in which the intellectual elite attain a special status over others. From Latin, *merere* = to deserve, earn + -cracy.

> *The classes that wash the most are those that work the least.*
> —G. K. Chesterton

QUIZ 48

Match the definitions with the words on the left.

___ 1.	mawkish	a.	beggar dependent on charity
___ 2.	megalomaniac	b.	apt to change moods
___ 3.	melancholy	c.	depressed
___ 4.	mendacious	d.	falsely attractive
___ 5.	mendicant	e.	given to lying
___ 6.	mephitic	f.	influenced by a desire for gain
___ 7.	mercenary	g.	one deluded with power
___ 8.	mercurial	h.	showing feeling in false ways
___ 9.	meretricious	i.	where the intellectual elite rule
___10.	meritocracy	j.	with a bad or poisonous odor

GRISLY LIST 49

"I say we pass out guns and take to the streets!" the **militant** woman exploded.

The members of the Women's Coalition for Change were upset that the police, in the process of arresting one of the protesters for trespassing, had broken her arm. Jennifer was angry too, but it seemed the protest was getting out of hand.

"Won't that **militate** against our objective?" she asked.

But she was drowned out when another screamed with **minatory** zeal, "This is **misfeasance**. **Misogynous** pigs! Men are all **misogynous** pigs!" the **misandrists** shouted.

Several **misologists** screamed, "Pass out the guns!"

A soft-spoken girl in a tie-dyed shirt stood up. "But wasn't it a female cop who broke our leader's arm? Aren't we really talking about hatred against all of humankind, not just women? Isn't this truly **misanthropy** that we are contending with? We can't resort to violence; if we do, wouldn't we then be guilty of **misoneism** ourselves?"

Several **minacious** protesters pounced on the hapless hippie and threw her off the stage. Jennifer picked up her books and, as quietly as she could, sidled out the back.

1. **militant** grunt mil′i-tənt A militant person is willing to fight, perhaps too willing to fight. It can be used as a noun to describe someone willing to use violence to further a cause. From Latin, *miles* = soldier.

> *Governments need to have both shepherds and butchers.*
> —*Voltaire*

2. **militating** troublemaker mil′i-tā-ting To militate is to work against something. From Latin, *militat* = to serve as a soldier.

> *An open foe may prove a curse*
> *but a pretended friend is worse.*
> —*John Gay*

3. **minacious** vulture mi-nā′shəs A minacious person is threatening or hostile. From Latin, *minari* = to threaten < *minae* = projecting points of walls.

> *It only takes my little fingers to blow you away.*
> —*Elvis Costello*

4. **minatory** mogul min′ə-tôr-ē Anyone minatory is threatening or menacing. From Latin, *minari* = to threaten.

> *You can get more with a kind word and a gun*
> *than you can with a kind word alone.*
> —*Al Capone*

5. **misanthropic** crank mis-ən-throp′ik A misanthrope hates humankind; hence, anyone misanthropic despises humankind. Don't confuse this with *misandrist*, one who hates men. From Greek, *misein* = to hate + *anthropos* = man.

> *Hell is other people.*
> —*Jean-Paul Sartre*

6. **misandrous** iceberg mis-an′drəs A misandrous person is a misandrist—someone who hates men, hence practices misandry. From Greek, *miso* = hate + *andr-* = man; imitative after *misogynous* in the 1940s.

> *If you catch a man, throw him back.*
> —*Women's Lib slogan*

7. **corrupt** *misfeasor* mis-fē′zər A misfeasor does a lawful act in an unlawful way that ends up hurting others. From Medieval English, *mis-* = ill, wrong + Latin, *facere* = to do.

> *I have never seen a situation so dismal*
> *that a policeman couldn't make it worse.*
> —*Brendan Behan*

8. **misogynous** browbeater mi-soj′ə-nəs A misogynous person is a *misogynist*—someone who hates women. This is the adjective form of misogyny. From Greek, *miso* = hatred + *gyno-* = female.

> *Some of us are becoming the kind of men*
> *we always wanted to marry.*
> —*Gloria Steinem*

9. **pigheaded *misologist*** mi-sol'ə-jəst Don't try to reason with a misologist, or some-one who practices misology. This one hates or distrusts reason or enlightenment. From Greek, *miso* = to hate + *logos* = a word, thought.

> *He who refuses to learn deserves extinction.*
> —Hillel ha-Babli

10. **bullheaded *misoneist*** mis-ə-nē'ist A misoneist hates innovation, change, or any-thing new. From Greek, *miso* = to hate + *neos* = new.

> *He has a first-rate mind until he makes it up.*
> —Violet Bonham-Carter

QUIZ 49

Match the definitions with the words on the left.

____ 1.	militant	a.	does a lawful act in an illegal way that hurts others
____ 2.	militate		
____ 3.	minacious	b.	hateful of women
____ 4.	minatory	c.	hating mankind
____ 5.	misanthropic	d.	one who hates innovation
____ 6.	misandrous	e.	one who distrusts reason
____ 7.	misfeasor	f.	one who hates men
____ 8.	misogynous	g.	threatening (fits two words)
____ 9.	misologist	h.	to work against something
____ 10.	misoneist	i.	willing to fight

GRISLY LIST 50

The **mountebank** gleefully counted out the take for the day, "A dollar for you. A dollar for me. One dollar, two dollars, three for me."

His **morose** stooge looked down at the dollar, and in a **monotonous** tone, asked:

"Why do I only get a dollar?"

His counterpart quipped, "What? I'm **mortified**. Do you accuse me of cheating you? You accuse me, who was so good enough to bring you into my little scam when you were nothing more than a **moribund** goner. I'm hurt. I'm very hurt."

His **mulish** stooge repeated, "Why do I only get a dollar?"

With his **mordacious** tongue, the con man blurted out, "Because, my dear friend, it's simple percentages: I do ninety percent of the work and you do ten: ergo, I get ninety percent of the proceeds."

His **monomaniac** companion nodded and said again, "Why do I only get a dollar?"

"Because, my dear dimwit," the con man shrieked with **mordant** flair, "I'm the brains and you're the brawn. It takes brains to run this scheme, which you don't have."

The dull man's blunt fist met, with considerable accuracy, the sharper man's chin. He grabbed the dollars out of the toppled con man's pockets as he stood over him, but this time his monotone voice conveyed a **mortiferous** edge.

"A dollar for you, a dollar for me. One dollar, two dollars, three for me."

1. **mad *monomaniac*** mon-ə-mā′nē-ak Monomania is a partial insanity focused on one idea; hence, a monomaniac is obsessed with one thing and one thing only, forever fixated on that elusive thing, person, or idea. From Greek, *monos* = alone, combined with *mania* = madness.

   Adhesion to one idea is slavery.
   —Christian Bovee

2. ***monotonous* lowbrow** mə-not′n-əs Anyone monotonous is tiresome because his/her voice doesn't vary and drones on interminably. Monotonous can also describe anything lacking in variety. From Greek, *mono* = one + *tonos* = strain, tone, mode.

   He is not only dull himself, he is the cause of dullness in others.
   —Samuel Johnson

3. ***mordacious* joker** môr-dā′shəs The mordacious person has a keen or biting wit, or maybe just likes to bite. From Latin, *mordacitas* = given to biting.

   True wit is nature to advantage dressed,
   What oft was thought but ne'er so well expressed.
   —Alexander Pope

4. ***mordant* wisecracker** môr′dənt Anything mordant is either biting and sarcastic or corrosive. From Latin, *mordere* = to bite.

   Sharp wits, like sharp knives, do often cut their owner's fingers.
   —Sinclair Lewis, Arrowsmith

5. ***moribund* has-been** môr′ə-bund Anyone moribund is dying, checking out, kicking the bucket, fading fast, petering out, biting the dust. From Latin, *moribundus* = dying.

   Either this man is dead or my watch has stopped.
   —Groucho Marx

6. ***morose* drag** mə-rōs′ A morose person is sullen and gloomy. From Latin, *morosus* = peevish, fretful.

   The only cure for grief is action.
   —G. H. Lewes

7. **mortiferous strangler** môr-tif'ə-rəs Beware! One who is mortiferous is deadly. From Latin, *mortiferus* = death-bearing.

> *We kill everybody, my dear.*
> *Some with bullets, some with words*
> *and everybody with our deeds.*
> *We drive people into their graves*
> *and neither see it nor feel it.*
> —*Maxim Gorky*

8. **mortified scapegoat** môr'tə-fīd To mortify is to punish oneself by self-denial, or to humiliate. Anyone mortified has been humiliated. From Latin, *mortificare* = to kill, destroy.

> *My one regret in life is that I'm not someone else.*
> —*Woody Allen*

9. **double-dealing *mountebank*** moun'tə-bangk A mountebank is a charlatan, a fake. In the past, a mountebank sold fraudulent remedies in public places, such as a town square. From Italian, *montimbanco* = one who climbs on a bench.

> *Quacks pretend to cure other men's disorders,*
> *but fail to find a cure for their own.*
> —*Cicero*

10. ***mulish* stick-in-the-mud** myoo'lish Anyone mulish is like a mule: stubborn. Mule comes from Latin, *mulus*.

> *There are two kinds of fools:*
> *those who can't change their opinions*
> *and those who won't.*
> —*Josh Billings*

QUIZ 50

Match the definitions with the words on the left.

____ 1. monomaniac	a.	charlatan, a fake
____ 2. monotonous	b.	deadly
____ 3. mordacious	c.	dying
____ 4. mordant	d.	humiliated
____ 5. moribund	e.	obsesses over one thing
____ 6. morose	f.	stubborn
____ 7. mortiferous	g.	sullen and gloomy
____ 8. mortified	h.	something (or someone's voice) that doesn't vary
____ 9. mountebank		
____ 10. mulish	i.	with biting wit (fits two words)

REVIEW 10

MATCH EACH QUOTE WITH THE APPROPRIATE WORD.

1. Every murderer is probably somebody's old friend.
—Agatha Christie

2. The artistic temperament is a disease that afflicts amateurs.
—G. K. Chesterton

3. A man's worst enemy can't wish him what he thinks up for himself.
—Yiddish proverb

4. Men's vows are women's traitors.
—Shakespeare

5. A man may build himself a throne of bayonets but he can't sit on it.
—William Ralph Inge

____ a. mercurial   ____ d. mendacious
____ b. mortiferous   ____ e. martial
____ c. masochistic

6. Join the army, see the world, meet interesting people, and kill them.
—Antiwar slogan

7. Always tell the truth in the form of a joke.
—Armenian proverb

8. One dies only once, and it's for such a long time!
—Molière

9. The reason men oppose progress is not that they hate progress,
but that they love inertia.
—Elbert Hubbard

____ f. mercenary   ____ h. misoneist
____ g. mordacious   ____ i. moribund

10. Any girl can be glamorous;
all you have to do is stand still and look stupid.
—Hedy Lamarr

11. He that flings dirt at another dirties himself most.
—English proverb

12. When a man is intoxicated by alcohol, he can recover,
but when intoxicated by power, he seldom recovers.
—James F. Byrnes

13. For it's "Tommy this an' Tommy that,"
and "Chuck 'im out, the brute."
But it's "Savior of 'is country," when
the guns begin to shoot.
—Rudyard Kipling

____ j. militant   ____ l. malign
____ k. meretricious   ____ m. megalomaniac

Chapter 11

*Those things for which we find words
are things we have already overcome.*
—Friedrich Nietzsche

IT IS ONE THING TO RECOGNIZE A WORD ON A
TEST. It is another thing to use it correctly in your speech. But it is another jump to use it in your writing. And if you want to improve your
writing, then you have to write. So take the time to write sentences using
the words below. Make the sentences as ridiculous or as serious as you
want. This will help your memory of the words, your spelling, and your
craft as a writer.

Are you the type that falls behind in your letter-writing? Yes? Then why
not use this book as a way to catch up? Just grab a bunch of postcards,
some stamps, this book, and sit down to write. Don't be too verbose.
Keep it simple, like: "Hi, Mom. Everything's great here except for the
pathological killer that crept into my apartment last night. Kisses, your
loving son." Or how about, "Dear Dad, I ran into some pedestrian
clone. Send money." You get the idea. Have fun with it.

GRISLY LIST 51

The **mutinous** mob began to creep up on the captain, **mussitating** their
hatred for the man who had led them on this wild goose chase that would
probably end in their deaths. They joined him to search for gold, but now had
been brought to such **necessitous** ends that they were eating their own boots.
Their once proud faces had grown ugly, like **Neanderthals**.

The captain's **myopic** leadership, aided by liquor, had led them adrift
somewhere in the North Atlantic. His **narcissistic** obsession for fame had re-
sulted in nothing but doom.

Suddenly the cabin boy jumped between his illustrious mentor and the
mundane sailors.

"Stop! I see land. I see land, I tell you!"

The mob stopped as the **naïve** boy peered through the telescope at the
horizon. In the distance, a **nebulous** patch of land became clearer and
clearer. Soon they were almost upon it.

"See! I told you, you idiots: the lost island of Atlantis," the **nefarious** captain screamed. "I'll have you all flogged."

As they passed by the iceberg, the cabin boy quipped:

"Okay. You can kill him."

1. **mundane commoner** mun-dān' Literally, mundane means "of the world," but it also
refers to anything ordinary. From Latin, *mundus* = world.

An ox remains an ox, even if driven to Vienna.
—*Hungarian proverb*

2. **mussitating** mob mus′ə-tā-ting To mussitate is to mumble and grumble almost silently. You see the mouth move but you can't quite make out what's being said. From Latin, *mussitare* = to mutter.

> *When people cease to complain, they cease to think.*
> —Napoleon Bonaparte, I

3. **mutinous** mobocracy myo͞ot′n-əs Anyone mutinous is revolting against authority. From Old French, *meute* = a riot.

> *In revolutions there are only two sorts of men,*
> *those who cause them and those who profit by them.*
> —Napoleon Bonaparte, I

4. **myopic** old maid mī-op′ik Literally, myopic means near-sighted, but it also denotes a lack of foresight or a preoccupation with the minor details. From Greek, *myops* = blinking.

> *Looking at small advantages*
> *prevents great affairs from being accomplished.*
> —Confucius

5. **naïve** schnook nī-ēv′ Anyone naïve is childlike and foolishly simple; hence, gullible. From Latin, *nativas* = natural.

> *One woman I was dating said,*
> *"Come on over, there's nobody home."*
> *I went over—nobody was home.*
> —Rodney Dangerfield

6. **narcissistic** mimbo när-si-sis′tik A narcissistic person is excessively self-centered, self-absorbed, and self-infatuated. In Greek mythology, Narcissus fell in love with his own reflection. It is coupled with **mimbo** = slang for a male bimbo.

> *There but for the grace of God, goes God.*
> —Winston Churchill

7. **lowbred** *Neanderthal* nē-an′dər-thôl A Neanderthal is a prehistoric subspecies of humans. It can also refer to any brutish person. From German, it literally means "Neander Valley," where the Neanderthal was first discovered.

> *While Darwinian Man, though well behaved,*
> *at best is only a monkey shaved.*
> —Sir William Gilbert

8. **nebulous** cipher neb′yə-ləs Nebulous describes anything that is unclear, vague, or indefinite. A nebula is a vast, indistinct cloud of stars too far away to be seen clearly. Here it is combined with the word **cipher**, which can mean either zero or a person of no influence; a nonentity. From Latin, *nebula* = vapor, mist, cloud.

> *I'm trying to arrange my life so that I don't even have to be present.*
> —Unknown

9. **necessitous** street urchin nə-ses′i-təs Anyone necessitous is needy. From Latin, *necessarius* = needful.

> *It is no disgrace to be poor, but it might as well be.*
> —Jim Grue

10. **nefarious** scoundrel nə-fâr′ē-əs A nefarious person is wicked and immoral. From Latin, *nefarius* = impious, abominable.

> *Evil enters like a needle and spreads like an oak tree.*
> —Ethiopian proverb

QUIZ 51

Match the definitions with the words on the left.

____ 1. mundane	a.	a prehistoric subspecies of humans
____ 2. mussitate	b.	childlike and foolishly simple
____ 3. mutinous	c.	in love with oneself
____ 4. myopic	d.	mumble almost silently
____ 5. naïve	e.	near-sighted
____ 6. narcissistic	f.	needful
____ 7. Neanderthal	g.	ordinary
____ 8. nebulous	h.	revolting against authority
____ 9. necessitous	i.	unclear, vague, or indefinite
____ 10. nefarious	j.	wicked

GRISLY LIST 52

The **nihilist** continued, "Don't you see? It's the **nepotistic** politicians that are our **nemeses**. Their **nocent** policies have wreaked havoc on the middle class and poor alike. To politicians we are but **negligible** cannon fodder, **nescient** dupes to sell their products to, to clean their bathrooms, to work in their factories. The **niddering** elite **niggardly** withhold from us the fruit of our labor. Our trade unions are nothing to them but a **nettling** nuisance. This construct is a sad leftover from a **Noachian** age. It is time for change. It is time for us to change."

His mother put his dinner plate on the table, "It's time for you to get a job."

1. ***negligible* figurehead** neg'li-jə-bəl Anyone or anything negligible is disregarded and unimportant. Don't confuse this with negligent. When one is *negligent*, one has failed in some task due to carelessness or inattention. From Latin, *neg-* = not + *legere* = to pick up + -ible.

> *He had the sort of face that, once seen, is never remembered.*
> *—Oscar Wilde*

2. **deadly *nemesis*** nem'i-sis A nemesis is a lifelong enemy, especially one that is unbeatable. It can also be anything that causes a vengeful act of justice. In Greek mythology, Nemesis is the god of retribution.

> *He hasn't an enemy in the world—but all his friends hate him.*
> *—Eddie Cantor*

3. ***nepotistic* politician** nep-ə-tis'tik To be nepotistic is to show favoritism, especially to relatives. From Latin, *nepos* = grandson + *potis* = nephew.

> *If the camel once gets his nose in the tent,*
> *his body will soon follow.*
> *—Arabic proverb*

4. ***nescient* nitwit** nesh'ənt Lacking any clue, a nescient person is ignorant and lacks experience. From Latin, *nesciens* = to be ignorant.

> *Only two things are infinite:*
> *the universe and human stupidity,*
> *and I'm not sure about the former.*
> *—Albert Einstein*

5. ***nettling* nag** net'ə-ling The nettle is a plant that stings; hence, to nettle is to irritate. A nettling person is irritating and annoying. From Medieval English, *netlen*.

> *Better to live on a corner of the roof*
> *than to share a house with a quarrelsome wife.*
> *—Proverbs 21:9*

6. ***niddering* ninny** nid'ər-ing Anyone who is niddering is a mean or cowardly person. From Icelandic, *nithingr* = to act basely.

> *Cowards never use their might*
> *But against such as will not fight.*
> *—Samuel Butler*

7. ***niggardly* spender** nig'ərd-lē Niggardly can mean stingy or insufficient in number. From Norwegian, *gnigga* = to be stingy.

> *He read in the paper that it takes ten dollars a year*
> *to support a kid in India. So he sent his kid there.*
> *—Red Buttons*

8. ***nihilistic* activist** nī-ə-lis'tik Nihilism is the denial of any basis for truth, the rejection of morality or religion. In politics, a nihilist believes that only violent overthrow can change the existing social structure. From Latin, *nihilum* = nothing.

There is no gravity. The earth sucks.
—Graffito

9. ***Noachian* hermit** nō-ā'kē-ən Noachian means of the time of Noah or ancient. It's from the biblical flood story related in Genesis 6–8. From Hebrew, *Noah* = rest, comfort.

I prefer old age to the alternative.
—Maurice Chevalier

10. ***nocent* hellion** nō-sənt Nocent means harmful, injurious, or criminal. From Latin, *nocens* = doing harm.

A thief believes everybody else steals.
—Ed Howe

QUIZ 52

Match the definitions with the words on the left.

_____ 1. negligible
_____ 2. nemesis
_____ 3. nepotistic
_____ 4. nescient
_____ 5. nettling
_____ 6. niddering
_____ 7. niggardly
_____ 8. nihilistic
_____ 9. Noachian
_____ 10. nocent

a. ancient
b. denying any basis for truth; rejecting morality and religion
c. disregarded as unimportant
d. harmful, injurious, or criminal
e. ignorant
f. irritating and annoying
g. lifelong enemy
h. mean or cowardly
i. showing favoritism to relatives
j. stingy

GRISLY LIST 53

Dear Mr. Eisenhower,

I'm writing this letter to tell you I think your book stinks! Why someone would write such a **noxious** book like this is beyond me. Its promise as an educational tool is **nugatory** at best. I can only deduce that you must be one of the most **nocuous** persons on the face of this planet. With the educational climate at a **notoriously** all-time low, why would you write a book that can only have a **noisome** influence on our poor children?

You probably will dismiss me as some **nondescript** complainer, a nagging **nonentity** who hasn't kept up with the times, but when I stumbled upon my precious little daughter actually reading your filthy description of a **nymphomaniac** I was so **nonplussed** I had to take off three weeks from work just to recuperate.

If your intention was to try to improve people's understanding of vocabulary, then let me say you have failed miserably. The only ray of hope that I can see is that I can sue you for **nonfeasance** of the worst sort.

Signed,
Nice Nelly

1. ***nocuous* hatchet man** nok′yoo-əs Anything nocuous is poisonous, harmful to health, noxious. From Latin, *nocere* = to hurt, injure.

EPITAPH:
*His concoction was meant to poison his wife
but she got wiser and gave him the knife*

2. ***noisome* nudnik** noi′səm A noisome person is harmful and/or smells bad. From a Latin phrase, *in odio* = in ill will > annoy > noy + -some. It is coupled with **nudnik =** Yiddish, a stupid, annoying pest.

*The drug he gave me, which he said was precious and cordial to me,
have I not found it murd'rous to th' senses?*
—Shakespeare

3. ***nondescript* drone** non-di-skript′ Anyone nondescript has no definite class or type. There is nothing that distinguishes this drone from the crowd. From Latin, *non-* = not + *descriptus* = described.

*One could not even dignify him with the name of stuffed shirt.
He was simply a hole in the air.*
—George Orwell

4. **forgettable *nonentity*** non-en′ti-tē Nonentity means something is not existing, but it can also describe a person of little or no importance. From Latin, *non-* = not + *entitas* = being.

Glory is fleeting, but obscurity is forever.
—Napoleon Bonaparte

5. ***nonfeasant* official** non-fē′zənt One who is guilty of nonfeasance has failed to do what duty requires. From Latin, *non-* = not + *facere* = to do.

He who holds the ladder is as bad as the thief.
—German proverb

6. ***nonplussed* chump** non-plust′ To be nonplussed is to be so utterly perplexed that one is unable to speak or act further. From Latin, *non-* = not + *plus* = further.

*At six I was left an orphan.
What on earth is a six-year-old supposed to do with an orphan?*
—Anonymous

7. ***notorious* mobster** nō-tôr'ē-əs A notorious person is bad to the bone and famous for it. From Late Latin, *notoria* = news, information.

> *The popularity of the bad man is as treacherous as he is himself.*
> —Pliny the Younger

8. ***noxious* blight** nok'shəs Anyone or anything noxious causes injury to health and/or morals. From Latin, *nocere* = to hurt, injure. Here it is coupled with **blight** = a pestilence; any person or thing that withers one's hopes or ambitions.

> *If it tastes good, it's trying to kill you.*
> —Roy Qualley

9. ***nugatory* wannabe** nōō'gə-tôr-ē Anyone or anything that is nugatory is worthless. From Latin, *nugae* = trifles.

> *You may marry the man of your dreams,*
> *but 15 years later you're married to a reclining chair that burps.*
> —Roseanne Barr

10. **naughty *nymphomaniac*** nim-fo-mā'nē-ak A nymphomaniac is a woman who has an uncontrollable desire for sex. The word derived from Greek, *nymph* = a nature goddess + *mania* = madness.

> *You can lead a horticulture, but you can't make her think.*
> —Dorothy Parker

QUIZ 53

Match the definitions with the words on the left.

____ 1. nocuous	a.	completely perplexed
____ 2. noisome	b.	failing to do one's duty
____ 3. nondescript	c.	famous and bad
____ 4. nonentity	d.	harmful to health
____ 5. nonfeasant		(fits three words)
____ 6. nonplussed	e.	having no definite class
____ 7. notorious	f.	worthless
____ 8. noxious	g.	not existing
____ 9. nugatory	h.	a woman who has an
____ 10. nymphomaniac		uncontrollable desire for sex

GRISLY LIST 54

Dear Nice Nelly,
  You're not nice at all. In fact, it's **objurgating obscurants** like you who are ruining this country. What makes you think I would be interested in you

obtrusively shoving your **obstipated** opinion down my throat? But I guess that wouldn't cross the mind of someone as **obdurate** as you. Did you really think that writing me a letter would turn me into some kind of **obsequious** twit? I think not. I wrote this book to help the poor souls who have to contend with **obstreperous** nuts like you.

Furthermore, don't **obfuscate** the truth by bringing up your daughter. Blaming me for your poor parenting skills won't make a lick of difference. And yes, I do think you are behind the times. When you're ready to leave your **obsolete** views behind and join the rest of the world, let us all know. Until then, keep your **obese** butt out of decent people's lives.

Sincerely,

P. E.

1. **obese tub of lard** ō-bēs' To be obese is to be so overweight that it is a health risk. From Latin, *obedere* = to devour.

> He must have had a magnificent build
> before his stomach went in for a career of its own.
> —Margaret Halsey

2. **obdurate numbskull** ob'dŏŏ-rit To be obdurate is to be hardheaded, stubborn, with a mulish attitude. From Latin, *obdurare* = to harden.

> I refuse to admit I'm more than fifty-two,
> even if that does make my sons illegitimate.
> —Nancy Astor

3. **obfuscating oddball** ob'fə-skāt To obfuscate is to cloud, confuse, bewilder, or stupefy. From Late Latin, *obfuscatus* = darkened.

> I wish people who have trouble communicating would just shut up.
> —Tom Lehrer

4. **objurgating mocker** ob'jər-gāt To objurgate is to criticize severely. From Latin, *objugare* = chastise, rebuke.

> The blow of a whip raises a welt,
> but a blow of the tongue crushes bones.
> —Ecclesiasticus 28:27

5. **narrow-minded obscurant** ob-skyŏŏr'ənt An obscurant tries to stop the spread of knowledge. From Latin, *obscurus* = dark.

> Pedantry crams our heads with learned lumber,
> and takes out our brains to make room for it.
> —Charles Caleb Colton

6. **obsequious twit** ob-sē'kwē-əs To be obsequious is to be overly submissive, much too willing to serve. From Latin, *obsequi* = to comply with.

> Servitude debases men to the point where they end up liking it.
> — Marquis Luc de Clapiers Vauvenargues

7. **obsolete** pawn ob-sə-lēt′ Anything obsolete is no longer needed. Of course, you can always use the word *obsolescent*, which means something is in the process of becoming obsolete. From Latin, *obsolescere* = to go out of use.

> It is better to be looked over than be overlooked.
> —Mae West

8. **obstipated** stiff ob′sti-pā-tid To be obstipated is to be obstinately constipated. Give him some prunes. From Late Latin, *obstipatio* = close pressure.

> People who never get carried away should be.
> —Malcolm Forbes

9. **obstreperous** stinkard ob-strep′ər-əs Anyone or anything obstreperous resists restraint and is unruly. From Latin, *obtrepere* = to roar at.

> If a child shows himself to be obstreperous,
> he should be quietly beheaded at the age of twelve,
> lest he grow to maturity, marry, and perpetuate his kind.
> —Don Marquis

10. **obtrusive** busybody ob-trōo′siv Anyone obtrusive intrudes or interferes without invitation. It can also mean something is conspicuous or blatant. From Latin, *ob* = toward + *trudere* = to thrust.

> I can't remember your name, but don't tell me.
> —Alexander Woollcott

QUIZ 54

Match the definitions with the words on the left.

_____ 1. obese
_____ 2. obdurate
_____ 3. obfuscate
_____ 4. objurgate
_____ 5. obscurant
_____ 6. obsequious
_____ 7. obsolete
_____ 8. obstreperous
_____ 9. obtrusive
_____ 10. obstipated

a. cloud over and muddle
b. so fat as to pose a health risk
c. hardheaded, stubborn
d. intruding or interfering without invitation; blatant
e. noisy and unruly
f. no longer needed, out of use
g. overly submissive
h. one who tries to stop the spread of knowledge
i. obstinately constipated
j. to criticize severely

GRISLY LIST 55

Pierre could just barely make out the **ominous** shadow of the scaffold that loomed out of the prison window. He could barely see it, but he could hear the screams of the **ochlocratic** rabble cheering with every chop-chop here and chop-chop there. Unfortunately, this was not the most gruesome aspect of prison life, nor was it the **opprobrious** distinction of knowing his head would soon be severed from his shoulders. It was the **odious** task of having to listen to his prison roommate, an **officious** gent whose **obtuse** outer shell belied his **oleaginous** inner slime.

"They say that when your head drops in the basket, for a few seconds your brain can think and sometimes if it bounces up you can see the guy who chopped it off."

"Yeah, but then they're idiots."

"No. Really. They say there are people who have talked after the decapitation."

"Shut up!"

Of course, this never stopped his fork-tongued, **ophidian** cellmate. Day after day, it had been Pierre's **onerous** misfortune to have to listen to this insanity in the **opaque** gloom of the prison walls. But it was after this particular "shut up" that his interrogator came in.

"Pierre, we give you one last chance to give us the name of the leader of the underground. You have my word that your life will be spared."

Pierre sighed as if he were unloading an enormous burden and eyed his cellmate.

"It's him!"

1. **obtuse ogre** ob-tōōs′ To be obtuse is to be blunt or intellectually slow. From Latin, *obtusus* = to be blunted, dull.

> *It is the dull man who is always sure,*
> *and the sure man who is always dull.*
> —H. L. Mencken

2. **ochlocratic rabble** ok-lə-krat′ik Ochlocratic means run by a riotous mob. From Greek, *ochlos* = mob.

> *The tyranny of the multitude is multiplied tyranny.*
> —Edmund Burke

3. **odious stalker** o′dē-əs An odious person is hated and fills others with disgust. From Latin, *odium* = hatred.

> *One should hate nobody whom one cannot destroy.*
> —Johann Wolfgang von Goethe

4. **officious** snoop ə-fish′əs An officious person is meddlesome, always offering unwanted advice. From Latin, *officiosus* = conformable to duty.

> *You will always find some Eskimos*
> *ready to instruct the Congolese*
> *on how to cope with heat waves.*
> —Stanislaw J. Lec

5. **oleaginous** sneak ō-lē-aj′ə-nəs Oleaginous means to have the nature of oil or to be unctuous, objectionably debonair and charming or smooth. From Latin, *oleaginus* = of the olive.

> *You're where you should be all the time*
> *and when you're not*
> *you're with a wife of a close friend.*
> —Carly Simon

6. **ominous** shadow om′ə-nəs Anything ominous is threatening and sinister, foreshadowing the evil, dread, or death that lurks just ahead. From Latin, *ominosus* = portentous.

> Likely comment:
> *Your days are numbered.*
> Your response:
> *Well, it's a good thing I can't count.*

7. **onerous** leech on′ər-əs Anything onerous is an incredible burden. From Latin, *onus* = a load.

> *It is not the load but the overload that kills.*
> —Spanish proverb

8. **opaque** flunky ō-pāk′ Anything opaque is impervious to light, loosely transparent, or stupid. From Latin, *opacus* = shady.

> *When you go to a mind reader, do you get half price?*
> —Ben Creed

9. **ophidian** conspirator ō-fid′ē-ən Anything ophidian is like a snake. From Greek, *ophis* = snake, serpent.

> *You snakes! You brood of vipers!*
> —Jesus of Nazareth, Luke 23:33

10. **opprobrious** sellout ə-prō′brē-əs Anything opprobrious is shameful, disgraceful, or conveys ridicule, contempt, or severe condemnation. From Latin, *opprobrius* = reproach.

> *One of the misfortunes of our time*
> *is that in getting rid of false shame*
> *we killed off so much real shame as well.*
> —Louis Kronenberger

QUIZ 55

Match the definitions with the words on the left.

_____ 1. obtuse	a.	burdensome
_____ 2. ochlocratic	b.	government run by riotous mob
_____ 3. odious	c.	hated
_____ 4. officious	d.	impervious to light
_____ 5. oleaginous	e.	blunt or dull
_____ 6. ominous	f.	offering unwanted advice
_____ 7. onerous	g.	of or like snakes
_____ 8. opaque	h.	oily, greasy
_____ 9. ophidian	i.	shameful, disgraceful
_____ 10. opprobrious	j.	threatening and sinister

REVIEW 11

MATCH EACH QUOTE WITH THE APPROPRIATE WORD.

1. Rebellion to tyrants is obedience to God.
—Thomas Jefferson

2. Whenever nature leaves a hole in a person's mind, she generally plasters it over with a thick coat of self-conceit.
—Henry Wadsworth Longfellow

3. By the pricking of my thumbs, something wicked this way comes.
—Shakespeare

4. It is the enemy whom we do not suspect who is the most dangerous.
—Fernando Rojas

____ a. nemesis   ____ c. nefarious
____ b. narcissistic   ____ d. mutinous

5. The most infamous are fond of fame;
and those who fear not guilt,
yet start at shame.
—Charles Churchill

6. That woman speaks eighteen languages, and can't say no in any of them.
—Dorothy Parker

7. No one is as deaf as the man who won't listen.
—Jewish proverb

8. Warm up a frozen snake and she will bite you.
—Armenian proverb

____ e. nymphomaniac   ____ g. obdurate
____ f. notorious   ____ h. ophidian

9. If I die, I forgive you; if I live, we'll see.
—Spanish proverb

10. A mob is the scum that rises upmost when the nation boils.
—John Dryden

11. I count him lost, who is lost to shame.
     —*Plautus*

12. Awkward, embarrassed, stiff, without the skill
     Of moving gracefully or standing still,
     One leg, as if suspicious of his brother,
     Desirous seems to run away from t'other.
     —*Charles Churchill*

____ i. opprobrious

____ j. ominous

____ k. ochlocratic

____ l. maladroit

Chapter 12

All words are pegs to hang ideas on.
—*Henry Ward Beecher*

IT IS HELPFUL TO LOOK AT THE ETYMOLOGY OF A PARTICULAR WORD to help you remember the word, but it is also helpful to go over the linguistic derivation of a word so you can use the word more precisely. Sometimes the etymon (root or origin) of a word isn't helpful, e.g. roguish < *rogare* = to beg; other times it's curious, e.g. salacious < *salaci* = to leap. However, at times the original word can help you see how best to use it, as in roister < *ruistre* = ruffian. Review this book, this time looking at all the etymons for each word. Focus on words that you find interesting and unique.

GRISLY LIST 56

Dear Mr. Eisenhower,

All of us down here at the Puppy Hills Accounting Firm want to thank you for getting rid of Nice Nelly for three weeks. It was the first vacation we've had in years. You're right; she isn't nice at all. She's one of the most **oppugnant** secretaries on our floor. Her **paranoid** delusions of persecution have made her the **pariah** of our department. If she were actually a good worker we might be able to put up with her, but she's an **otiose** slob. Unfortunately, she has seniority so we have to listen to her constant **palavering** about her nymphomaniac daughter (to whom she **panders** incessantly) and, moreover, she never seems to notice the **oscitant** effect it has on us. When she isn't going on about her daughter, she's constantly displaying the **ostentatious** jewelry she's gleaned from her daughter's many boyfriends. Moreover, she's the most **parsimonious** vulture any of us have ever met. She somehow always manages to sneak out without ever paying her share of the tab.

But here's the problem: she's back. Please forgive us for being such **ovine** cowards, but could you please get rid of her again?

In your debt,

The staff of the Puppy Hills Accounting Firm

1. **oppugnant** thug ə-pug′nənt Anyone oppugnant is hostile and antagonistic. From the same Latin word as pugnacious, *pugna* = a fight.

> *The world is a madhouse,*
> *so it's only right that it is patrolled by armed idiots.*
> —*Brendan Behan*

2. ***oscitant* lummox** os′i-tənt Oscitancy is the action of yawning or the condition of being drowsy or dull. An oscitant person is drowsy and dull. From Latin, *oscitant* = yawning.

> *Life is one long process of getting tired.*
> —Samuel Butler

3. ***ostentatious* yuppie** os-ten-tā′shəs Anyone ostentatious shows a pretentious display of wealth. From Latin, *ostendere* = to show.

> *If you stay in Beverly Hills too long you become a Mercedes.*
> —Robert Redford

4. ***otiose* baggage** ō′shē-ōs One who is otiose is useless, worthless, or lazy. From Latin, *otium* = leisure.

> *Many are idly busy. Domitian was busy,*
> *but then it was at catching flies.*
> —Jeremy Taylor

5. ***ovine* oaf** ō′vīn Anyone ovine is like a sheep. From Latin, *ovis* = sheep.

> *Make thyself a sheep and the wolf is ready.*
> —Russian proverb

6. ***palavering* putz** pə-lav′ər To palaver either means to chat idly or to charm or cheat someone by talking. From Portuguese, *palavra* = a word, speech.

> EPITAPH:
> *Though his words were quite sweet*
> *The cannibals need meat*
> *So they munched on his hide*
> *From his head to his feet*

7. ***pandering* pimp** pan′də-ring This pimp tries to cater to your vile, evil, incestuous desires. The word *pander* comes from the Greek name Panderos, a character in the Homer's *Iliad* who acted as a romantic intermediary for Troilus and Cressida.

> *I see the devil's hook, and yet cannot help nibbling at his bait.*
> —M. Adams

8. ***paranoid* loony** par′ə-noid One who is paranoid is overly suspicious, with delusions of persecution. From Greek, *para* = beside + *nous* = the mind.

> *When dealing with the insane, the best method is to pretend to be sane.*
> —Hermann Hesse

9. **exiled *pariah*** pə-rī′ə This outcast is despised and rejected by the community. Originally, a pariah was the lowest class in India, an untouchable. From Tamil, *parai* = a drum: the pariah was the hereditary drumbeater.

> *Loneliness is the ultimate poverty.*
> —Abigail Van Buren

10. **parsimonious** penny pincher pär-sə-mō′nē-əs A parsimonious person is excessively frugal and fearful of being wasteful. From Latin, *parcere* = to spare.

> *Save a little money each month and at the end of the year*
> *you'll be surprised at how little you have.*
> —*Ernest Haskins*

QUIZ 56

Match the definitions with the words on the left.

____ 1. oppugnant	a.	an outcast
____ 2. oscitant	b.	cater to vile, evil desires
____ 3. ostentatious	c.	drowsy and dull
____ 4. otiose	d.	excessively frugal
____ 5. ovine	e.	hostile and antagonistic
____ 6. palaver	f.	lazy
____ 7. pander	g.	like sheep
____ 8. paranoid	h.	having delusions of persecution
____ 9. pariah	i.	an affected show of wealth
____ 10. parsimonious	j.	to cheat another by one's talk

GRISLY LIST 57

"He has got to be the most **pathetic pedant** on campus," thought Alice as she tried to crouch behind her textbook. No matter how many sweaters she wore, her teacher gawked like a **Pavlovian** dog at her chest, as if it was his **pathological** perversion. And whenever he passed by her desk, he always had to put his **pedicular** paw on her shoulder. She couldn't stand it. She couldn't stand his **patronizing**.

"So, Miss Alice," her teacher began in his usual **pedagogic** style, "If you've read your text, kindly give us your opinion on what Fitzgerald is suggesting about the **peccable** nature of man: Are we noble, or is each of us capable of **peculating**, murdering, exploiting others if the right situation arises?"

She hadn't read her text but thought she could pull this off if she played it just right.

"Fitzgerald is never interested in the **pedestrian** man; he's always pointing out the evil in those with power and how they use it to abuse and exploit the ones beneath them."

For the rest of the class he didn't as much as glimpse at Alice for one split second, which suited her just fine.

1. ***pathetic* puppet** pə-thet′ik Someone or something pathetic is either pitiful or miserably inadequate. From Greek, *pathos* = suffering.

> *Women live like bats or owls, labor like beasts, and die like worms.*
> —Margaret Cavendish

2. ***pathological* liar** path-ə-loj′i-kəl Pathological is anything related to disease, or it can also describe anyone governed by an excessive compulsion because of a mental disease. From Greek, *pathos* = suffering, disease.

> *I don't buy temporary insanity as a murder defense.*
> *'Cause people kill people. That's an animal instinct.*
> *I think breaking into someone's home and ironing*
> *all their clothes is temporary insanity.*
> —Sue Kolinsky

3. ***patronizing* wiseacre** pā′trə-nī-zing To patronize is to treat another in a condescending way. From Latin, *patronus* = a protector.

> EPITAPH:
> *He talked down to others like he was the rave*
> *Now dogs look down as they piss on his grave*

4. ***Pavlovian* dog** pav-lō′vē-ən Ivan Pavlov was a Russian physiologist who studied behavior by training dogs to salivate at the sound of a bell, but it can be a wonderful slur for anyone who reacts predictably to stimuli.

> *He's the kind of a man a woman would have to marry to get rid of.*
> —Mae West

5. ***peccable* sot** pek′ə-bəl A peccable person is liable to sin or error. Don't confuse this with *peccant*, which means one is already sinning. From Latin, *peccare* = to sin.

> *Oh Lord, help me to be pure, but not yet.*
> —St. Augustine

6. ***peculating* trustee** pek′yə-lā-ting To peculate is to steal money entrusted to one's care; embezzle. From Latin, *peculari* = to embezzle < *peculium* = private property < *pecus* = cattle.

> *Is it a bigger crime to rob a bank or to open one?*
> —Ted Allan

7. ***pedagogic* egomaniac** ped-ə-goj′ik A pedagogue is a teacher, but pedagogic usually denotes one who is pedantic and/or dogmatic. From Greek, *paidagogos* = a boy's tutor.

> *Deep versed in books, and shallow in himself.*
> —John Milton

8. ***pedantic* prig** pə-dan′tik A pedantic person stresses the trivial points of learning. From French, *pedant* = schoolmaster. It is coupled with **prig** = one who is overly precise, proper, and haughty in following rules.

> *Academic tenure encourages pedants to become fossils.*
> —Leo Rosten

9. ***pedestrian* clone** pə-des′trē-ən A pedestrian is one who travels on foot, but it can also describe something or someone who is ordinary or run-of-the-mill. From Latin, *pedester* = on foot.

> *The trouble with some women*
> *is that they get all excited about nothing*
> *—and then marry him.*
> *—Cher*

10. ***pedicular* booboisie** pə-dik′yə-lər Literally, pedicular means "filled with lice," but it also describes one considered "lousy," as in crummy. From Latin, *pedis* = louse. It is coupled with **booboisie** = the social class of the stupid and gullible, a term coined by vicious journalist H. L. Mencken.

> *The lean lice bite most.*
> *—Polish proverb*

QUIZ 57

Match the definitions with the words on the left.

____ 1.	pathetic	a.	compulsive from mental illness
____ 2.	pathological	b.	a pedantic teacher
____ 3.	patronizing	c.	treat in a condescending way
____ 4.	Pavlovian	d.	filled with lice; lousy
____ 5.	peccable	e.	liable to sin or error
____ 6.	peculate	f.	ordinary
____ 7.	pedagogue	g.	pitiful or miserably inadequate
____ 8.	pedantic	h.	reacting predictably to stimuli
____ 9.	pedestrian	i.	rob cash trusted to one's care
____ 10.	pedicular	j.	stressing trivial points of learning

GRISLY LIST 58

"Are you aware, Ms. Jeffers, that if you don't answer truthfully, you could be guilty of **perjury?**"

The **pert** and **persnickety** Ms. Jeffers sat tall in her seat with her hands folded on her lap. "I swear it's the truth. Mr. Riley has never laundered any money. And I've been in his service for seven years."

The **perfidious** Mr. Riley arrogantly grinned.

"No further questions," a disappointed prosecutor said in a **perfunctory** fashion.

"Of course, he can be **pelting**." She chimed in **peevishly**.

"Thank you, no further questions."

Ms. Jeffers, her **pejorative** testimony on a roll, blithered on. "Seven years without a raise! I'd call that **penurious**, wouldn't you?"

The judge pounded his gavel. "Ms. Jeffers, if you don't have any criminal charges to make, then please step down. This court has no interest in whether Mr. Riley gave you a raise, provided that he did pay you."

"Oh, he always paid me. He's stingy but honest. Every Friday he paid me, in cash."

"Cash?" asked the prosecutor, seeing the **pernicious** crack in the defendant's smile.

"Yes," Ms. Jeffers beamed, "Mr. Riley always pays everyone in cash from the trunks he keeps in the basement."

1. ***peevish* prune** pē'vish A peevish person is impatient and hard to please. From Medieval English, *pevish* = spiteful.

> *My license plate says PMS. Nobody cuts me off.*
> —*Wendy Liebman*

2. ***pejorative* nitpicker** pi-jôr'ə-tiv Pejorative is usually applied to words whose meanings have changed for the worse, but it can also be used to describe someone who is disparaging, derisive, or the like. From Latin, *pejore* = to make worse.

> *When one is not good oneself,*
> *one likes to talk of what is wrong with others.*
> —*Slavic proverb*

3. ***pelting* plutocracy** pel'ting Don't confuse pelting with the verb *pelt*, which means to attack with repeated blows or missiles; its origin is obscure but it connotes anyone who is mean and/or miserly. From Danish, *pjalt* = rags. It is coupled with **plutocracy** = government by the wealthy.

> EPITAPH:
> *They rode in style in long limousines*
> *But the ride was cut short by the guillotine.*

4. ***penurious* cheapskate** pə-noor'ē-əs Penurious can mean stingy or poor, or stingy *and* poor. From Latin, *penuria* = want.

> *Man hoards himself when he has nothing to give away.*
> —*Edward Dahlberg*

5. ***perfidious* fiend** pər-fid'ē-əs Perfidy is the premeditated breaking of faith. A perfidious fiend is treacherous. From Latin, *perfidios* = faithless, dishonest.

> *Alas, they had been friends in youth;*
> *but whispering tongues can poison truth.*
> —*Samuel Taylor Coleridge*

6. ***perfunctory* grubber** pər-fungk'tə-rē Anything perfunctory is done in a routine fashion, without care. From Latin, *perfungi* = to get rid of. It is coupled with **grubber** = one who toils for his/her daily bread.

> *Most men in a brazen prison live,*
> *Where, in the sun's hot eye,*
> *With heads bent o'er their toil, they languidly*
> *Their lives to some unmeaning taskwork give,*
> *Dreaming of naught beyond their prison wall.*
> —Matthew Arnold, "A Summer Night"

7. ***perjuring* pretender** pûr'jər-ing To perjure is to lie under oath. From Latin, *perjurus* = breaking oath.

> *His face was filled with broken commandments.*
> —John Masefield

8. ***pernicious* parasite** pər-nish'əs Anyone or anything pernicious is harmful by insidiously weakening you. From Latin, *perniciosus* = destructive.

> *Destroy the seed of evil, or it will grow up to your ruin.*
> —Aesop

9. ***persnickety* fusspot** pər-snik'i-tē One who is persnickety is too precise and fussy. From Scottish, perhaps derived from a child's word for particular, *pertickie*.

> *Nancy Reagan fell down and broke her hair.*
> —Johnny Carson

10. ***pert* prima donna** pûrt A pert person is bold, saucy, and forward. From Old French, *apert* = open, free; hence, impudent < Latin, *apertus* = open.

> EPITAPH:
> *She wanted a world on her own terms*
> *Now she's food for maggots and worms.*

QUIZ 58

Match the definitions with the words on the left.

____ 1.	peevish	a.	bold, saucy, and forward
____ 2.	pejorative	b.	disparaging, derisive
____ 3.	pelting	c.	hard to please, impatient
____ 4.	penurious	d.	insidiously weakening
____ 5.	perfidious	e.	in a routine way, without care
____ 6.	perfunctory	f.	lie under oath
____ 7.	perjure	g.	mean, miserly
____ 8.	pernicious	h.	stingy and/or poor
____ 9.	persnickety	i.	too precise and fussy
____ 10.	pert	j.	treacherous

GRISLY LIST 59

Dear Puppy Hills Accounting Firm Staff,

Sure. I'd love nothing better than to help you get rid of this **pesky** and **pertinacious** problem. First, introduce me to the daughter. That'll send her over the edge. Instead of giving the mother jewelry, I'll pawn off any **picayunish** gewgaws I've got hanging around on her. While I'm keeping the **philandering** daughter busy (or she's keeping me busy), keep dropping my book on Nice Nelly's desk when she's not watching. Now, if you've got the stomach for some really **perverse** humor, convince the **pestiferous** pain to videotape the office to catch any slackers; she'll like this. Then hire a **pettifogger** and threaten to sue the company over the harassment you've put up with from this **pettish** troublemaker. Make it clear that you'll be willing to settle for nothing if they get rid of the **petulant** hag. If they hesitate, show them the video of your **phlegmatic** overseer not doing her job. She'll be out of the office in a New York second.

Viciously yours,

P. E.

1. **pertinacious zealot** pûr-tn-ā'shəs Stubborn to the end, a pertinacious person never says die. From Latin, *pertinacia* = stubbornness.

> *In the friendship of an ass expect nothing but kicks.*
> —*Indian proverb*

2. **perverse flasher** pûr-vûrs' To be perverse is to deviate from what is considered right or good, or to be stubborn in what is wrong. From Latin, *pervertare* = to pervert.

> *Nothing is good for him for whom nothing is bad.*
> —*Baltasar Gracian*

3. **pesky critter** pes'kē A pesky person is annoying and troublesome. The word is a blend of pes(t) + (ri)sky.

> *Never lend your car to anyone to whom you have given birth.*
> —*Erma Bombeck*

4. **pestiferous rogue** pe-stif'ər-əs Anything pestiferous is diseased, evil, or simply mischievous. From Latin, *pestes* = a plague + *ferre* = to bear.

> *Disease is the retribution of outraged nature.*
> —*Hosea Ballou*

5. **pettifogging mouthpiece** pet'ē-fog-ging A pettifogger is a lawyer who handles petty cases unethically; a cheater; a quibbler. From Middle Dutch, *voeger* = one who arranges things.

> *Two farmers each claimed to own a certain cow.*
> *While one pulled on its head and other pulled on its tail,*
> *the cow was milked by a lawyer.*
> —*Jewish parable*

6. ***pettish* hen** pet'ish Originally pettish meant "like a pet," that is, like a spoiled child. Now it signifies one who is cross and peevish. From French, *petit* = little, used as an endearment, *mon petit* = my little one.

> Famous last lines:
> *Either they go, or I do.*
> —*Oscar Wilde, on his bedroom curtains*

7. ***petulant* snot** pech'ə-lənt One who is petulant is peevish, froward, and impatient. From Latin, *petulant* = impudent.

> *Keep your paws off. He's mine.*
> —*Amanda,* Melrose Place

8. ***philandering* playboy** fi-lan'də-ring To philander is to love insincerely, to flit from affair to affair, especially when married. From Greek, *philos* = loving + *andros* = a man.

> *Never make the big pitch until the second date.*
> *If her eyes don't quite track, it's a sign of a sure kill.*
> —*International swordsman*

9. ***phlegmatic* slug** fleg-mat'ik Think of phlegm, mucus, snot! This one is sluggish and stolid. In medieval times it was believed that phlegm was one of the four humors that controlled the human personality. From Greek, *phlegma* = a flame; hence, an inflammation.

> *When I feel like exercising I just lie down until the feeling goes away.*
> —*Robert M. Hutchins*

10. ***picayunish* tightwad** pik-ə-yoon'ish One who is picayunish is either worthless or concerned with unimportant details. From French, *picaillan* = small change.

> Likely comment:
> *Gee. When our dinner bill is $1.29,*
> *how do we split the check evenly?*
> Your response:
> *Right between your eyes.*

Match the definitions with the words on the left.

____ 1. pertinacious	a.	annoying and troublesome
____ 2. perverse	b.	an unethical lawyer
____ 3. pesky	c.	peevish (fits two words)
____ 4. pestiferous	d.	diseased, evil, or mischievous
____ 5. pettifogger	e.	like snot: sluggish and stolid
____ 6. pettish	f.	make love insincerely
____ 7. petulant	g.	of little value
____ 8. philander	h.	stubborn to the end
____ 9. phlegmatic	i.	deviate from what is right
____ 10. picayune		

GRISLY LIST 60

Albert was not the brave sort; in fact, he was more the gutless **poltroon** type and **pinguid** to boot. He stood shivering in his new jail cell and tried to face his new cellmate, a bulky, **pockmarked** brute.

"What are you in for?" the brute asked.

"**Plagiarizing**."

"What's that?"

"It's a kind of **pilfering**."

His cellmate scowled.

"**Pillaging!**" Albert blurted out trying as best he could to give his words an air of **pococurante pomposity**. "Raping, murdering people, blowing up banks. When I'm under that drunken **piscine** influence, I get **polemic** and dangerous. What are you in for?"

The brute took a drag from his cigarette. "Passing bad checks."

Albert gave a sigh of relief, "Whew. For a minute I thought I might not live through the night. I was just kidding about the murder and other stuff. Passing bad checks? You should be out of here in no time."

"Twenty years!"

"Twenty years for passing bad checks?"

"It's my second offense," the ugly man put out his cigarette in the palm of his hand. "My first was for beating a man to death."

1. ***pillaging* pirate** pil'ij-ing To pillage is to violently strip property or money from a victim. From Middle French, *pillar* = to rob.

> *Hitler is a monster of wickedness,*
> *insatiable in his lust for blood and plunder . . .*
> *So now this bloodthirsty guttersnipe*
> *must launch his mechanized armies*
> *upon new fields of slaughter, pillage and devastation.*
> —*Winston Churchill*

2. ***pilfering* purse snatcher** pil'fər-ing A pilfering person steals small items and usually steals habitually. From Middle French, *pelfre* = stolen goods.

> *He without benefit of scruples*
> *His fun and money soon quadruples*
> —*Ogden Nash*

3. ***pinguid* porker** pin'gwid One who is pinguid is fat. From Latin, *pinguis* = fat.

> *If you want to look young and thin, hang around old fat people.*
> —*Jim Eason*

4. ***piscine* sponge** pis'īn Literally, piscine means "like or resembling a fish," but it connotes drunkenness (someone who drinks booze like a fish drinks water). From Latin, *piscis* = fish.

> *I can't die until the government finds a safe place for my liver.*
> —*Phil Harris*

5. ***plagiarizing* copycat** plā'jə-rī-zing To plagiarize is to take other's ideas and pass them off as one's own. From Latin, *plagiarius* = kidnapper.

> *A plagiarist should be made to copy the author a hundred times.*
> —*Karl Kraus*

6. ***pockmarked* palooka** pok'märkt To be pockmarked is to be scarred and pitted from pimples, smallpox, and the like. From Old English, *poc* = a pustule.

> *Now there's a face for radio.*
> —*Paul Attanasio,* Quiz Show

7. **useless *pococurante*** pō-kō-kōō-ran'tē In Italian, a pococurante is indifferent and careless. The word can be used as an adjective or a noun. From Latin, *paucus* = few + *cura* = care.

> *He did nothing in particular, and did it very well.*
> —*W. S. Gilbert*

8. ***polemic* partisan** pə-lem'ik Anyone polemic (or polemical) is either controversial or argumentative. From Greek, *polemos* = a war.

> *People generally quarrel because they cannot argue.*
> —*G. K. Chesterton*

9. **gutless** *poltroon* pol-trōōn′ A poltroon is a contemptible coward. From Old Italian, *poltrone* = idler, coward; literally, one who lies in bed.

> *There is nothing that makes more cowards and feeble men than public opinion.*
> —*Henry Ward Beecher*

10. *pompous* **autocrat** pom′pəs A pompous person is full of self-importance, overly serious, or grandiloquent. From Greek, *pompe* = solemn procession.

> *Don't remind a vain man of his pimples.*
> —*Russian proverb*

QUIZ 60

Match the definitions with the words on the left.

_____ 1. pillage

_____ 2. pilfer

_____ 3. pinguid

_____ 4. piscine

_____ 5. plagiarize

_____ 6. pockmarked

_____ 7. pococurante

_____ 8. polemic

_____ 9. poltroon

_____ 10. pompous

a. a coward

b. controversial; argumentative

c. fat

d. full of self-importance

e. like or resembling a fish; drunk

f. steal

g. tardy, late

h. to be scarred from pimples

i. take another's ideas and pass them off as one's own

j. to violently strip property or money from a victim

REVIEW 12

MATCH EACH QUOTE WITH THE APPROPRIATE WORD.

1. Behind every argument is someone's ignorance.
—*Louis D. Brandeis*

2. Borrowed thoughts, like borrowed money, only show the poverty of
the borrower.
—*Lady Blessington*

3. He that falls into sin is a man; that grieves at it, is a saint; that boasteth
of it, is a devil.
—*Thomas Fuller*

4. Violence is the last refuge of the incompetent.
—*Isaac Asimov*

5. Brimful of learning, see the pedant stride,
bristling with horrid Greek, and puffed with pride!
A thousand authors he in vain has read,
and with their maxims stuffed his empty head;
and thinks that without Aristotle's rules,
reason is blind, and common sense a fool!
—*Nicolas Boileau*

6. Women still remember the first kiss after men have forgotten the last.
—*Remy de Gourmont*

____ a. oppugnant
____ b. peccable
____ c. philanderer

____ d. plagiarize
____ e. polemic
____ f. pedagogue

7. Bureaucracy is a giant mechanism operated by pigmies.
—*Honoré de Balzac*

8. Education: the inculcation of the incomprehensible into the indifferent
by the incompetent.
—*John Maynard Keynes*

9. Men are not punished for their sins, but by them.
—*Frank McKinney Hubbard*

10. The best way to put an end to the bugs is to set fire to the bed.
—*Mexican proverb*

11. Treachery, though at first very cautious, in the end betrays itself.
—*Livy*

12. Woe unto them that call evil good, and good evil.
—*Isaiah 5:20*

____ g. peccant
____ h. pedantic
____ i. perfidious

____ j. perverse
____ k. pestiferous
____ l. functionary

Chapter 13

When ideas fail,
words come in very handy.
—Johann Wolfgang von Goethe

NOW THAT YOU HAVE A STRONGER COMMAND OF LANGUAGE, you are less likely to be fooled by it. We live in a society where lawyers and politicians mince words about what the word *is* means. In this society, those who can skillfully use rhetoric to communicate with others are valued, but so are those who can obscure information with craft and subtlety.

The beauty of words like *pulchritudinous* and *doughty* is that even when others know what those words mean, they don't necessarily know what you mean. One word means "beautiful" and the other means "brave." Depending upon how you use them, they could be insults or a compliments. No one will know for sure. Now why is that important? Well, the gift of language is not only to make things clear but also to make things ambiguous when, for example, you are subtly insulting someone or writing poetry. However you use these words, you will benefit by improving your vocabulary.

GRISLY LIST 61

Natasha took the extra moment to **preen** in front of the living room mirror. She was **precociously** gorgeous, and the green gown clung tightly to her. To her right, the **porcine** man sat firmly in the recliner downing his vodka. He was old, even **preadamic** and, as she painted her full lips red, he **pontificated** with growing, **precipitous** passion.

"Young people these days, they have no respect. In my day you treated your elders with honor, with dignity, with proper decorum."

"Don't wait up for me. I'll be out very late, past your bedtime." Natasha asserted **presumptuously**, in a thick Russian accent.

The doorbell rang and Natasha pouted at the old man, who **ponderously** got up to answer the door. It opened to reveal a young fellow complete with acne and a corsage.

"I'll kill him. I'll kill him." The old man waved his **potvaliant** fists with **predatory** fervor at the boy.

Natasha brushed him aside as she grabbed her corsage and exited. The boy tried to appease him.

"I'll have your daughter home by eleven."

"Daughter?!" he screamed, "That's my wife!"

1. ***ponderous* plodder** pon'dər-əs Anything ponderous is heavy and bulky or labored and dull. From Latin, *pondus* = a weight.

> *If the human being is condemned and restricted*
> *to perform the same functions over and over again,*
> *he will not even be a good ant,*
> *not to mention a good human being.*
> —Norbert Wiener

2. ***pontificating* windbag** pon-tif'i-kā-ting To pontificate is to speak in a pompous and dogmatic style. From Latin, *pontifex* = pontiff (a pope or bishop), implying a pontiff is likely to be pompous and dogmatic.

> *A closed mouth gathers no feet.*
> —Unknown

3. ***porcine* fatso** pôr'sīn Anything porcine is involving or resembling a pig. From Latin, *porcus* = a hog.

> *Outside every fat man there is an even fatter man trying to close in.*
> —Kingsley Amis

4. ***potvaliant* scrapper** pot'val-yənt Anyone who is potvaliant is brave because he/she is drunk. From English slang, *potted* = drunk + *valiant* = brave.

> *They were red-hot with drinking,*
> *so full of valor that they smote the air.*
> —William Shakespeare

5. ***preadamic* caveman** prē-ə-dam'ik To be preadamic is to have existed before the biblical Adam. It also refers to those who believe man existed before Adam. From Hebrew (Genesis 2:7), *adha'm* = man, human being < *adha'ma'h* = earth.

> *Old men and comets have been reverenced for the the same reason;*
> *their long beards, and pretences to foretell events.*
> — Jonathan Swift

6. ***precipitous* grouch** pri-sip'i-təs Precipitous indicates something that is steep, but it can also imply a rash or hasty disposition. From Latin, *praeceps* = headlong.

> *I'm not crazy. I've just been in a very bad mood for forty years.*
> —Robert Harling, Steel Magnolias

7. ***precocious* jailbait** pri-kō'shəs A precocious person is more mature than is usual for someone at a particular age; especially said of a child or teenager. From Latin, *praecoci* = early, ripe.

> *Men aren't attracted to me by my mind, but what I don't mind.*
> —Gypsy Rose Lee

8. ***predatory* savage** pred'ə-tôr-ē One who is predatory lives by preying on others. From Latin, *praedari* = to plunder.

> *Don't jump on a man unless he's down.*
> —Finley Peter Dunne

9. ***preening* peacock** prē′ning To preen is to trim one's feathers or adorn oneself. From Medieval English, *preonen* = prick with a pin.

The smaller the mind, the greater the conceit.
—Aesop

10. ***presumptuous* whippersnapper** pri-zump′choo-əs Anyone who is presumptuous takes too much for granted. From Latin, *praesumere* = to undertake beforehand.

No young man believes he will ever die.
—William Hazlitt

QUIZ 61

Match the definitions with the words on the left.

____ 1. ponderous	a.	brave because one is drunk
____ 2. pontificate	b.	preying; exploiting, plundering
____ 3. porcine	c.	bulky, or labored and dull
____ 4. potvaliant	d.	of or like a pig
____ 5. preadamic	e.	old; existed before Adam
____ 6. precipitous	f.	pompous and dogmatic
____ 7. precocious	g.	premature
____ 8. predatory	h.	steep; rash or hasty in disposition
____ 9. preen	i.	takes too much for granted
____ 10. presumptuous	j.	to trim one's feathers, or to vainly adorn oneself

GRISLY LIST 62

The **Procrustean** king reached to punch the trap door that would send the **prodigal profligate** hurtling to the **primordial** jaws of the alligators below.

"Wait!" the doomed man shrieked. "You don't want to do that."

"I don't?" the king asked.

"No." He looked around the courtroom, grasping at straws, hoping someone would show mercy. The **pretentious**, superior sneer on the queen's face didn't help, and her manly, **priapic** guards were no better. His crime was so small; he'd **profaned** the name of the king's dog.

"Were you going to tell me where my enemies are hiding?"

"Uh. . ."

The king toyed with him with his **proleptic** jest. "Because if you were, I should let you know that I already know where they are."

"Uh, well, no. But—"

"You're not **prevaricating**, are you?"

The poor wretch had no idea what **prevaricate** meant, but when the king reached toward the button one more time, he cried out:

"I know a good joke!"

"This could be good," the king laughed and sat back. "Tell me your joke. I might let you live after all."

He could only remember one joke, but he knew that if he could make it through one, he could remember a million more. Hope was renewed in his heart, for his one redeeming quality was his ability to tell a good joke.

"There once was a queen in a ruckus . . ."

"Oh, stop **procrastinating**," the queen whined and pushed the button.

1. ***pretentious* diva** pri-ten'shəs A pretentious person is stuck-up, snobbish, and acts affectedly superior. From Middle Latin, *praetensus* = alleged.

> *An ounce of pretension is worth a pound of manure.*
> —*Steven E. Clark*

2. ***prevaricating* grifter** pri-var'i-kā-ting To prevaricate is to avoid telling the truth, to equivocate, to be evasive. From Latin, *praevaricatus* = to walk crookedly; hence, to stray from the proper path. It is coupled with **grifter** = one who operates a sideshow at a fair or a circus; in slang, a con man, a swindler.

> *The masses will more easily fall victim to a big lie than to a small one.*
> —*Adolf Hitler*

3. ***priapic* yutz** prī-a'pik Anyone priapic is overly concerned with virility or manliness. From Greek, *priapizein* = to be lewd < Priapus, the god of male reproduction.

> *In the past, it was easy to be a Real Man.*
> *All you had to do was abuse women,*
> *steal land from Indians,*
> *and find some place to dump the toxic waste.*
> —*Bruce Fierstein*

4. ***primordial* slime** prī-môr'dē-əl Anything primordial is out of the depths of time, from the very beginning; primitive. From Latin, *primus* = first + *ordiri* = to begin.

> *You remind me of my brother Bosco—only he had a human head.*
> —*Judy Tenuta*

5. ***procrastinating* idler** prō-kras'tə-nā-ting To procrastinate is to postpone a task. From Latin, *pro* = ahead + *crastinus* = belonging to tomorrow.

> *If it weren't for the last minute, nothing would get done.*
> —*Unknown*

6. ***Procrustean* Gestapo** prō-krus'tē-ən In Greek mythology, the giant, Procrustes, would stretch or amputate limbs of his victims so that they would fit his bed. Now Procrustean defines a person who ruthlessly forces control.

> *And if the population should treat us with indignation,*
> *we chop 'em to bits because we like our hamburgers raw.*
> —*Bertolt Brecht*

7. ***prodigal*** **squanderer** prod'i-gəl As an adjective, prodigal describes one who is wasteful or extravagantly wild. The noun denotes one who wastes his or her parents' money. From Latin, *prodigere* = to drive away, waste.

> *He's got a wonderful head for money. There's a long slit on the top.*
> —David Frost

8. ***profane*** **menace** prō-fān' Anyone profane shows disrespect for sacred things. From Latin, *profanare* = to desecrate.

> *With devotion visage, and pious action*
> *we do sugar o'er the devil himself.*
> —William Shakespeare

9. **reckless *profligate*** prof'li-git A profligate is shamelessly immoral or given to reckless extravagance From Latin, *profligare* = to strike to the ground.

> *A woman drove me to drink*
> *and I never had the courtesy to thank her.*
> —W. C. Fields

10. ***proleptic*** **wisenheimer** prō-lep'tik A prolepsis is an introduction that anticipates someone's argument. To be proleptic is to anticipate an argument so as to answer before the other person has had a chance to respond. From Greek, *prolepsis* = anticipation < *pro-* = forward + *lepsis* = to take.

> *The opposite of talking isn't listening.*
> *The opposite of talking is waiting.*
> —Fran Lebowitz

QUIZ 62

Match the definitions with the words on the left.

____ 1.	pretentious	a.	act affectedly superior
____ 2.	prevaricate	b.	anticipate another's argument
____ 3.	priapic	c.	existing from the beginning
____ 4.	primordial	d.	shamelessly immoral or given to
____ 5.	procrastinate		reckless extravagance
____ 6.	Procrustean	e.	overly concerned with virility
____ 7.	prodigal	f.	ruthlessly forcing control
____ 8.	profane	g.	disrespectful of sacred things
____ 9.	profligate	h.	to lie or evade the truth
____ 10.	proleptic	i.	to postpone a task
		j.	wasteful

GRISLY LIST 63

"It's a rather **prolix** speech."

"What the hell does that mean?" shouted the **pugnacious** athlete.

"It's wordy," the tutor said while wondering if this galoot spoke with anything other than a deafening roar.

"It's a speech! It's supposed to have words in it!"

"Well, yes. But it's **prosaic**." He could see this wasn't getting through. "**Prosy**, like prose? It's dull. You need to take out a good portion of this and then spice it up with some witty remarks so it's less **provincial**. And the **prurient** comments about the cheerleaders could get you into trouble."

The **pugilistic** bully slammed his fists on the table. "I worked hard on this! You said you'd help me!"

The tutor sized up the athlete's steroid-pumped biceps coupled with the **puerile** personality and considered his options for survival. He wondered if he could play the **pseudologist**.

"I'm just pulling your leg. Actually, it's great." The tutor watched the dummy's face quickly begin to beam.

"Really?"

"It's the best I've ever read. Trust me: You are going places." The tutor quickly darted out the door. A **puckish** smile crossed his face; when this speech would be presented, he'd be long gone.

1. ***prolix* prattler** prō′liks To be prolix is to be exasperatingly wordy. From Latin, *prolixus* = extended.

> *A chattering fool comes to ruin.*
> *—Proverbs 10:8*

2. ***prosaic* scribbler** prō-zā′ik Dull! Dull! Dull! A prosaic person's writing is like prose and hence, lacking the imagination of poetry. From Latin, *prosa* = straightforward (speech).

> *The Home Beautiful . . . is a play lousy.*
> *—Dorothy Parker*

3. ***prosy* piece of twaddle** prō′zē Anything prosy is dull and tedious because it resembles prose—not poetry. From Latin, *prosa* – straightforward (speech).

> *Some people stay longer in an hour*
> *than others do in a month.*
> *—William Dean Howells*

4. ***provincial* square** prə-vin′shəl Anyone who is provincial is rustic, narrow-minded, unsophisticated, and uninformed. From Latin, *provincia* = province.

> *Some fellers get credit for being conservative*
> *when they're only stupid.*
> *—Kin Hubbard*

5. ***prurient* rodent** prŏŏr'ē-ənt A prurient person is excessively lustful. From Latin, *prurire* = to itch.

> *There is nothing a young man can get by wenching*
> *but duels, the clap and bastards.*
> —Kathleen Winsor

6. **two-faced *pseudologist*** sŏŏ-dol'ə-jist A pseudologist is an ultimate liar. From Greek, *pseudes* = false + *logos* = word, speech.

> *There's one way to find out if a man is honest:*
> *ask him; if he says yes, you know he is crooked.*
> —Mark Twain

7. ***puckish* pain in the neck** puk'ish One who is puckish is mischievous. It comes from Puck, a mischievous spirit. From Old Norse, *puki* = a devil or a mischievous demon.

> *He that mischief hatcheth, mischief catcheth.*
> —William Camden

8. ***puerile* fly-by-nighter** pyŏŏr'əl A puerile person acts silly, immature, and childish. In psychology, puerile is used as a noun to describe people who are self-absorbed. From Latin, *puerilis* = boyish.

> *Boys will be boys, and so will a lot of middle-aged men.*
> —Kin Hubbard

9. ***pugilistic* blockhead** pyŏŏ-jə-lis'tik A pugilist is a professional boxer, or anyone who likes to fistfight; hence, anyone pugilistic likes to fight. From Latin, *pugil* = boxer.

> *Make yourself at home, Frank. Hit somebody.*
> —Don Rickles, to Frank Sinatra

10. ***pugnacious* pug** pug-nā'shəs Anyone pugnacious is belligerent, prone to fight or quarrel. From Latin, *pugnacitas* = combativeness.

> *My kid beat up your honor student.*
> —Bumper sticker

QUIZ 63

Match the definitions with the words on the left.

_____ 1. prolix	a. a professional boxer
_____ 2. prosaic	b. dull (fits two words)
_____ 3. prosy	c. prone to fight or quarrel
_____ 4. provincial	d. lustful
_____ 5. prurient	e. mischievous
_____ 6. pseudologist	f. one who lies
_____ 7. puckish	g. rustic, narrow-minded
_____ 8. puerile	h. silly, immature and childish
_____ 9. pugilist	i. too wordy
_____ 10. pugnacious	

GRISLY LIST 64

Dear Puppy Hills Accounting Firm Staff,

Since you haven't returned any of my calls, I've no choice but to write you this letter. It seems there were a few details you failed to bring me up to speed on regarding to my part with the (ahem) **pulchritudinous** daughter of the **punctilious** Ms. Nelly. I hate to sound too **querulous**, but did it occur to you that the **putrid** smell of this **quasi** human might be offensive? And forgive me if I'm sounding like a **pusillanimous** chicken or a **quailing** crybaby, but couldn't you have mentioned that Nelly's daughter is a professional boxer? Not to mention her penchant for **purloining** every single thing she can get her hands on. Give me a break! I find it hard to believe that you could be **purblind** enough not to notice these small imperfections. Ever since our little prank, I'm looking over my shoulder with every **quavering** step I take. Perhaps you could be so kind as to return the favor and free me of my particular burden.

Longing to hear from you,

P. E.

1. **pulchritudinous** babe pul-kri-tōōd′n-əs Strictly defined, pulchritudinous means "beautiful," but it is now often used in jest, meaning just the opposite. From Latin, *pulcher* = beautiful.

> *Beauty is only sin deep.*
> —*Saki (H H. Munro)*

2. **punctilious** pedant pungk-til′ē-əs A punctilious person is overly exacting in observing rules; you get the feeling this pedant has a clock that's wound a little too tight. From Latin, *punctillum* – a little point.

> EPITAPH:
> *Tried to control things a little too tightly*
> *When renal failure caused a death unsightly*

3. **purblind** automaton pûr′blīnd A purblind person lacks vision, insight, and/or intelligence. From Medieval English, *pur blind* = completely blind.

> *Where all think alike, no one thinks very much.*
> —*Walter Lippman*

4. **purloining** shoplifter pər-loin′ing To purloin is to steal, but it can have the added connotation of breaking faith in the act of stealing. From Old French, *purloigner* = remove < from Latin, *longus* = to put far off; hence, purloin developed the sense "to make off with."

> *Opportunity makes the thief.*
> —*English proverb*

5. **pusillanimous** cream puff pyōō-sə-lan′ə-məs A pusillanimous person is a coward. From Latin, *pusillus* = tiny + *animus* = the mind, courage.

> *It is better to die on your feet than live on your knees.*
> —*Talmud*

6. ***putrid* pile of tripe** py‾oo′trid Anything putrid is rotten and reeking an odor of decay. Putrid can also signify something that is corrupt and disgustingly bad. From Latin, *putris* = rotten.

> *She's like a rose to me. It smells and so does she.*
> —Homer Haynes

7. ***quailing* coward** kwā′ling To quail is to shrink, cower, draw back in fear. From Medieval English, *quail* = to fail. Quail's modern sense is probably derived from the very shy, timid bird of the same name.

> *It is easy to frighten a bull from the window.*
> —Italian proverb

8. ***quasi* intelligentsia** kwä′zē Anything quasi isn't real or true. It is often combined with a noun; for example, quasi academic, a quasi hero. From Latin, *quasi* = as if. It is coupled with **intelligentsia** = intellectuals, the educated class.

> *Everyone agreed that Clevinger was certain*
> *to go far in the academic world.*
> *In short, Clevinger was one of those people*
> *with lots of intelligence and no brains,*
> *and everyone knew it*
> *except those who soon found it out.*
> *In short, he was a dope.*
> —Joseph Heller, Catch 22

9. ***quavering* crybaby** kwā′və-ring To quaver is to tremble from fear or anxiety. It can also describe one who speaks in a trembling voice. From Medieval English, *cwafien* = to tremble. It may be a blend of qua(ke) and (wa)ver.

> *Cowards die many times before their deaths;*
> *the valiant never taste death but once.*
> —William Shakespeare, Julius Caesar

10. ***querulous* backseat driver** kwer′yə-ləs To be querulous is to be complaining and faultfinding. From Latin, *queri* = to complain.

> *Clean your finger before you point your finger at my spots.*
> —Benjamin Franklin

Match the definitions with the words on the left.

____ 1.	pulchritudinous	a.	beautiful (often used in jest)
____ 2.	punctilious	b.	complaining and faultfinding
____ 3.	purblind	c.	cowardly
____ 4.	purloin	d.	lacking vision, intelligence
____ 5.	pusillanimous	e.	overly exacting in observing rules
____ 6.	putrid	f.	not real or true
____ 7.	quail	g.	rotten, disgustingly bad
____ 8.	quasi	h.	steal
____ 9.	quaver	i.	to draw back in fear
____ 10.	querulous	j.	tremble

GRISLY LIST 65

"You wouldn't." Bobby stared at his sister in disbelief. His friends had been a bit **rambunctious**, a bit **raffish**, perhaps, but his sister had never turned on him before. The **Rabelaisian** leftovers of last night's party had left their parents' place a mess, but he'd clean it up before they got home.

"Most definitely," she **rabidly** fumed.

"Why? Why play the **quidnunc** now?"

"You brought that **rakish** creep in here with his despicable girlfriend."

Suddenly it dawned on him: His sister's ex had shown up with his new girlfriend. Last night he'd been too drunk to care, but now the thought had him **quivering** in his boots.

"Me? No. You only broke up with him last week; how would I know that you hadn't got back together?"

"Gee, I don't know. Maybe because he locked himself in your room with someone else."

Bobby knew he was done for. **Quibbling** hadn't worked. He'd better try something honest, even **quixotic**.

"You're right. I screwed up. I'm the **quisling** here. If you did that to me, I'd be steaming. I'll tell him to never come here again. Is there anything I can do to make it up to you?"

His sister gave a furtive glance at his '66 Mustang.

1. ***quibbling* dodger** kwib'ling To quibble is to evade the main point by emphasizing some petty detail. From Latin, *quibus* = to whom, as in "to whom it may concern"; this word was common in legal documents.

> *Be these juggling fiends no more believed,*
> *that palter with us in a double sense,*
> *that keep the word of promise to our ear,*
> *and break it to our hope.*
> —*William Shakespeare*

2. **eavesdropping *quidnunc*** kwid'nungk A quidnunc is a gossip or a nosy person. From Latin, *quid nunc* = what now?

> *Gossip is vice enjoyed vicariously.*
> —*Elbert Hubbard*

3. **deceitful *quisling*** kwiz'ling To call someone a quisling is to call him/her a traitor of the most despicable sort. Vidkun Quisling was a Norwegian politician who betrayed his country to the Nazis, and in exchange became a puppet dictator.

> *Treachery lurks in honeyed words.*
> —*Danish proverb*

4. ***quivering* blabbermouth** kwiv'ə-ring To quiver is to tremble. From Medieval Danish, *quiveren* = to tremble.

> *Coward: One who in a perilous emergency thinks with his legs.*
> —*Ambrose Bierce*

5. ***quixotic* knight** kwik-sot'ik Anyone quixotic is extravagantly chivalrous or impractical. It is derived from the novel *Don Quixote*, written by Miguel de Cervantes in 1605. Quixote, the hero, fought imaginary dragons for damsels of questionable virtue.

> EPITAPH:
> *He would have killed the deadly dragon*
> *If it hadn't been a Chevy wagon*

6. ***Rabelaisian* rascal** rab-ə-lā'zē-ən Anyone Rabelaisian is given to vulgar tastes. François Rabelais (1490?–1553) was a French satirist and humorist who favored coarse, vulgar humor.

> *I drink no more than a sponge.*
> —*François Rabelais*

7. ***rabid* sicko** rab'id Anyone rabid is raving, has rabies, or is acting as if he/she is affected by rabies, a disease that causes madness and loss of control. From Latin, *rabidus* = raving, furious < *rabere* = to be mad.

> *Whom the gods wish to destroy they first make mad.*
> —*Sophocles*

8. ***raffish* heel** raf'ish One who is raffish is rakish and vulgar. From Old French, *rif et raf* = every scrape.

> *Ooooh. Ahhhh. Get out.*
> —*Andrew Dice Clay's impression of a one-night stand*

9. ***rakish* wolf** rā′kish A rake is a Lothario, a Romeo, a Don Juan, a womanizer who lacks moral restraint. From Middle English, *rakel* = rash, wild.

> *My mother-in-law broke up my marriage.*
> *One day my wife came home early from work*
> *and found us in bed together.*
> —*Lenny Bruce*

10. ***rambunctious* riffraff** ram-bungk′shəs To be rambunctious is to be wild, rough, difficult to control, and noisy. The word is a blend of ram + bumptious. Check Chapter 3, Grisly List 12 for a description of **bumptious**.

> EPITAPH:
> *We had to play taps*
> *When the frat house floor collapsed*

QUIZ 65

Match the definitions with the words on the left.

_____ 1. quibble
_____ 2. quidnunc
_____ 3. quisling
_____ 4. quiver
_____ 5. quixotic
_____ 6. Rabelaisian
_____ 7. rabid
_____ 8. raffish
_____ 9. rakish
_____ 10. rambunctious

a. affected by rabies, raving, or out of control
b. a gossip
c. a traitor
d. evade the main point by stressing petty details
e. extravagantly chivalrous
f. given to vulgar tastes
g. lacking moral restraint
h. rakish and vulgar
i. tremble
j. wild, rough, hard to control

REVIEW 13

MATCH EACH QUOTE WITH THE APPROPRIATE WORD.

1. Fear has the largest eyes of all.
   —*Boris Pasternak*

2. The soul of this man is in his clothes.
   —*William Shakespeare*

3. What he says he doesn't mean, and what he means he doesn't say.
   —*Jewish proverb*

4. Macho doesn't necessarily mean mucho.
   —*Zsa Zsa Gabor*

____ a. preen   ____ c. quaver
____ b. prevaricate   ____ d. priapic

5. To a toad, what is beauty? A female with two pop eyes, a wide mouth, yellow belly, and spotted back.
   —*Voltaire*

6. For virtue's self may too much zeal be had; the worst of madness is a saint run mad.
   —*Alexander Pope*

7. What lies lurk in kisses.
   —*Heinrich Heine*

8. A faultfinder complains even that the bride is too pretty.
   —*Yiddish proverb*

____ e. pseudologist   ____ g. querulous
____ f. pulchritudinous   ____ h. Quixotic

9. A sneer is the weapon of the weak.
   —*J. R. Lowell*

10. The way to be nothing is to do nothing.
   —*Nathaniel Howe*

11. Punctuality is the virtue of the bored.
   —*Evelyn Waugh*

12. While pondering when to begin it becomes too late to do.
   —*Quintillian*

____ i. nonentity

____ j. patronize

____ k. procrastinate

____ l. punctilious

Chapter 14

Ill deeds are doubled with an evil word.
—Shakespeare

DON'T GET SO LOST IN ALL OF MY SUGGESTIONS

that you end up forgetting the main purpose of this book—to insult people! I want you to enjoy yourself; when the occasion arises, to puff your chest up with pride and spit out some slight that whittles some stultified schlemiel down to size.

Perhaps I should also mention some safety tips: Don't insult people who are bigger than you; don't insult people with guns, knives, or powerful lawyers; don't insult people who are psychotic, especially those who lead cults that have guns, knives, or powerful lawyers; and remember, many people who don't *look* psychotic *are* psychotic.

GRISLY LIST 66

The **recluse**, his **rebarbative** mien outdone by his **rank** odor, watched as the **recreants** made a mess of his shack, **rampaging** about as they looked for his fabled fortune.

"Where is it? Where is it?" one thug **ranted** as he throttled the **recalcitrant** hermit.

"Where is what?" the old hermit grinned.

The **rapacious** thugs gave up as quickly as they had started, their **raucous** racket echoing after them as they left the **recluse** in the rubble they had made of his little hovel. They had been there before and the **recidivistic** gang would be back again. The old codger picked up his bank statement from under the trash and chuckled, "You think I'd keep it here?"

1. ***rampageous* rioter** ram-pā'jəs A rampageous person is on a rampage; this one is characterized by raging behavior, violently rushing about. From Frankish, *rampon* = to creep or crawl < Germanic, *rampu* = a claw.

> *The public is a ferocious beast:*
> *one must either chain it up or flee from it.*
> —Voltaire

2. ***rank* beginner** rangk Rank can mean stinking, flagrant, absolute or growing excessively. Don't confuse this adjective with the noun *rank*, as in "He moved up in rank." From Icelandic, *rakkr* = straight, bold.

> *Nobody will use other people's experience,*
> *nor has any of his own till it is too late to use it.*
> —Nathaniel Hawthorne

3. ***ranting* bellyacher** ran'ting To rant is to scream and rave. From Dutch, *ranten* = to rave.

> *A cowardly cur barks more fiercely than it bites.*
> —Quintus Curtius Rufus

4. ***rapacious* monopolist** rə-pā'shəs A rapacious person is plundering and greedy. From Latin, *rapere* = to seize.

> *Avarice is the sphincter of the heart.*
> —Matthew Green

5. ***raucous* partiers** rô'kəs To be raucous is to be either loud and rowdy or harsh and strident. From Indo-European, *reu-* = to give hoarse cries.

> *You know your party is out of control*
> *when people you don't even know ask you how the shower works.*
> —Buddy Baron

6. ***rebarbative* tough** rē-bär'bə-tiv One who is rebarbative is repellent, irritating, and/or unattractive. From Middle French, *rebarber* = to face beard to beard, implying resisting the enemy.

> *Better an ugly face than an ugly mind.*
> —James Ellis

7. ***recalcitrant* brat** rē-kal'si-trənt To be recalcitrant is to obstinately resist authority, or refuse to comply. From Latin, *recalcitrare* = to kick back.

> *Students today are tyrants. They contradict their parents,*
> *gobble their food, and tyrannize their teachers.*
> —Socrates

8. ***recidivistic* delinquent** ri-sid-ə-vis'tik A recidivistic person habitually relapses into former criminal or antisocial behavior. From Latin, *recidivus* = relapse.

> *As the dog returns to his vomit so a fool repeats his own folly.*
> —Proverbs 26:11

9. **addlebrained *recluse*** rek'lōōs A recluse prefers to be alone, shut away from the rest of the world. From Latin, *recludere* = to enclose.

> *Happiness is having a large, loving, caring, close-knit family*
> *in another city.*
> —George Burns

10. ***recreant* rip-off artist** rek're-ənt A recreant is a coward and/or a traitor. From Old French, *recroire* = to surrender in a competition.

> *Thou kill'd him sleeping. O brave touch!*
> *Could not a worm, an adder, do so much?*
> —William Shakespeare, A Midsummer Night's Dream

Match the definitions with the words on the left.

_____ 1. rampage
_____ 2. rank
_____ 3. rant
_____ 4. rapacious
_____ 5. raucous
_____ 6. rebarbative
_____ 7. recalcitrant
_____ 8. recidivistic
_____ 9. recluse
_____ 10. recreant

a. cowardly and disloyal
b. habitually relapsing into former criminal behavior
c. loud and rowdy, or harsh and strident
d. one who prefers to be alone
e. not complying
f. plundering, greedy
g. repellent, irritating, and/or unattractive
h. stinking, flagrant, absolute
i. to scream, to rave
j. to violently rush about

GRISLY LIST 67

The hobgoblin tried to quiet the **restive** devils, goblins, gremlins, and sprites that bounced about the hellish lecture hall.

"All right, goblins, your task today is to hound the children's classrooms; please pay special attention to any **refractory** classes where substitute teachers are present. If any children are sent to the office, help them make **recriminations** against the teachers."

Several cheers went up from the goblins.

"And devils, there's talk of guards stopping a prison riot; we can't have that. Make sure things get thoroughly out of control. We have very special **reprobates** there and they need our support."

Applause broke out from the devil camp.

"Let's see . . . oh yes. This is important. There's the principal's speech today. I need a volunteer to make his speech especially **redundant**."

An especially **reprehensible** gremlin raised his hand.

"Thank you, Cliff. And now, sprites, once again we need someone to steal socks so that people can't find a decent pair."

Boos broke out from the sprite camp.

"Now, now," said the hobgoblin, "no **repining**. This is an important job."

A **repugnant** sprite cried out from the back, "**Reneger!**"

The hobgoblin zapped the screamer into smithereens with **remorseless** indifference and went on, "I know I've promised you some more mischievous tasks, but we need workers to soften up the weak underbelly. Prove yourself there and you'll get better jobs."

He stopped and looked down at his feet.

"All right. Who stole one of my socks?"

1. ***recriminating* birdbrain** ri-krim′ə-nā-ting To criminate is to accuse another of a crime. To recriminate is to make counter-accusations when confronted with someone accusing you. From Latin, *re-* = again, anew + *crimen* = offense.

> *One false knave accuses another.*
> *—English proverb*

2. ***redundant* hack** ri-dun′dənt To be redundant is to use more words than are needed, or to needlessly repeat something. From Latin, *redundare* = to overflow; hence, to be in excess.

> *That which is repeated too often becomes insipid and tedious.*
> *—Nicolas Boileau-Despreaux*

3. ***refractory* misfit** ri-frak′tə-rē A refractory person is hard to control and stubborn as a mule. From Latin, *refringere* = to turn aside.

> *Obstinacy and vehemency in opinion*
> *are the surest signs of stupidity.*
> *—Bernard Burton*

4. ***remorseless* tormenter** ri-môrs′lis One who is remorseless has no conscience, no mercy, no pity. From Latin, *remordere* = to bite again, the connotation being that a conscience bites afterwards + *-less*.

> *If your beard were on fire, he'd light his cigarette on it.*
> *—Armenian proverb*

5. ***reneging* scam artist** ri-neg′ing To renege is to make a promise, but then back out. From Latin, *re-* = again + *negare* = to deny.

> *Break the deal; face the wheel.*
> *—Tina Turner*
> *from the movie* Mad Max: Beyond Thunderdome

6. ***repining* neurotic** ri-pī′ning To repine is to fret, complain, or be fretfully discontented. From Old English, re- + *pinian* = to torment.

> *I broke up with my psychiatrist. I told him I had suicidal tendencies.*
> *He told me from now on I had to pay in advance.*
> *—Rodney Dangerfield*

7. ***reprehensible* kidnapper** rep-ri-hen′sə-bəl A reprehensible person is worthy of blame. From Latin, *reprehendere* = to hold back, restrain.

> *The more I see of my representatives*
> *the more I admire my dogs.*
> *—Alphonse de Lamartine*

8. **lowdown *reprobate*** rep'rə-bāt A reprobate is one who is rejected by God, a wicked person. From Latin, *reprobatus* = disapproved, rejected.

> God bears with the wicked, but not forever.
> —Miguel de Cervantes, Don Quixote

9. ***repugnant* pimpleface** ri-pug'nənt Repugnant can mean inconsistent or resistant; nowadays it more often connotes something distasteful and offensive. From Latin, *re* = back + *pugnare* = to fight.

> I never forget a face, but in your case
> I'll be glad to make an exception.
> —Groucho Marx

10. ***restive* tyke** res'tiv Restive has several meanings: to refuse to go forward; to be unruly; or to be restless, fidgeting. From Latin, *restive* = to stop, stand, rest.

> Never raise your hands to your kids.
> It leaves your groin unprotected.
> —Red Buttons

QUIZ 67

Match the definitions with the words on the left.

___ 1. recriminate	a.	back out of a promise
___ 2. redundant	b.	distasteful and offensive
___ 3. refractory	c.	hard to control; stubborn
___ 4. remorseless	d.	to use more words than are
___ 5. renege		necessary
___ 6. repine	e.	not complying
___ 7. reprehensible	f.	to be unruly or restless
___ 8. reprobate	g.	to fret or be fretfully unhappy
___ 9. repugnant	h.	to make counteraccusations
___ 10. restive	i.	without mercy or pity
	j.	worthy of blame

GRISLY LIST 68

The wife went about her business as the two men talked; her **reticence** had turned into quiet resignation whenever her husband began his usual **rhetorical rodomontade**.

"You see, I am a **revanchist**. Until we send the lake people back to their lake, there can be no peace," the husband asserted as he picked up his beer.

"You are right, my friend," his **ribald** pal agreed as he poured himself another drink. "If you are from the lake, all you do is take."

The husband spread his legs out to make more room for his **rotund** gut. "You have heard of evolution; this is devolution. As soon as they came and took over our country, it has been in a **retrogressive** condition."

"They are stupid; they can't help it," his **roguish** friend laughed as the **rugose** lines on his face deepened.

The **roisterous** pair laughed so hard that the husband barely noticed his wife heading to the door, a suitcase at her side.

"Honey?" he asked. "Where are you going?"

"To my parents' home at the lake."

1. ***reticent* doormat** ret'i-sənt Someone who is either habitually silent or unwilling to talk. From Latin, *reticere* = to be silent.

> *He knew the precise psychological moment when to say nothing.*
> *—Oscar Wilde*

2. ***retrogressive* jailbird** ret-rə-gres'iv To retrogress is to move back to a worse condition. From Latin, *retro* = backward + *gradus* = a step.

> EPITAPH:
> *He tried to jump bail*
> *But took a bullet in the tail*

3. **hardcore *revanchist*** rə-vän'chist A revanchist's vengeful spirit is motivated by the need to restore his/her country's territories, power, etc. lost earlier from an enemy. From French, *revanche* = revenge.

> *Revenge is a dish that should be eaten cold.*
> *—English proverb*

4. ***rhetorical* hot-air artist** ri-tôr'i-kəl Rhetoric is an effective use of words or a stagy display of language. From Greek, *rhetor* = to speak.

> *Whoever can speak well can also lie well.*
> *—Japanese proverb*

5. ***ribald* chap** rib'əld A ribald person is given to coarse and vulgar joking. From Old French, *ribauld* = debaucher.

> *Of all the griefs that harass the distressed,*
> *Sure the most bitter is a scornful jest.*
> *—Samuel Johnson*

6. ***rodomontading* hotshot** rod-ə-mon-tā'ding To rodomontade is to arrogantly brag. Rodomontade was a fictional character noted for his boasting in *Orlando Rurioso* (1516), an epic by the Italian poet Ariosto.

> *The noisiest drum has nothing in it but air.*
> *—English proverb*

7. **roguish rebel** rō′gish Anyone roguish is like a rogue: dishonest or playfully mischievous. Rogue was a 16th-century slang term possibly derived from the Latin word *rogare* = to ask, beg.

> *I prefer rogues rather than fools; for rogues occasionally take a break.*
> —Alexandre Dumas, père

8. **roisterous brat pack** roi′stə-rəs A roisterous pack parties hard, noisily, without restraint. They laugh. They fight. They swagger. They drink. From Medieval French, *ru(i)stre* = ruffian, boor < *ru(i)ste* = rustic.

> *I hate to advocate drugs, alcohol, violence, or insanity to anyone,*
> *but they've always worked for me.*
> —Hunter S. Thompson

9. **rotund dumpling** rō-tund′ Rotund means plump and rounded. From Latin, *rota* = a wheel.

> *She was so fat, he danced with her for half an hour*
> *before he realized she was still sitting down.*
> —Ed Wynn

10. **rugose fossil** rōō′gōs Anyone rugose is wrinkled or creased. It is usually describes leaves but that doesn't mean you can't refer to someone's face as being rugose. From Latin, *ruga* = wrinkle.

> *What is the worst of woes that wait on age?*
> *What stamps the wrinkle deeper on the brow?*
> *To view each loved one blotted from life's page,*
> *And be alone on earth, as I am now.*
> —George Gordon, Lord Byron

QUIZ 68

Match the definitions with the words on the left.

____ 1. reticent	a.	proudly brag in a stormy way
____ 2. retrogressive	b.	a stagy display of language
____ 3. revanchist	c.	dishonest, playfully ill-behaved
____ 4. rhetoric	d.	given to coarse, vulgar joking
____ 5. ribald	e.	habitually silent
____ 6. rodomontade	f.	moving backward to a worse
____ 7. roguish		condition
____ 8. roisterous	g.	noisy, without restraint
____ 9. rotund	h.	plump and rounded
____ 10. rugose	i.	vengeful to another country
	j.	wrinkled

GRISLY LIST 69

Lilly watched from her car as the two **rumbustious** friends made their way toward the barbed wire fence.

"What are you guys doing?"

Ian stopped and whispered, "Shhh. We're going to tip some cows. Don't wake them up."

"Why are you going to tip cows?"

"To get back at our boss."

"He's a **sadistic** slave driver," Carl hissed.

"That's not the cow's fault."

"Don't be a **saccharine** goody two-shoes," Ian said **sarcastically**.

"I'm not kidding. What did the cow ever do to you?"

"Come on, Ian, let's go," Carl whispered.

As the two **sackless** cow-tippers approached the first cow with **sanguinary** intent, Lilly honked her horn and screamed:

"Run away!"

And the cow did, taking her other bovine companions with her.

Carl kept chasing the herd while Ian came back.

"Why did you do that?"

"You know why."

He knelt down and **sacrilegiously** bowed, "O **sanctimonious** one, where is the golden calf that we might worship and adore him?"

"Get lost."

Ian saw that Carl was far away and smiled **salaciously** at Lilly, "You know, we could leave Carl here and go park at Lookout Mountain."

Lilly locked the doors, revved the engine, and with a **sardonic** sneer said, "Go tip a cow."

1. **rumbustious clod** rum-bus'chəs A rumbustious person is wild, unruly, and boisterous. This possibly comes from a blend of rum (the liquor) and rambunctious.

   You gotta fight for your right to party.
   —Beastie Boys

2. **saccharine goody two-shoes** sak'ər-in Anything saccharine is sweet, or perhaps artificially and exaggeratedly sweet or sentimental. From Latin, *saccharum* = sugar.

   Where does the ant die except in sugar?
   —Malay proverb

3. **sackless patsy** sak'lis Feeble-minded, a sackless person lacks energy. From Latin, *saccus* = bag + -less.

   Why don't you bore a hole in your head and let the sap run out?
   —Groucho Marx

4. **sacrilegious** **knave** sak-rə-lij'əs To be sacrilegious is to be disrespectful to anything sacred. From Latin, *sacrilegus* = temple robber. It has been coupled with **knave** = a dishonest person, a servant.

> *So if you worship me, it will all be yours.*
> —Satan, Luke 4:8

5. **sadistic** **slave driver** sə-dis'tik The word *sadism* came from the Marquis de Sade, a nut case who derived pleasure from giving others pain.

> *Every normal man must be tempted at times*
> *to spit on his hands, hoist the black flag,*
> *and begin slitting throats.*
> —H. L. Mencken

6. **salacious** **swinger** sə-lā'shəs Anyone who is salacious is lustful, perhaps crudely so. It comes from the Latin, *salacis* = to leap.

> *Sex is nobody's business except the three people involved.*
> —Anonymous

7. **sanctimonious** **hypocrite** sangk-tə-mō'nē-əs One who is sanctimonious struts around with a hypocritical show of piety. From Latin, *sanctimonia* = holiness.

> *The last Christian died on the cross.*
> —Friedrich Nietzsche

8. **sanguinary** **bloodsucker** sang'gwə-ner-e Sanguinary means being distended with blood, so it can connote something positive like rosy cheeks, but it also can imply bloodthirstiness. From Latin, *sanguis* = blood.

> *It is better to be wanted for murder than not to be wanted at all.*
> —Marty Winch

9. **sarcastic** **shrew** sär-kas'tik To be sarcastic is to give sneering, cutting remarks that mean the opposite of what they seem to say. From Greek, *sarkazein* = to rend (flesh) to sneer.

> *If my dog had your face, I'd shave his butt*
> *and teach him to walk backwards.*
> —Jamie Farr

10. **sardonic** **cut-up** sär-don'ik Someone who disdainfully sneers at others with scorn and sarcasm. From Greek, *sardanios* = bitter, scornful.

> *A man who lacks judgment derides his neighbor.*
> —Proverbs 11:12

Match the definitions with the words on the left.

___ 1. rumbustious	a.	distended with blood or
___ 2. saccharine		bloodthirsty
___ 3. sackless	b.	wild, unruly, and boisterous
___ 4. sacrilegious	c.	disrespectful to the sacred
___ 5. sadist	d.	feeble-minded; lacking energy
___ 6. salacious	e.	making sneering remarks
___ 7. sanctimonious		(fits two words)
___ 8. sanguinary	f.	lustful
___ 9. sarcastic	g.	one who gets pleasure from
___ 10. sardonic		giving pain
	h.	sweet or too sweet
	i.	with an insincere piety

GRISLY LIST 70

Rhonda glanced out the window at the **saucy** tramp lounging around the pool. This other **sciolistic** "assistant" had a salary that dwarfed hers. She was tired of **scrimping**, and so the **saturnine** assistant plucked up her courage to face her **scrooge** of a boss:

"I need a raise!"

"A raise!" the boss scoffed. "If you need money, you can drop your drawers. I'll pay you good money for that."

He threw his magazine at her feet. It was the most **scabrous** smut rag on the market. The business tycoon had made his fortune on a motto proclaiming that the more **scatological** his paper, the more money he'd make. He was, after all, the biggest and richest **satyromaniac** in New York.

She thought of something **scathing** to say, but bit her tongue. Should she quit now or just leave him a message?

"No, thanks."

"Suit yourself. Now listen, I need those legal papers to go out today or I'm in big trouble. And have a limo ready for my day in court."

A **scampish** idea crossed her mind.

"Don't worry about a thing."

1. **saturnine grumbler** sat'ər-nīn To be saturnine is to be sluggish and gloomy. It comes from the planet Saturn, because of its distance and sluggish movement. From Old French, *saturnin* = of Saturn; of lead, heavy.

> *Noble deeds and hot baths are the best cures for depression.*
> —Dodie Smith

2. **reckless *satyromaniac*** sat-ər-ō-mā′nē-ak A male sexual addict. a satyromaniac is the male counterpart to a nymphomaniac. In Greek mythology, a satyr—an attendant to Bacchus—had horns on his head and the legs of a goat and was given to lechery.

> *Sex between a man and a woman can be wonderful*
> *provided you get between the right man and woman.*
> *—Woody Allen*

3. **saucy tease** sô′sē A saucy person is rude and impudent or sexually suggestive in a playful way. From Latin, *salsus* = salted.

> *The fastest way to a man's heart is through his chest.*
> *—Roseanne Barr*

4. **scabrous guttermouth** skab′rəs Scabrous means rough, hard to handle, or lewd, indecent, and shocking. From Latin, *scaber* = scurfy (rough, harsh).

> *It doesn't matter what you do in the bedroom as long as you don't*
> *do it in the street and frighten the horses.*
> *—Mrs. Patrick Campbell*

5. **scampish squirt** skam′pish One who is scampish is mischievous, puckish, or impish. From Medieval French, *escamper* = to flee.

> *A child is a curly, dimpled lunatic.*
> *—Ralph Waldo Emerson*

6. **scathing satirist** skā′thing Scathing speech is harsh and mean-spirited. From Greek, *skethos* = injury.

> *She doesn't need a steak knife. Rona cuts her steak with her tongue.*
> *—Johnny Carson on Rona Barrett*

7. **scatological slime bucket** skat-l-oj′i-kəl To be scatological is to be fixated with excrement or obscenity. From Greek, *skat-* = excrement + *-logy* = a word, thought.

> Likely comment:
> *Once there was a lady from Nantucket*
> Your response:
> *Who said you're a scatological slime bucket.*

8. **sciolistic doofus** sī-ə-lis′tik A sciolistic person has only a superficial knowledge of the facts. From Late Latin, *sciolus* = one who knows little.

> EPITAPH:
> *He tried to balloon*
> *Way up to the moon*
> *But died before noon*

9. ***scrimping* dregs of society** skrim'ping To scrimp is to save money to try to make ends meet. From Danish, *skrumpe* = to shrivel.

> *Debt is the worst poverty.*
> —M. G. Lichtwer

10. **tight-fisted *scrooge*** skrōōj One who is a scrooge is a cheap, stingy, and mean person. Ebenezer Scrooge is a character noted for his miserly behavior in Charles Dickens' novella *A Christmas Carol.*

> *Who will not feed the cats,*
> *must feed the mice and rats.*
> —German proverb

QUIZ 70

Match the definitions with the words on the left.

_____ 1. saturnine
_____ 2. satyromaniac
_____ 3. saucy
_____ 4. scabrous
_____ 5. scampish
_____ 6. scathing
_____ 7. scatological
_____ 8. sciolistic
_____ 9. scrimp
_____ 10. scrooge

a. a cheap, stingy, mean person
b. a male sexual addict
c. fixated with excrement or obscenity
d. harsh and mean-spirited
e. having a superficial knowledge of the facts
f. mischievous
g. rough, hard to handle, or lewd, indecent, and shocking
h. rude and impudent
i. sluggish and gloomy
j. to try to make ends meet

REVIEW 14

MATCH EACH QUOTE WITH THE APPROPRIATE WORD.

1. As we must render an account of every idle word,
so we must of our *idle silence.*
—Saint Ambrose

2. Great men may jest with saints; 'tis wit in them; but,
in the less foul profanation.
—*William Shakespeare*

3. He who is in evil, is also in the punishment of evil.
—*Emanuel Swedenborg*

4. Lizzie Borden took an axe
And gave her mother forty whacks;
When she saw what she had done,
She gave her father forty-one!
—*Anonymous*

5. The man who is fond of complaining, likes to remain amid the objects
of his vexation. It is at the moment that he declares them insupportable
that he will most strongly revolt against every means proposed for his de-
liverance. This is what suits him. He asks nothing better than to sigh over
his position and to remain in it.
—*Francois Guizot*

____ a. sanguinary   ____ d. reticent
____ b. repine   ____ e. ribald
____ c. reprobate

6. He that studieth revenge keepeth his own wounds green,
which otherwise would heal and do well.
—*Francis Bacon*

7. Hypocrites do the devil's drudgery in Christ's livery.
—*Matthew Henry*

8. Television is a whore: Any man who wants her full favors can have
them in five minutes with a pistol.
—*Anonymous hijacker (quoted in* Esquire, *1977)*

9. To save the state the expense of a trial, your honor,
my client has escaped.
—*Chon Day*

10. The head is always the dupe of the heart.
—François, Duc de la Rochefoucauld

11. What you shout out will only echo back in the same way.
  —*Russian proverb*

____ f. sanctimonious   ____ i. revanchist
____ g. rant   ____ j. maleficent
____ h. recidivistic   ____ k. infatuated

Chapter 15

Speak clearly, if you speak at all;
Carve every word before you let it fall.
—Oliver Wendell Holmes

ARISTOTLE SAID THAT WIT IS EDUCATED INSO-
LENCE. If this is true, then it is important to practice being insolent
and to study those who have mastered the art of being witty. It certainly
helps to have a masterful command of words, but it is even more important that one knows how to put those words together. Sometimes,
just a few words will do. Winston Churchill was known for having that
kind of wit. At a dinner party, a gossip seated next to him said, "Mr.
Churchill, I have placed a bet that I can get more than two words out of
you." Mr. Churchill replied, "You lose."

Groucho Marx was another great wit. A guest of his, upon leaving,
turned to Groucho and said, "I'd like to say good-bye to your wife."
Groucho quipped, "Wouldn't we all." There are plenty of times we wish
we had made the right remark at the right moment, but, like anything
else, that takes practice. If you take the time to study the great wits as
you do the vocabulary, you might be surprised at just how witty you
can be.

GRISLY LIST 71

"You're sure?" the genie asked.

"That's what I want. Remove all **sectarian** groups in every country, include any **seditious** groups as well, and send them to Australia."

"You've got three wishes and this is what you want."

"That's it."

The genie eyed his oily, **sebaceous** master, who seemed so **sedentary,** as if
he were born in the chair he was sitting in, and thought, "Thirteen hundred
years waiting in the dark and this is what I get."

"Any reason in particular that you want them to go to Australia? I mean,
do you have a special beef with Australians?"

"No. I like Australians. It's just that that is where they belong."

"Great," the genie thought. "This **senescent** dope is **senile** as well."

He tried another tack. "You know, most men wish for things like gold,
fame, or gorgeous women."

"Oh, I've got too much **adulation** as it is."

The genie looked around at the ramshackle house and then back at his
sebiferous host. "Have you ever wanted to be someone else, to look different
than you do now?"

"No way."

"And your other two wishes?"

"I really don't like people that are **sententious**."

"Sententious."

"Or **sequacious**. They should go to Australia, too."

"Could you fill me in on how you found the bottle I came in?"

"Let's see, it was in this box I found in the attic. To tell you the truth, it was so much trouble to open, I wish I'd never found it."

1. **sebaceous pus bucket** si-bā'shəs A sebaceous person oozes oil and fat out of every pore. From Latin, *sebum* = tallow, fat.

> *I never eat more than I can lift.*
> —Miss Piggy

2. **sebiferous blimp** si-bif'ər-əs To be sebiferous is to secrete fat. From Latin, *sebum* = tallow, fat.

> EPITAPH:
> *They say his heart went kerplop*
> *When second helpings made him drop*

3. **sectarian faction** sek-târ'ē-ən A sectarian group is narrow-minded. It can also be used as a noun; e.g. that dimwitted sectarian. From Latin, *secta* = a path, faction.

> *Beware of the man of one book.*
> —St. Thomas Aquinas

4. **sedentary bump on a log** sed'n-ter-ē Anyone sedentary doesn't budge and is always sitting. From Latin, *sedentarius* = sitting.

> *A sedentary life is the real sin against the Holy Spirit.*
> —Friedrich Nietzsche

5. **seditious instigator** si-dish'əs A seditious group stirs up discontent. From Latin, *sadire* = to go aside; hence, to rebel.

> *Let the ruling classes tremble at a Communist revolution.*
> *The proletarians have nothing to lose but their chains.*
> *They have a world to win. Working men of all countries, unite!*
> —Karl Marx and Friedrich Engels

6. **self-adulating jerk** self-aj'ə-lā-ting To adulate means to show excessive devotion, flattery, or admiration in a servile way. A self-adulator excessively praises him- or herself. From Latin, *adulatus* = to fawn upon.

> *I have nothing to declare except my genius.*
> —Oscar Wilde, to a customs inspector

7. **senescent geezer** si-nes'ənt Anyone senescent is growing or acting old. From Latin, *senex* = old.

> *You know you're growing old when everything hurts.*
> *And what doesn't hurt doesn't work.*
> —Hy Gardner

8. **senile** nutcase sē'nĭl One who is senile has deteriorated in strength or mental ability due to old age. From Latin, *senex* = old.

> *I'm in the prime of my senility.*
> —*Benjamin Franklin*

9. **sententious** smart aleck sen-ten'shəs A sententious person can be pithy or is full of pompous moral sayings. From Latin, *sententia* = way of thinking, opinion.

> *Platitudes are the Sundays of stupidity.*
> —*Unknown*

10. **sequacious** sheep si-kwā'shəs Lacking will, a sequacious person tends to follow a leader. From Latin, *sequi* = to follow.

> *People, like sheep, tend to follow a leader*
> —*occasionally in the right direction.*
> —*Alexander Chase*

QUIZ 71

Match the definitions with the words on the left.

_____ 1. sebaceous
_____ 2. sebiferous
_____ 3. sectarian
_____ 4. sedentary
_____ 5. seditious
_____ 6. self-adulate
_____ 7. senescent
_____ 8. senile
_____ 9. sententious
_____ 10. sequacious

a. doesn't move; always sitting
b. deteriorated in strength or mental ability due to old age
c. growing old
d. narrow-minded
e. oily and fatty (fits two words)
f. full of pompous moral sayings
g. stirring up discontent
h. tending to follow
i. show excessive devotion to oneself

GRISLY LIST 72

Thor punched in the coordinates for the Vinoori star system and leaned back as the stars whizzed by. With a **simpering** smile, he winked at the **sinuous** concubine licking his ear.

"This is the life," mused Thor. "I'm so lucky that this is written by a **sexist** sci-fi writer. I've got it made: **servile**, half-human babes waiting hand and foot on me with their **serpentine** tongues. It's a **sinecurist** life for me!"

He pulled his favorite concubine closer to give her a squeeze, but then stopped short; her face had suddenly morphed into that of a **simian** beast.

"What?" he screamed, too late, for everything had changed: He now kneeled before the Monkey-God.

"You are accused, foul **simoniac**, of selling the sacred stones of Chimp! How do you plead?"

Thor broke free and began the **Sisyphean** struggle to crawl off the page. He had to know what **sinister** plot twist had turned his perfect world inside out. As he reached the edge of page one, a voice shook the universe:

"Yeah, Bob. I'm not happy about it either, but it looks like a page one rewrite."

1. *serpentine* **temptress** sûr'pən-tīn To be serpentine is to be like a serpent, especially in terms of movement, winding and sinuous. However, it also connotes being cunning and devious. From Latin, *serpens bestia* = a creeping or gliding beast.

> *The prince of darkness is always a gentleman.*
> —*William Shakespeare,* King Lear

2. *servile* **conformist** sûr'vəl To be servile is to act like a slave. From Latin, *servus* = a slave.

> *One sheep follows another.*
> —*English proverb*

3. *sexist* **pig** sek'sist Anyone sexist discriminates against the opposite sex, believing it to be inferior. From a combination of *sex* and *racism*.

> *I don't mate in captivity.*
> —*Gloria Steinem (She's married now)*

4. *simian* **dork** sim'ē-ən A simian is an ape or a monkey or something like an ape or a monkey. From Latin, *simia* = an ape.

> *Man is more an ape than many of the apes.*
> —*Friedrich Nietzsche*

5. **slick** *simoniac* sī-mō'nē-ak A simoniac is anyone trying to buy or sell sacred things for dishonest reasons. In Acts 8:18, Simon the magician offers money to the disciples of Jesus Christ in exchange for their spiritual power.

> *What price salvation now?*
> —*George Bernard Shaw,* Major Barbara

6. *simpering* **sap** sim'pə-ring A simpering person wears a silly and stupid smile. From German *zimpfer* = elegant, delicate.

> *Whatever it is, wherever he is, whatever he is doing,*
> *he smiles; it is a malady he has.*
> —*Gaius Valerius Catullus*

7. **lazy** *sinecurist* si'ni-kyŏŏr-ist A sinecure is any paying job that requires no work. A sinecurist is the lazy (or lucky) slob who gets a job like this. From a Latin phrase, *sine cura* = without care.

> *Office hours are from 12 to 1 with an hour off for lunch.*
> —*George S. Kaufman, speaking of the U.S. Senate*

8. **sinister cabal** sin'i-stər Anyone or anything sinister is devious and wicked. From Latin, *sinister* = of the left hand. It is coupled with **cabal** = a conspiratorial group of plotters.

> *Where trust is greatest, there treason is in its most horrid shape.*
> —John Dryden

9. **sinuous seducer** sin'yōō-əs A sinuous one is either gracefully winding or devious. From Latin, *sinuosus* = bending in and out; hence, serpentine.

> *Hell can lie between the eyelashes of a beautiful woman's eyes.*
> —Anonymous

10. **Sisyphean workhorse** sis-ə-fē'ən Anything Sisyphean is endlessly difficult. Sisyphus is a mythical Greek whose fate was to eternally roll a stone up a hill, only to watch it slip and roll down again.

> *To crush . . . a man utterly . . .*
> *one need only give him work of an absolutely,*
> *completely useless and irrational character.*
> —Fyodor Dostoevsky

QUIZ 72

Match the definitions with the words on the left.

____ 1. serpentine	a. devious and wicked
____ 2. servile	b. discriminates against other sex
____ 3. sexist	c. like an ape
____ 4. simian	d. like a slave
____ 5. simoniac	e. one trying to buy or sell sacred things for dishonest reasons
____ 6. simper	f. one with a paying job that requires no work
____ 7. sinecurist	g. pointlessly or endlessly difficult
____ 8. sinister	h. smile in a silly and stupid way
____ 9. sinuous	i. winding; devious (fits two words)
____ 10. Sisyphean	

GRISLY LIST 73

Liz glared at her **slovenly** image in the mirror and began to cry. She had wanted something edgy, something sexy, but her ghoulish gown hadn't worked. In fact, it sucked. She looked like a **slattern**, and a **smirchy** one at that, a **slothful** twenty-dollar hooker **slavishly** working the streets, **skulking** in dark alleyways with **slavering** customers lurking nearby.

She plopped down on her bed and wiped away the tears. She had only minutes before Greg would be there to pick her up. She could hear the **smarmy** voice of her older sister saying "I told you so." Then she saw it, her mother's prom dress, with the pleated skirt. Her **sleekit** mother had **skittishly** laid it on her bed when she was in the shower. She tried it on and smiled. With her green hair and her red high-tops, it worked.

1. ***skittish* pushover** skit′ish A skittish person is easily frightened, very fickle, or playfully coy. From Scandinavian, *skite* = to dart about.

> *We poison our lives with fear of burglary and shipwreck and, ask anyone,*
> *the house is never burgled and the ship never goes down.*
> —*Jean Anouilh*

2. ***skulking* creep** skul′king To skulk is to move about in a sneaking or cowardly way, or to hide and wait for some evil purpose. From Low German, *schulken* = to play truant, or from Dutch, *skulke* = to skulk.

> *Even though a snake enters a bamboo tube, it still is apt to slither.*
> —*Chinese proverb*

3. ***slatternly* sow** slat′ərn-lē A slattern is either an untidy woman or a harlot; hence, to be slatternly is to be untidy, sloppy, or sluttish. Possibly from Medieval English, *slatter* = to slash or slit (clothes).

> *Of all the tame beasts, I hate sluts.*
> —*John Ray*

4. ***slavering* dullard** slav′ɔ-ring To slaver is to drool, fawn, or flatter in a slobbering way. From Icelandic, *slafra* = to slobber.

> *Flatterers are cats that lick before and scratch behind.*
> —*German proverb*

5. ***slavish* brown-noser** slā′vish Anyone slavish acts like a slave. From Old Bulgarian, *Slovene* = inhabitant name for Slavic populace, so named given that many Slavs were enslaved in the Middle Ages.

> *Many men die at twenty-five*
> *and aren't buried until they are seventy-five.*
> —*Benjamin Franklin*

6. ***sleekit* smuggler** slek′it Anyone sleekit is sneaky. From Old English, *slician* = to make smooth.

> *Wolves can't catch what dogs do not expose.*
> —*Jean de la Fontaine*

7. ***slovenly* spud** sluv′ən-lē A sloven is one who is careless in appearance, so one who is slovenly is habitually dirty and untidy. From Medieval Dutch, *slof* = lax, limp.

> *Women were made to give our eyes delight;*
> *A female sloven is an odious sight.*
> —*Edward Young*

8. *slothful* **do-nothing** slôth'fəl A sloth is an animal that moves so slowly it appears to be half-asleep; hence, a slothful person is one who is either slow or lazy. Sloth is also one of the seven deadly sins. From Old English, *slaw* = slow.

> A little sleep, a little slumber,
> a little folding of the hands to rest,
> and poverty will come upon you like a vagabond,
> and want like an armed man.
> —Proverbs 6:10 11

9. *smarmy* **sugar daddy** smär'mē A smarmy person flatters in an oily, insincere way. From English, *smarm* = to smear, gush.

> Learn that every flatterer lives at the flattered listener's cost.
> —Jean de la Fontaine

10. *smirchy* **little rugrat** smûr'chē One who is smirchy is dirty and grimy. Smirchy can also mean dishonored. It is possibly a blend of smear, from German, *schmer* = grease and smut from Middle High German, *smutz* = to smear, or from Old French, *esmorcher* = to hurt.

> In Köln, a town of monks and bones
> And pavements fanged with murderous stones,
> And rags, and hags, and hideous wenches;
> I counted two and seventy stenches.
> —Unknown

QUIZ 73

Match the definitions with the words on the left.

____ 1. skittish	a.	careless in appearance, habitually dirty and untidy
____ 2. skulk	b.	dirty, and grimy
____ 3. slatternly	c.	easily frightened, very fickle
____ 4. slaver	d.	flattering in an oily, devious way
____ 5. slavish	e.	like a slave
____ 6. sleekit	f.	cowardly sneak about
____ 7. slovenly	g.	slobber, drool, and/or fawn
____ 8. slothful	h.	slow or lazy
____ 9. smarmy	i.	untidy or sluttish
____ 10. smirchy	j.	sneaky

GRISLY LIST 74

"That's a **specious** argument!"

"No, really—how do I know you really exist? I'm not trying to be **sophistical** here," the smaller man **sniveled**.

"Don't give me that **solipsistic** crap. I'm in a **splenetic** mood, as it is. Even the most **sodden** drunk on the planet knows that others exist. Anyone who ascribes to that only the self exists' nonsense is a **sophomoric** geek."

"Ain't so."

"Is so, my **solecistic** chum."

"Well, I'm not all that gung-ho about your **sordid** nihilism. That **soporific** stuff makes me yawn."

"So where's my money?"

"Like I said, how do I know you really exist?"

"'Cuz it'll hurt when I put my foot in your face."

The smaller man nodded. "I got your money right here."

1. **sniveling small fry** sniv'ə-ling Snivel has several meanings: it can mean to whine, or to have snot drip from your nose, or to make an audible sound by drawing up snot into your nose, or to speak while your nose is running, or to pretend you're crying. It is from Old English, *snofl* = mucus.

> *Babies: a loud noise at one end*
> *and no sense of responsibility at the other.*
> —*Father Ron Knox*

2. **sodden souse** sod'n Anything sodden is soaked with liquid, but it can refer to one soaked in too much liquor. From the past participle of seethe = to boil; to soak, < Old Norse, *sauthr* = a burnt offering.

> *I drink too much.*
> *The last time I gave a urine sample there was an olive in it.*
> —*Rodney Dangerfield*

3. **solecistic lightweight** sol-i-sis'tik Anyone solecistic is characterized by making errors in grammar. From Greek, *soloikos* = speaking incorrectly.

> *A writer who can't write in a grammarly manner better shut up shop.*
> —*Artemus Ward*

4. **solipsistic egoist** sol-ip-sis'tik A solipsistic person waxes philosophical about how only the self exists. From Latin, *solus* = alone.

> *The more you speak of yourself, the more you are likely to lie.*
> —*Johann Zimmerman*

5. **sophistical snake** sə-fis′ti-kəl A sophist is one who uses deceptive reasoning. In Ancient Greece, a sophist was a skilled teacher of reasoning, but as time passed, these sophists began to use ingenuity and sly, misleading arguments. From Greek, *sóphistes* = sage, a wise man.

> *Sophistry is like a window curtain:*
> *it pleases as an ornament,*
> *but its true use is to keep out the light.*
> —Edmund Burke

6. **sophomoric geek** sof-ə-môr′ik One who is sophomoric is annoyingly immature. From Greek, *sophos* = wise + *moros* = foolish.

> *The highlight of my childhood was making my brother*
> *laugh so hard that food came out of his nose.*
> —Garrison Keillor

7. **soporific poet** sop-ə-rif′ik Anything soporific induces drowsiness or sleep, or it is boring and dull. From Latin, *sopire* = to send to sleep.

> *I never sleep comfortably*
> *except when I am at a sermon or when I pray to God.*
> —François Rabelais

8. **sordid poison peddler** sôr′did Anyone sordid displays the most horrible characteristics of human personality; depravity, avarice, self-centeredness. It can also mean something is filthy and wretched. From Indo-European, *swordo* = black, dirty.

> *Man is god in ruins.*
> —Ralph Waldo Emerson

9. **specious argument** spē′shəs Anything specious looks good, but in actuality is false, deceptive. From Latin, *specios* = fair, beautiful.

> *Some so speak in exaggerations and superlatives*
> *that we need to make a large discount from their statements*
> *before we can come at their real meaning.*
> —Tyron Edwards

10. **splenetic cur** spli-net′ik To be splenetic is to be irritable, peevish, and spiteful. Long ago, doctors thought that using leeches to bleed patients was a good idea, because they thought the spleen caused people to be testy or irritable. From Latin, *spleen* = spleen.

> *A tart temper never mellows with age.*
> —Washington Irving

Match the definitions with the words on the left.

____ 1. snivel	a. believing only the self exists
____ 2. sodden	b. making errors in grammar
____ 3. solecistic	c. filthy and wretched
____ 4. solipsistic	d. having the appearance of being
____ 5. sophistical	right but actually being wrong
____ 6. sophomoric	e. immature
____ 7. soporific	f. soaked with liquid; drunk
____ 8. sordid	g. testy, irritable, peevish
____ 9. specious	h. tending to produce sleep; boring
____ 10. splenetic	i. to make an audible sound by
	drawing up snot into your nose
	j. using deceptive reasoning

GRISLY LIST 75

The **steatopygous** woman **spluttered** into the officer's face, "Tho I thath to him: I don't want any tholen property."

Detective Thompson looked at the stolen car that sat in the **stagnant** pool that covered the front yard.

"So how did the car end up in your driveway?"

"Beath me. Thith ith the firtht time I've theen it."

If she'd only had a dime for every **spurious** excuse she heard. Thompson wasn't **squeamish**, but the stench coming from this **squalid** pigsty made her sick. The Cottonwood area had been **stigmatized** as having the highest crime rate in the country and not much had changed.

"It looks like it's been here for some time."

"Someone thpoliated it and left it here."

"**Spoliated?**"

"Thpoliated." She nodded.

"You didn't buy a stolen car?"

"No, my huthband alwayth thquandererth hith paycheck."

"**Squanders?**"

"He'th not good with money."

"May I speak with your husband?"

Thompson thought, "Finally, someone who won't spit on me. He's got to be easier to interview than this dimwit."

The old buzzard slowly came to the door and then, with the most ear-splitting, **stentorian** voice Thompson had ever heard, he boomed:

"HELLO. CAN I HELP YOU?"

1. ***spluttering* head case** splut'ə-ring From a blend of splash and sputter, to splutter is to make a spitting sound or speak incoherently, or to speak incoherently while spitting.

> *Great talkers are like leaky pitchers—everything runs out of them.*
> *—English proverb*

2. ***spoliating* burglar** spō'lē-ā-ting To spoliate is to steal, plunder, or despoil. From Latin, *spoliare* = to spoil.

> *Old burglars never die, they just steal away.*
> *—Glen Gilbreath, facing his 13th robbery charge*

3. ***spurious* spinmeister** spyŏŏr'ē-əs If something is spurious it is false, or deceitfully false. From Latin, *spurius* = illegitimate.

> *In much of your talking, thinking is half-murdered.*
> *—Kahlil Gibran*

4. ***squalid* pigsty** skwol'id Anything squalid is dirty, filthy, and wretched. From Latin, *squalere* = to be foul or filthy.

> *I hate housework! You make the bed; you do the dishes;*
> *and six months later you have to start all over again.*
> *—Joan Rivers*

5. ***squandering* spendthrift** skwon'də-ring To squander is to spend wastefully. The derivation of squander is uncertain, but it was popularized after Shakespeare's play *The Merchant of Venice* (1600).

> *Who more than he is worth does spend,*
> *he makes a rope his life to end.*
> *—English proverb*

6. ***squeamish* pipsqueak** skwē'mish Thin-skinned, a squeamish person is easily sickened or offended. From Anglo-French, *escoimous* = disdainfully shy.

> *He who is afraid of every nettle should not piss in the grass.*
> *—Thomas Fuller*

7. ***stagnant* sweathog** stag'nənt Anything stagnant is foul and putrid from not moving. From Latin, *stagnum* = a swamp.

> *The only difference between a rut and a grave is the depth.*
> *— Unknown*

8. ***steatopygous* lardass** stē-at-ə-pī'gəs One who is steatopygous has an extremely fat butt. From Greek, *steat* = fat + *pyge* = buttocks.

> Likely comment:
> *Gentlemen come from miles around just to see me.*
> Your response:
> *That's because it takes them miles to get around you.*

9. **stentorian** **big mouth** sten-tôr′ē-ən Anyone stentorian is excessively loud, speaking with a deafening roar. It is akin to the Greek word *stenein* = to rumble or roar. Stentor was a Greek herald in the Trojan War, as recounted in Homer's *Iliad*.

> *They that are loudest in their threats are the weakest in the execution of them.*
> *It is probable that he who is killed by lightning hears no noise;*
> *but the thunder-clap which follows, and which most alarms the ignorant,*
> *is the surest proof of their safety.*
> —Charles Caleb Colton

10. **stigmatized** **maggot** stig′mə-tīzd A stigma was a mark cut or burned into the skin of a criminal or slave in the 1400s. Hence, stigmatized is to be branded as disgraced. Stigmata refers to the hands and feet of those who, out of religious devotion, are thought to bleed from the palms and ankles or feet, like Jesus. From German, *stizein* = to prick.

> *One speck of rat's dung spoils a whole pot of rice.*
> —Chinese proverb

QUIZ 75

Match the definitions with the words on the left.

_____ 1.	splutter	a.	dirty, filthy, and wretched
_____ 2.	spoliate	b.	easily sickened
_____ 3.	spurious	c.	excessively loud
_____ 4.	squalid	d.	false, illegitimate
_____ 5.	squander	e.	having an extremely fat butt
_____ 6.	squeamish	f.	branded as disgraced
_____ 7.	stagnant	g.	not moving
_____ 8.	steatopygous	h.	spend wastefully
_____ 9.	stentorian	i.	to speak incoherently
_____ 10.	stigmatized	j.	to steal, plunder, or despoil

REVIEW 15

MATCH EACH QUOTE WITH THE APPROPRIATE WORD.

1. A fixed point of view kills anybody who has one.
—Brooks Atkinson

2. Fixed like a plant on his peculiar spot.
To draw nutrition, propagate, and rot.
—Alexander Pope

3. God hates those who praise themselves.
—St. Clement

4. What an ugly beast is the ape, and how like us.
—Cicero

5. You can always rely on a society of equals taking it out on the woman.
—Alan Sillitoe

___ a. sectarian   ___ d. sexist
___ b. sedentary   ___ e. simian
___ c. self-adulate

6. A disagreeable smile distorts the lines of beauty,
and is more repulsive than a frown.
—John Casper Lavater

7. A man takes a drink, then the drink takes a drink,
and the next drink takes a man.
—Japanese proverb

8. If you sleep with a dog you will rise full of fleas.
—Greek proverb

9. When a crook kisses you, count your teeth.
—Anonymous

___ f. sinister   ___ h. sodden
___ g. smirchy   ___ i. simper

10. A sweet disorder in the dress
kindles in clothes a wantonness.
—Robert Herrick

11. If the chief party, whether it be the people, or the army, or the nobility, which you think most useful and of most consequence to you for the conservation of your dignity, be corrupt, you must follow their humor and indulge them, and in that case honesty and virtue are pernicious.
—*Niccolò Machiavelli,* The Prince

12. Violence in the voice is often only the death rattle of reason in the throat.
—*John Frederick Boyes*

13. We will bury you.
—*Nikita S. Khrushchev*

____ j. stentorian

____ k. Machiavellian

____ l. oppugnant

____ m. slattern

Chapter 16

*Satire should,
like a polished razor keen,
Wound with a touch
that's scarcely felt or seen.*
—Lady Mary Wortley Montagu

THERE ARE VISUAL LEARNERS, those who learn primarily by seeing; aural learners, those who learn primarily by hearing; and kinesthetic learners, those who learn primarily by doing. However, all learners benefit in some way from all three approaches. When you read the words on the page, you are visually learning. When you sound them out, you are aurally learning. If you write them down or draw a picture, you are kinesthetically learning. The process is now in your muscle memory. Take time to write these words down to fix them in your muscle memory.

Furthermore, try keeping a list of your favorite words, words that you are most likely to use because they appeal to you. These words will be easier for you to memorize and add to your speech. You don't need to spend more than few minutes each day looking them over. In no time at all, you will find them deeply imbedded in your long-term memory.

GRISLY LIST 76

The mayor of Mousetown, with a **supercilious** air, patted Willy on the back.

"My good fellow, it is the role of the **subservient** mouse to face the cat and get the cheese."

Willy could see the cat, his **stolid** hulk lounging beneath the table, and on top of the table, a **superfluous** pile of cheese, enough to last a lifetime.

In a **sullen** tone he whined, "I'm not really hungry."

"Not hungry! What if every mouse said 'I'm not hungry.' Civilization would crumble. That is why it's important that we follow **stringent** rules for mouse survival. All for one and one for all and you for us."

"So why don't *you* go?"

The **stultified** mayor hemmed and hawed. "Remember the proverb: The generous mouse does not **stint**, but shares with the tribe."

But then a small mouse, a **stunted** chap, chimed in, "Yeah, why don't the mayor go?"

The mayor's **superficial** concern for Mousetown suddenly evaporated. "I'm not hungry either."

1. *stinting* **slumlord** stin'ting One who stints is stingy and sparing. From Medieval English, *stinten* = to stint, cease, stop.

> *He's so stingy that if he gave you the measles,*
> *it would be one measle at a time.*
> —*Irish proverb*

2. ***stolid* dunderhead** stol'id A stolid person is impassive and shows no feeling whatsoever. From Latin, *stolidus* = firm, slow, stupid.

> *I didn't know he was dead; I thought he was British.*
> —*Unknown*

3. ***stringent* killjoy** strin'jənt To be stringent is to impose rigorous standards and rigid control. From Latin, *stringere* = to draw tight.

> *I know a man who gave up smoking, drinking, sex, and rich food.*
> *He was healthy right up to the time he killed himself.*
> —*Johnny Carson*

4. ***stultified* schlemiel** stul'tə-fīd To stultify is to make someone look foolish or stupid. From Latin, *stultus* = foolish + *facere* = to make. It is coupled with **schlemiel** = from Yiddish, a habitual bungler.

> *A schlemiel falls on his back and breaks his nose.*
> —*Yiddish proverb*

5. ***stunted* hillbilly** stun'tid Something stunted has been slowed down in growth or development. From Old English, *stunt* = dull, stupid.

> *You have the brain of a four-year-old,*
> *and I bet he was glad to get rid of it.*
> —*Groucho Marx*

6. ***subservient* schlep** səb-sûr'vē-ənt A subservient person is totally submissive. From Latin, *sub-* = under + *servus* = a slave. It is coupled with **schlep** = (noun) an ineffectual person, (verb) to drag or carry something in a laborious way.

> *It is dangerous to free people who prefer to be slaves.*
> —*Niccolò Machiavelli*

7. ***sullen* wet blanket** sul'ən A sullen person is depressed, morose, sulky. From Latin, *solus* = alone.

> EPITAPH:
> *He was so depressed and out of sorts*
> *and thought his life a wreck*
> *He tried to jump off of a bridge*
> *but slipped and broke his neck*

8. ***supercilious* upstart** soo-pər-sil'ē-əs Supercilious means "to act disdainful and haughty." From Latin, *superciliam* = eyebrow; hence, with one's eyebrows raised. It is coupled with **upstart** = one whose recent wealth or power has led to presumptuous, pretentious behavior.

> *I can't help it. I was born sneering.*
> —*Gilbert and Sullivan,* The Mikado

9. **superficial** *phony* soo-pər-fish'əl One who is superficial lacks depth. Whatever you see on the surface, that's it! From Latin, *superficies* = the fact of being positioned on top, surface < *super-* = above, beyond + *ficies* = face.

> *I'm a deeply superficial person.*
> —Andy Warhol

10. **superfluous** *chatterbox* soo-pûr'floo-əs Anything superfluous is excessive and needless to what is required. From Latin, *super-* = over + *fluere* = to flow.

> *To go beyond is as wrong as to fall short.*
> —Confucius

QUIZ 76

Match the definitions with the words on the left.

___ 1.	stinting	a.	depressed, morose, sulky
___ 2.	stolid	b.	disdainful and haughty
___ 3.	stringent	c.	more than what is required
___ 4.	stultified	d.	hindered in growth
___ 5.	stunted	e.	impassive, showing no feeling
___ 6.	subservient	f.	rigidly controlling
___ 7.	sullen	g.	shallow
___ 8.	supercilious	h.	stingy and sparing
___ 9.	superficial	i.	to look foolish or stupid
___ 10.	superfluous	j.	totally submissive

GRISLY LIST 77

The doctor looked at his **tabescent** patient. Once, the dying man had been the talk of the town, another high muck-a-muck, a member of the **Sybaritic** aristocracy, complete with **sycophants** hanging on his every word. Now he was quite **taciturn**; his affable nature had become **surly** and **tactless** even with his own family. Once, he'd been a **taurine** force to be reckoned with; now he was a debilitated shell, an obituary notice waiting to happen.

And when he did speak, instead of wit, the people heard **tangential** discourses, **tautological** demands that eventually drove everyone away. He looked for hope; he hoped for death.

The doctor felt his faint pulse and whispered **surreptitiously** to the nurse, "Bleed him."

1. **surly** little punk sûr′lē A surly person is bad-tempered with a touch of arrogance. From Early English, *sirly* = like a lord.

> The best time I had with Joan Crawford
> is when I pushed her down the stairs.
> —Bette Davis

2. **surreptitious** spy sûr-əp-tish′əs To be surreptitious is to act in a secret, stealthy way. From Latin, *surreptitius* = stolen, clandestine.

> A man chases a woman until she catches him.
> —Anonymous

3. **Sybaritic** jet-setter sib-ə-rit′ik A Sybarite loves luxury to the point of self-indulgence. It comes from Sybaris, an ancient Greek city noted for its wealth and luxury.

> On the soft bed of luxury most kingdoms have expired.
> —Edward Young

4. **lying** *sycophant* sik′ə-fənt A sycophant is a self-seeking flatterer. The adjective is sycophantic. From Greek, *sykophantes* = informer.

> Sycophant: One who says things to your face
> that he wouldn't say behind your back.
> —Anonymous

5. **tabescent** string bean tə-bes′ənt A tabescent person is emaciated, generally as a consequence of a persistent illness. From Latin, *tabescent* = dwindling.

> His eyes were like the eyes of a fish not in the best of health.
> —P. G. Wodehouse

6. **taciturn** milquetoast tas′i-tûrn One who is taciturn is almost always silent. From Latin, *tacere* = to be silent. It is coupled with **milquetoast,** a timid and spineless person.

> Silence is argument carried on by other means.
> —Ernesto "Che" Guevara

7. **tactless** witling takt′lis Offensively blunt; undiplomatic. To have tact is just the opposite: you have a keen sense of what to say or do in difficult situations. From Latin, *tactus* = sense of touch + -less. It is coupled with **witling,** one who tries to be witty but lacks the talent.

> Likely comment:
> *(shouting at a VIP party)*
> *Hey, how's the diarrhea?*
> Your response:
> *Fine. How's the impotence?*

8. **tangential jawsmith** tan-jen'shəl A tangent is a line that connects to but doesn't cross or intersect another line. To be tangential is to stray off the topic of discussion on a subject matter only slightly related but not germane to the conversation. From Latin, *tangere* = to touch. It is coupled with **jawsmith,** one who talks too much.

> *The tongue of a fool carves a piece of his heart to all that sit near him.*
> —*English proverb*

9. **taurine bulldozer** tôr'īn Anyone taurine is like a bull. From Latin, *taurus* = a bull.

> *Don't help a bull out of a ditch,*
> *for when he's out he'll butt.*
> —*Malagasy proverb*

10. **tautological earbinder** tô-tə-loj'ə-kəl Tautological means to be redundant or needlessly repeat an idea using different words. From Greek, *tauto* = same + *logos* = a word.

> EPITAPH:
> *While on earth his tongue never ceased*
> *Now that he's dead, we can rest in peace*

QUIZ 77

Match the definitions with the words on the left.

_____ 1. surly
_____ 2. surreptitious
_____ 3. Sybaritic
_____ 4. sycophant
_____ 5. tabescent
_____ 6. taciturn
_____ 7. tactless
_____ 8. tangential
_____ 9. taurine
_____ 10. tautological

a. almost always silent
b. bad-tempered; arrogant
c. emaciated
d. like a bull
e. loves luxury self-indulgently
f. needlessly repeating an idea by using different words
g. secretive, stealthy
h. self-seeking flatterer
i. straying off the topic onto a topic not germane to the conversation
j. offensively blunt; undiplomatic

GRISLY LIST 78

"It's you," the salesman beamed as he handed the **termagant** a mirror to see her new earrings. This had been a **temerarious** gamble: The **tetched** woman had been notorious with salesmen everywhere as the most difficult customer ever. Peter had made the **thrasonical** challenge that he could outsell anyone and someone had thrown down the gauntlet of Ms. Addleson, the **tempestuous** wildcat of Colton County.

"You like these? Tell me the truth; you'd buy these for your wife?" She grimaced as she held the earrings up to her ear.

"These are my wife's favorite," he **tergiversated**. The truth was that he wasn't married and these were the most **tawdry** things he'd ever seen, but he simply had to make the sale. "But she only said that after seeing Julia Roberts wearing them."

"Julia Roberts wears these?"

"Forgive me for being **tendentious**, but they look much better on you."

Ms. Addleson put them on but, to the surprise of the salesman, a metamorphosis took place: Her **teratoid** features gave way and an inner beauty came forth, and her **testy** personality seemed to die, only to be reborn as an angel.

Later that night, the salesman left feeling as if he had been the dupe, because he had no explanation for what he had seen. The next day, the **testiest** woman of Colton County went out on the town and people marveled at the radical change in her appearance and demeanor. The salesman, on the other hand, got married and opened up a drugstore.

1. **tawdry tramp** tô'drē One who is tawdry is cheap, showy and sleazy. It derives from the St. Audrey's fair in Norwich, England, where cheap, showy neckpieces were sold.

> *A lot of women are getting tattoos. Don't do it. That's sick.*
> *That butterfly looks great on your breast when you're 20, 30.*
> *When you get to be 70, 80, it stretches into a condor.*
> —Billy Elmer

2. **temerarious half-wit** tem-ə-râr'ē-əs A temerarious person is foolishly bold. From Latin, *temere* = rashly, blindly.

> *Always goes as if he had a spare neck in his pocket.*
> —R. S. Surtees

3. **tempestuous wildcat** tem-pes'chōō-əs One who is tempestuous is violent and stormy. From Latin, *tempestes* = calamity, storm.

> *Of all the wild beasts of land or sea, the wildest is woman.*
> —Menander

4. **tendentious twit** ten-den'shəs A tendentious person is biased or overly opinionated. From Latin, *tendens* = to extend.

> *Everyone has a right to my opinion.*
> —Madonna

5. **teratoid horror** ter'ə-toid Anything teratoid resembles a monster. From Greek, *teras* = a monster, wonder.

> *Her face was her chaperone.*
> —Rupert Hughes

6. **tergiversating scamp** tər-jiv′ər-sā-ting To tergiversate is to desert a cause or a party, to be a traitor, or to equivocate or use evasions to hide the truth. From Latin, *tergiversari* = to turn one's back, decline.

> *False in one thing, false in everything.*
> *—Unknown*

7. **plug-ugly termagant** tûr′mə-gənt In medieval times, Christians believed (wrongly) that a termagant was a Muslim deity. Christians introduced it into their morality plays as a violent, overbearing person in long robes. Now termagant means "a scolding, quarrelsome woman."

> *My wife was too beautiful for words, but not for arguments.*
> *—John Barrymore*

8. **testy relic** tes′tē A testy person is irritably impatient and touchy. From Old French, *teste* = the head.

> *Why be disagreeable, when with a little effort you can be impossible?*
> *—Douglas Woodruff*

9. **tetched old kook** techt A tetched person is a tad demented, a little crazy. From Late Medieval English, *teche* = a mark.

> *If a patient is poor he is committed to a public hospital as a "psychotic."*
> *If he can afford a sanatorium, the diagnosis is "neurasthenia."*
> *If he is wealthy enough to be in his own home under the constant watch*
> *of nurses and physicians, he is simply "an indisposed eccentric."*
> *—Pierre Janet*

10. **thrasonical gasbag** thrā-son′i-kəl One who is thrasonical likes to brag. From Greek, *thrasos* = too bold > Thrason, a braggart in the Roman playwright Terrence's play *Eunuch*.

> Likely comment:
> *I have five sports cars.*
> Your response:
> *Then get in one and drive away.*

Match the definitions with the words on the right.

____ 1. tawdry
____ 2. temerarious
____ 3. tempestuous
____ 4. tendentious
____ 5. teratoid
____ 6. tergiversate
____ 7. termagant
____ 8. testy
____ 9. tetched
____ 10. thrasonical

a. a little crazy
b. a quarrelsome woman
c. bragging
d. cheap, showy, and sleazy
e. to desert a cause or a party or be evasive
f. foolishly bold
g. irritably impatient
h. very opinionated
i. resembling a monster
j. violent and stormy

GRISLY LIST 79

Adrian walked into the bathroom and saw the would-be robber, a **tyro** if ever there was one, stuck in the window. His **torpid** figure hung almost lifelessly with his head over the toilet. His soft belly was **turgid** from being stuck there for some indeterminate time, bulging and red along the windowsill. Possibly, he'd been there for days.

"What's going on here?" Adrian asked **truculently**.

All the robber could see was the owner's **troglodytic** legs and feet.

"What?" He suddenly came to life and put on his best **treacly** tone. "I'm sorry. I thought this was my apartment. I was drunk. I got lost."

"Don't give me that crap!" Adrian screamed at the **timorous** robber. "You were trying to rob this place, weren't you?"

"No. I swear I was drunk. I swear. I swear." His **truckling** cries pleaded with Adrian to help him out.

"I should snap your neck."

"No. Please," he begged **tremulously**, "I've been stuck here all night long, for days. I can't even go to the bathroom, man. Don't hurt me, please!"

"Maybe I'll just take a couple of pictures and send them to your mom and some of your friends," his **traducer** laughed.

The robber raised his head.

"Dad?"

1. **timorous tenderfoot** tim'ər-əs To be timorous is to tremble, to be fearful, to be tentative. From Latin, *timor* = fear.

EPITAPH:
His ticker stopped ticking
and gave up the fight
When kittens so tiny
mewled in the night

2. **torpid vegetable** tôr'pid To be torpid is to be sluggish and/or apathetic. From Latin, *torpere* = to be numb or sluggish.

The biggest sin is sitting on your ass.
—Florence Kennedy

3. **traducing pile of rubbish** trə-dōō'sing To traduce is to slander, to make a mockery of others. Traducer is the noun. From Latin, *traducere* = to exhibit as a spectacle.

Alas, they had been friends in youth;
but whispering tongues can poison truth.
—Samuel T. Coleridge

4. **treacly brainwasher** trē'klē A treacly person is given to overly sweet talk or sentiment. Treacle was a concoction used as an antidote for poison. In the 17th century, when molasses was added to many remedies, treacle took on the overly sweet connotation. From Latin, *theriaca* = antidote for poison.

Honeyed speech often conceals poison and gall.
—Danish proverb

5. **tremulous tinhorn** trem'yə-ləs Trembling with fear or anxiety, someone tremulous shakes like a bowl of Jell-O. From Latin, *tremere* = tremble.

I was so timid I was beaten up by Quakers.
—Woody Allen

6. **troglodytic hulk** trog-lə-dī'tik A troglodyte is someone who lives in a cave, or a person of primitive or brutal character. From Greek, *troglodytes* = one who creeps into holes.

Man is the missing link between the ape and the human being.
—Anonymous

7. **truckling dipwad** truk'ling A truckle is a small wheel, but because of its low place it can imply servility or obsequiousness. From Greek, *trokhos* = a wheel.

Servitude debases men to the point where they end up liking it.
—Luc de la Clapiers Vauvenargues

8. **truculent lunk** truk'yə-lənt A truculent person is vicious in both manner and speech. From Latin, *truculentus* = ferocious, cruel.

Man is still a savage to the extent
that he has little respect
for anything that cannot hurt him.
—Edgar Watson Howe

9. **turgid** motormouth tûr'jid Turgid means swollen and can also be used metaphorically, being "swollen," as in bombastic and pompous. From Latin, *turgere* = to swell.

> *If only I had a little humility, I would be perfect.*
> —Attributed to Ted Turner

10. **tongue-tied** *tyro* tī'rō A tyro is a rank beginner, one who is just starting to learn something. From Latin, *tiro* = a young soldier.

> *A good man is always a beginner.*
> —Martial

QUIZ 79

Match the definitions with the words on the right.

____ 1.	timorous	a.	a beginner
____ 2.	torpid	b.	a caveman
____ 3.	traduce	c.	a small wheel; servile, cringing,
____ 4.	treacly		or obsequious
____ 5.	tremulous	d.	overly sweet
____ 6.	troglodyte	e.	savage, vicious
____ 7.	truckling	f.	slander, make a mockery
____ 8.	truculent	g.	sluggish and apathetic
____ 9.	turgid	h.	swollen; pompous
____ 10.	tyro	i.	trembling (fits two words)

GRISLY LIST 80

"No," the woman spewed with **unbridled** fury. " I could never in a million years be interested in such an **unconscionable** worm as you."

"But—"

"The thought of sleeping with such an **uncouth** animal as you makes my skin crawl."

"I—"

"Forget it!" she repeated her **unbitted** attack, "Even seeing you this close with your **ugsome** filth on my doorstep makes me want to take a bath and scrub the sidewalk."

"If—"

"I want a man, not some **unfledged** wannabe."

"You—"

"**Unctuous** slobs like you **undermine** a woman's faith in finding a good man."

"Sugar! I want to borrow some sugar!" the man shouted.

"What?"

"Sugar. I just came over to borrow some sugar from my new neighbor. That's all."

"Oh."

"What **ulterior** motives did you think I had?"

"I'm so sorry. Oh, I'm sorry. I'm so embarrassed! You must think I'm a raving lunatic. I'm so sorry. Sugar? Uh, no. I'm sorry. I haven't gone shopping yet."

"Well, it's okay," He smiled and leaned in her doorway. "Since your cupboards are bare, come on over to my place and I'll cook something up for you."

The man had had other doors slam in his face, but as he held his bleeding nose and walked back to his apartment, he couldn't remember one being slammed as hard and as fast.

"Talk about being **umbrageous!**"

1. **ugsome perpetrator** ug'səm Anyone ugsome is loathsome and horrid. From Medieval English, *uggen* = to fear, cause loathing.

> *I have found little that is good about human beings.*
> *In my experience most of them are trash.*
> —Sigmund Freud

2. **ulterior motive** ul-tîr'ē-ər Anything ulterior is undisclosed or hidden. Someone with an ulterior motive is concealing his or her true intention. From Latin, *ultra* = beyond.

> *He can best avoid a snare that knows how to set one.*
> —Publilius Syrus

3. **umbrageous powder keg** um-brā'jəs To be umbrageous is to take offense too easily. From French, *ombrageux* = shy, suspecting.

> EPITAPH:
> *A little too touchy,*
> *A little too hurt,*
> *Now he won't take offense,*
> *Under six feet of dirt*

4. **unbitted Delilah** un-bit'd A bit is the metal mouthpiece used to control a horse; hence, to be unbitted is to be wild and uncontrolled. From Old English, un- = not + *bitan* = bite.

> *Give a woman an inch and she'll park her car on it.*
> —E.P.B. White

5. **unbridled battle-ax** un-brīd'ld A bridle is the headpiece used to control a horse. To be unbridled is to be unrestrained. From Old English, un- = not + *bregdan* = to pull, turn.

> *When passion is on the throne, reason is out of doors.*
> —M. Henry

6. **unconscionable** worm un-kon'shə-nə-bəl An unconscionable person has no morals and no conscience. From Latin, *un-* = without + *conscientia* = moral sense.

> Pity was invented by the weak.
> —Mendele Mocher Serforim

7. **uncouth** animal un-kōōth' Anyone uncouth is clumsy and crude. From Old English, *uncuth* = unknown.

> There is a vast difference between the savage and the civilized man,
> but it is never apparent to their wives until after breakfast.
> —Helen Rowland

8. **unctuous** manipulator ungk'chōō-əs Unctuous means oily or smooth and deceitful. From Latin, *unctum* = ointment.

> In the mouths of many men soft words are like roses
> that soldiers put into the muzzles of their muskets on holidays.
> —Henry Wadsworth Longfellow

9. **undermining** heckler un-dər-mī'ning To undermine is to dig underneath, to wear away at the base, or to weaken by some insidious means. From Old Icelandic, *undir* = under + Gaelic, *mein* = ore, mineral.

> Why do you heckle me? For all you know, I'm your father.
> —Jack White

10. **unfledged** novice un-flejd' An unfledged novice is immature and untried. From Medieval English, *un-* = not + *flegge* = ready to fly.

> Youth is a disease that only time can cure.
> —P. Snurd

QUIZ 80

Match the definitions with the words on the right.

___ 1. ugsome	a.	concealing one's true motive
___ 2. ulterior	b.	horrid and loathsome
___ 3. umbrageous	c.	immature and untried
___ 4. unbitted	d.	smooth and deceitful
___ 5. unbridled	e.	clumsy and crude
___ 6. unconscionable	f.	take offense too easily
___ 7. uncouth	g.	weaken insidiously
___ 8. unctuous	h.	wild, unrestrained
___ 9. undermine		(fits two words)
___ 10. unfledged	i.	with no morals or conscience

REVIEW 16

MATCH EACH QUOTE WITH THE APPROPRIATE WORD.

1. No mask like open truth to cover lies,
As to go naked is the best disguise.
—*Congreve*

2. He is looking for the donkey while sitting on it.
—*Armenian proverb*

3. The larger the income, the harder it is to live within it.
—*Richard Whately*

4. Without tact you can learn nothing.
—*Benjamin Disraeli*

____ a. stultified ____ c. unctuous
____ b. Sybaritic ____ d. tactless

5. Three may keep a secret, if two of them are dead.
—*Benjamin Franklin*

6. Some men, like dogs, will only fawn the more when repulsed,
but will pay little heed to a friendly caress.
—*Abd-el-Kader*

7. The bigger the man's head, the worse his headache.
—*Persian proverb*

____ e. truckling ____ g. surreptitious
____ f. supercilious

8. By means of a whorish woman a man is brought to a piece of bread.
—*Proverbs 6:26*

9. With audacity one can undertake anything, but not do everything.
—*Napoleon I*

10. A truth that's told with bad intent
Beats all the lies you can invent.
—*William Blake*

11. We must interpret a bad temper as a sign of an inferiority complex.
—*Alfred Adler*

12. They brag most that do the least.
—*English proverb*

___ h. thrasonical ___ k. temerarious
___ i. testy ___ l. salacious
___ j. traduce

Chapter 17

*A healthy ear
can stand hearing sick words.*
—Senegalese proverb

MALCOLM X WAS STUCK IN JAIL. He could have let his mind rot, but he didn't: he read! He read every book he could get his hands on. He even read all the way through the dictionary. Is it any wonder that he went on to become one of the most powerful and influential speakers of his era? People still debate his legacy, but no one can dismiss his power as a speaker to influence people. Which brings us to you. No one can dismiss you either. The rest of your life is an open book. And the key to what may make you a force to be reckoned with might be the next book you pick up.

What I'm suggesting is this: your love of language should go beyond this book. It never hurts to pick up another vocabulary book and whisk through it. One word book makes the next easier, and so on. Soon you'll make yourself a word sleuth. The easier each book becomes, the less frustrating it is to study. In time, you might end up skimming through the book to see if there is anything you don't already know.

GRISLY LIST 81

I scanned the bar, littered with the usual **unregenerate** types: **ungainly** bums and **unkempt** tarts. But I was looking for just one, the **usurious** Sammy the Loan Shark. If I was going to find this **unseemly** scumbag, I'd have to sift through every **unsavory** saloon this side of town.

This time I was lucky, for the **unwitting** sleaze sat in the corner of this godforsaken tavern. It was Sammy, all right: the **unkempt** hair, the **unscrupulous** eyes. Sammy looked up at me and spat out the usual **untoward** comment:

"You? The **unmitigated** gall. Fancy seeing you here."

I took Sammy's cigarette and blew a smoke ring, "Mom, it's time to come home."

1. **ungainly stumblebum** un-gān'lē Ungainly means uncoordinated and unattractive. From Old Norse, *un-* = not + *gegn* = straight, fit.

> *He had a profile like a flight of steps.*
> —*Rudyard Kipling, on King Edward VII*

2. **_unkempt_ mutt** un-kempt′ Uncombed and untidy, an unkempt person looks shabby. From Middle English, *un-* = not + *kembe* = to comb.

> There was a young belle of old Natchez
> Whose garments were always in patchez.
> When comment arose
> On the state of her clothes,
> She drawled, When Ah itchez, Ah scratches.
> —Ogden Nash

3. **_unmitigated_ cuckoo** un-mit′i-gā-tid Anything unmitigated is absolute or not lessened: an unmitigated cuckoo is an out-and-out lunatic. From Middle English, *un-* = not, the opposite of + *mitigare* = to make mild.

> EPITAPH:
> *Get me out of here!!*

4. **_unregenerate_ ruck** un-ri-jen′ər-it Literally, unregenerate means not born again, but it signifies an obstinate, recalcitrant, profane, or heathen person. From Latin, *in-* = not + *re-* = again + *generare* = to create. It is coupled with **ruck** = a mass of common people.

> I'm a born-again atheist.
> —Gore Vidal

5. **_unsavory_ lowlife** un-sā′və-rē To be unsavory is to have a bad taste or odor, but it can also mean morally bad. From Old French, *un-* + *savoure* = tasty.

> If man is only a little lower than the angels, the angels should reform.
> —Mary Wilson Little

6. **_unscrupulous_ warmonger** un-skroo′pyə-ləs An unscrupulous person is without morals or conscience. From Latin, *in-* = without + *scrupus* = a sharp pebble or stone.

> I propose getting rid of conventional armaments
> and replacing them with reasonably priced hydrogen bombs
> that would be distributed equally throughout the world.
> —Idi Amin

7. **_unseemly_ sleaze** un-sēm′lē To be unseemly is to be rude, indecent, improper. From Medieval English, *un-* = not + *semlich* = fitting.

> Want of decency is want of sense.
> —Wentworth Dillon

8. **_untoward_ remark** un-tôrd′ Untoward can mean an unfortunate remark or, more likely, an unseemly remark. From Old English, *un-* = not + *toweard* = in the direction of, facing.

> I've been around so long, I knew Doris Day before she was a virgin.
> —Groucho Marx

9. **unwitting tool** un-wit'ing Completely unaware, an unwitting person could end up being the unintentional accomplice of others. From Old English, *un-* = not + *witan* = to know.

> *Ignorance, when voluntary, is criminal.*
> —Samuel Johnson

10. **usurious loan shark** yōō-zhōōr'ē-əs Anyone usurious lends money at exorbitantly high interest. From Latin, *usuria* = use.

> *A legal thief, a bloodless murderer,*
> *A fiend incarnate, a false usurer.*
> —Joseph Hall

QUIZ 81

Match the definitions with the words on the right

_____ 1. ungainly
_____ 2. unkempt
_____ 3. unmitigated
_____ 4. unregenerate
_____ 5. unsavory
_____ 6. unscrupulous
_____ 7. unseemly
_____ 8. untoward
_____ 9. unwitting
_____ 10. usurious

a. absolute or not lessened
b. completely unaware
c. indecent (fits two words)
d. uncoordinated; unattractive
e. lends money at high interest
f. profane, heathen, obstinate
g. morally bad or tastes bad
h. uncombed and untidy, shabby
i. without morals or conscience

GRISLY LIST 82

"If you hadn't got us lost, we wouldn't be in this mess," the **vainglorious** woman hissed while she whacked her **uxorious** husband upside the head.

The sad, slight man rasped, "Yes, dear."

He had taken this kind of abuse for so many years that he seemed more like a shriveled **vagabond** who hadn't had a decent night's sleep in years— and he hadn't. Although his eyes had been blue and bright when he was younger, all that remained was the **vacuous** expression of a ghost. Now the mismatched couple together faced the ugly menace of a **vagrant** with a knife who seemed bent on robbing them, or worse.

The wife whacked her husband again and growled, "Well, give the **venal** mongrel something to make him go away."

"Yes, dear." The man droned with **vapid** regularity and gently tossed his wallet to the man.

"Not the whole wallet!" she screamed.

The **vagrant** quickly slipped the wallet into his pocket and, with a **venerious** gleam in his eye, grabbed her purse as well.

"Oh, no, you don't," the self-**vaunted** scold laughed, "not with me you don't."

The two struggled for a brief moment until her wiry husband leaped between them. As the **vagrant** ran away, purse in hand, the husband fell down, a knife in his belly.

"Oh, my god! Oh, my god! You've been stabbed!" the woman screamed.

Her husband looked down at the gaping wound with a **vagarious** grin on his face. Then, with a peaceful sigh, he whispered his last words: "Yes, dear."

1. **uxorious dunce** uk-sôr'ē-əs An uxorious man is submissively devoted to his wife. From Latin, *uxor* = wife.

> *A husband is what's left of a man after the nerve has been extracted.*
> —*Helen Rowland*

2. **vacuous groupie** vak'yoo-əs Anyone vacuous is empty, shallow, lacking intelligence. From Latin, *vacuus* = to be empty + -ous.

> *I locked my keys in the car*
> *and had to break the windshield to get my wife out.*
> —*Red Skelton*

3. **road-weary vagabond** vag'ə-bond A vagabond is a hobo, one who moves from place to place. From Latin, *vagari* = to wander.

> *I'm dating a homeless woman.*
> *It was easier to talk her into staying over.*
> —*Garry Shandling*

4. **vagarious eccentric** və-gar'ē-əs Vagarious means to express odd and eccentric behavior. From Latin, *vagari* = to wander.

> *Shirley MacLaine could go to group therapy all by herself.*
> —*Cynthia Nelms*

5. **flea-bitten vagrant** vā'grənt A vagrant is a hobo, someone who wanders from place to place. From Latin, *vagari* = to wander.

> *They say the homeless are homeless by choice. That's true.*
> *I was walking down Bleecker Street at two in the morning,*
> *and I just had that burning desire to go to sleep right there.*
> —*Scott Blakeman*

6. **vainglorious show-off** vān-glôr'ē-əs A vainglorious person is high and mighty, boastful and conceited. From Latin, *vana gloria* = empty boasting.

> *Who knows himself a braggart, let him fear this;*
> *for it shall come to pass that every braggart shall be found an ass.*
> —*Shakespeare*, All's Well That Ends Well

7. ***vapid* socialite** vap'id To be vapid is to be dull and/or tasteless. From Latin, *vapidus* = stale, insipid.

> *Being popular is important. Otherwise, people might not like you.*
> —Mimi Pond

8. **self-*vaunting* know-it-all** vôn'ting To vaunt is to boast or brag about one's success. From Latin, *vanus* = empty, vain.

> *Self-praise smells bad.*
> —Swedish proverb

9. ***venal* self-promoter** vē'nəl Anyone venal is capable of being bribed or corrupted. From Latin, *venalis* = for sale.

> *A conscience, which has been bought once, will be bought twice.*
> —Norbert Wiener

10. ***venerious* bedhopper** və-nēr'ē-əs Venery has two meanings. From Latin, venery comes from Venus = goddess of love; hence, it means lustful. It also comes from Latin, *vener* = to hunt. So it can depict one given to hunting or one on the hunt for sex.

> *He said he got the misery, but he had a lot of fun.*
> —Little Richard

QUIZ 82

Match the definitions with the words on the right.

____ 1. uxorious
____ 2. vacuous
____ 3. vagabond
____ 4. vagarious
____ 5. vagrant
____ 6. vainglorious
____ 7. vapid
____ 8. vaunt
____ 9. venal
____ 10. venerious

a. a hobo (fits two words)
b. boastfully conceited
c. capable of being bribed
d. dull and/or tasteless
e. empty; lacking intelligence
f. submissively devoted to one's wife
g. full of eccentric behavior
h. lustful; given to hunting
i. to boast

GRISLY LIST 83

"I'll catch him," Olivia grinned with **vengeful** hate.

She lay prostrate under her boyfriend's bed and waited for him to come home. "What **virulent** thing can I say to him when I catch him?" she wondered. "Better yet, what **vilipending** thing can I say to her?"

It had all started three weeks prior, when they were talking on the phone. He'd just complained that she was too **verbose,** and she asked, "What's that mean?" when he stopped and said:

"Olivia, hold on for just a second."

It was muffled, but she could've sworn she heard way in the background: "Precious, give me a kiss."

"Who was precious?" That **vexatious** thought had been driving her crazy. "How long has this been going on?"

And so, here she was, under the bed, feeling absolutely **villainous** breaking into her boyfriend's apartment. This was not like her at all, but everything had been so perfect. For years she had been **vicariously** experiencing her friends' weddings, all the while waiting for the one she would marry. The one she would have children with. Finally she thought she had found him. What tramp had **vitiated** her chances?

The door opened.

"Hey, baby doll," he called out.

"Baby doll!" she **venomously** fumed. "He never calls me baby doll."

"How's my little precious?"

"Little!" she thought. "Oh, no! Her **vindictive** plan had failed: she'd suffer the humiliation of seeing her competition look thin and beautiful.

She could see his feet as he strode into the room before he plopped down on the bed.

"Where are you going, precious?"

A small kitten jumped down and peeped under the bed.

"Where you going, kitty? Come back up here."

1. **vengeful stalker** venj'fəl Vengeful literally means "full of venge," which is an archaic word meaning "avenge." From Old French, *venger* = to avenge.

> *Revenge is sweet and not fattening.*
> —*Alfred Hitchcock*

2. **venomous villain** ven'ə-məs Anything venomous is poisonous, full of venom, the toxic liquid created by an animal to stop prey or defend itself. It can also describe one who is spiteful. From Latin, *venenum* = a poison.

> *The man recovered of the bite.*
> *The dog it was that died.*
> —*Oliver Goldsmith*

3. **verbose yenta** vər-bōs Anyone verbose simply uses too many words. From Latin, *verbum* = word. It is coupled with **yenta** = Yiddish for an annoying, gossipy woman.

> *Open your mouth only to change feet.*
> —*Stanley Ralph Ross*

4. **vexatious in-laws** vek-sā'shəs Anyone vexatious is annoying. From French, *vexer* = to torment < Latin, *vexare* = to shake, agitate.

> *People who think they know everything*
> *are very irritating to those of us who do.*
> —*Anonymous*

5. **vicarious voyeur** vī-kâr'ē-əs A vicarious person is thrilled by imagined participation watching another's experience, as when a fan gets a thrill watching a sports team win a game. From Latin, *vicarius* = substituting.

> *An orgy looks particularly alluring*
> *seen through the mists of righteous indignation.*
> —*Malcolm Muggeridge*

6. **vilipending snitch** vil'ə-pen-ding To vilipend is to treat others with low regard or speak slanderously about them. From Latin, *vili* = cheap.

> *Accuse. To affirm another's guilt or unworthiness;*
> *most commonly as a justification of ourselves of having wronged him.*
> —*Ambrose Bierce*

7. **villainous mugger** vil'ə-nəs Anyone villainous is criminal or wicked. From Vulgar Latin, *villanus* = a farm worker.

> *A man cannot become perfect in a hundred years;*
> *but he may become corrupt in less than one day.*
> —*Chinese proverb*

8. **vindictive viper** vin-dik'tiv Watch your back! A vindictive person wants revenge. From Latin, *vindicare* = avenge, to claim.

> *She always tells stories in the present vindictive.*
> —*Tom Peace*

9. **virulent arsonist** vîr'yə-lənt Someone or something virulent is poisonous or infectious. Virulent can also be used to describe one who is spiteful. From Latin, *virulentus* = full of poison.

> *What does not poison fattens.*
> —*Italian proverb*

10. **vitiated varmint** vish'ē-ā-tid Literally, vitiated means spoiled, but it can also describe one who has been weakened morally. From Latin, *vitiare* = to spoil.

> *Corruption is like a ball of snow:*
> *whence once set a-rolling it must increase.*
> —*Charles Caleb Colton*

Match the definitions with the words on the right.

____ 1. vengeful	a.	annoying
____ 2. venomous	b.	criminal or wicked
____ 3. verbose	c.	experienced through another
____ 4. vexatious		person via imagination
____ 5. vicarious	d.	poisonous (fits two words)
____ 6. vilipend	e.	spoiled; weakened morally
____ 7. villainous	f.	to slander
____ 8. vindictive	g.	using too many words
____ 9. virulent	h.	revengeful (fits two words)
____ 10. vitiated		

GRISLY LIST 84

"You see, Mr. Eisenhower," he opined with a **vulpine** twinkle in his eyes, "your book is simply too **vitriolic**, too **vituperative** for our audience."

I wanted to scream, to **vociferously** blare out: "You just used two of the words in my book!" But instead, I pushed my **volatile** nerves deep inside my belly where they would one day give me cancer, and whimpered,

"Well, uh, you can use the words in a positive, helpful way."

That sucked. That really sucked, but what could I say?

"And, quite frankly, some of your quotes . . ."

He then jammed a sandwich in his mouth and proceeded to chew **voraciously** while I waited for him to finish his sentence.

". . . they have such a **wanton** edge that only a **vulgarian** would find them amusing."

"Vulgarians need love too."

"You're not serious, are you?" he said sternly.

I **waffled** and said, "I, uh, no, well, uh, yes, kind of."

He took another bite of his sandwich, so I said, "I take it you're not interested."

He laughed **waggishly**. "No, we love it; I was just kidding you. Didn't you notice how I used vocabulary from your book?"

1. **vitriolic tongue-lasher** vit-rē-ol'ik Anyone vitriolic is sharp, bitter, and biting. Oil of vitriol is sulfuric acid. From Latin, *vitreus* = glassy, because of the oil's glassy appearance.

> *Any fool can criticize, and many of them do.*
> —C. Garbett

2. ***vituperative* vermin** vī-tōō′pər-ə-tiv A vituperative person hurls abuse, spits out accusations, rants and raves. From Latin, *vituperare* = to blame.

> *By blackening another you do not whiten yourself.*
> *—Romanian proverb*

3. ***vociferous* griper** vō-sif′ər-əs To be vociferous is to be loud or clamorous. From Latin, *vociferare* = to shout, to cry out noisily.

> *What he lacks in substance he makes up for in volume.*
> *—Unknown*

4. ***volatile* vixen** vol′ə-tl Volatile has several meanings: able to fly, vaporizing quickly, or fickle, unstable, and explosive. If you're a volatile person you're likely to explode at any time. From Latin, *volare* = to fly.

> *The advantage of emotions is that they lead us astray.*
> *—Oscar Wilde*

5. ***voracious* vamp** vô-rā′shəs Voracious usually means greedy (a voracious appetite), but it also signifies one who is immoderate, as in, "His voracious lust for power was his undoing." From Latin, *vorare* = to devour.

> *Big mouthfuls often choke.*
> *—Italian proverb*

6. **foul-mouthed *vulgarian*** vul-gâr′ē-ən A vulgarian is given to coarse tastes—indecent, crude, and shows a lack of good breeding. From Latin, *vulgus* = the general public.

> *Maintain your rank, vulgarity despise.*
> *To swear is neither brave, polite, nor wise.*
> *—William Cowper*

7. ***vulpine* opportunist** vul′pīn Vulpine means like a fox. So a vulpine opportunist is a crafty person who sees a chance to get ahead and takes it. From Latin, *vulpes* = fox.

> *The fox changes his skin but not his habits.*
> *—Suetonius*

8. ***waffling* wimp** wof′ling To waffle is to speak in an indecisive way or perhaps in a purposely vague way in order to equivocate. Probably from wave, which is from Indo-European, *webh* = to fluctuate.

> *His indecision is final.*
> *—Anonymous*

9. ***waggish* clown** wag′ish A wag is one given to droll, roguish humor. The origin of wag is uncertain, but it may come from Middle English, *wag-halter* = a gallows bird. (A gallows bird was anyone who deserved hanging.)

> *A hooker told me she'd do anything I wanted for fifty bucks.*
> *I said, "Paint my house."*
> *—Henny Youngman*

10. **wanton womanizer** won'tən Wanton can mean unmanageable, sexually loose, or senseless. From Medieval English, *wantowen* = undisciplined.

> *Don't accept rides from strange men,*
> *and remember that all men are strange.*
> —Robin Morgan

QUIZ 84

Match the definitions with the words on the right.

____ 1.	vitriolic	a.	able to fly; vaporizing quickly;
____ 2.	vituperative		or fickle, unstable, explosive
____ 3.	vociferous	b.	greedy
____ 4.	volatile	c.	given to droll, roguish humor
____ 5.	voracious	d.	hurling abuse, ranting
____ 6.	vulgarian	e.	like a fox
____ 7.	vulpine	f.	loud, clamorous
____ 8.	waffle	g.	one given to coarse tastes
____ 9.	waggish	h.	sharp, bitter, and biting
____ 10.	wanton	i.	speak in a purposely vague way
		j.	unmanageable; sexually loose

GRISLY LIST 85

The **wizened** old man limped down the alley, looking this way and that to get his bearings, until he stood behind the pet food store.

"Damn!" he yelled, seeing the lock on the trash bin.

Then, patiently and tenderly, he pulled the small pup out of his jacket and laid him at his feet. The tiny thing gazed up at his master with **woebegone** eyes, as if the lugubrious look could **wheedle** some food out of his empty trousers.

The man scanned the alley for a tool of some kind but all he could find was a small block of concrete. Then, with **willful** determination, he pounded at the lock with all his might.

"Damn!" he **winced** as he cut his hand. He then slumped down on the ground and began to cry.

Another **wastrel** came out of his shelter to see what all the commotion was about, and the two **xenophobes** glared at each other until they finally lost interest.

The little dog licked the blood off his master's hand and then scurried around the side of the trash bin until he sniffed out the small hole that corrosion had made near the back of the bin. The **wily** little critter barked once.

His master crawled to the hole. With a **wry** grin, he reached inside and pulled out a can. It was cat food, but his dog wouldn't care. He stuffed his pockets with as much pet food as he could, put his dog back in his coat and, with a **whimsical** gait, limped back through the alley.

1. **wretched *wastrel*** wā′strəl A wastrel has wasted his/her money, life, and essence. From Latin, *vastus* = empty, waste.

   > *The greater cantle of the world is lost with very ignorance,*
   > *we have kissed away kingdoms and provinces.*
   > —Shakespeare, Antony and Cleopatra

2. ***wheedling* briber** hwēd′ling To wheedle is to try to influence by flattery or guile. From German, *wedein* = to wag a fan or tail; thus, to flatter < *wedel* = a fan or tail.

   > *He who knows how to flatter*
   > *also knows how to slander.*
   > —Napoleon Bonaparte

3. ***whimsical* dabbler** hwim′zi-kəl A whimsical person is capricious, fanciful, odd. Possibly from Old Norse, *hvima* = to let one's eyes wander.

   > *Some have at first for wits,*
   > *then poets passed;*
   > *turned critics next,*
   > *and proved plain fools at last.*
   > —Alexander Pope

4. ***willful* bigot** wil′fəl Willful can mean two things: it can mean "voluntary," or it can mean "unreasonable" or "stubborn." From Indo-European, *wel* = to wish, to choose.

   > *O sir, to willful men, the injuries that they themselves procure*
   > *must be their schoolmasters.*
   > —Shakespeare, King Lear

5. ***wily* gremlin** wī′lē A wily person is crafty and sly. From Old Norse *vél* = craft + -y.

   > *In order to be the master, the politician poses as the servant.*
   > —Charles de Gaulle

6. ***wincing* simp** win′sing To wince is to shrink back involuntarily from pain or fear. From Medieval English, *wincen* = to kick.

   > *Hollow men, like horses hot at hand,*
   > *make gallant show and promise of their mettle;*
   > *but when they should endure the bloody spur,*
   > *they fall their crests, and like deceitful jades sink in the trial.*
   > —Shakespeare, Julius Caesar

7. ***wizened* old leper** wiz′ənd Wizened means shriveled, dried up, withered. From Icelandic, *visna* = to wither.

   > *I wasted time, and now doth time waste me.*
   > —William Shakespeare

8. **woebegone** stray wō'bi-gôn Woebegone means "filled with sorrow." From Middle English, *wo* = great sorrow + *begon* = to go around.

> *Man's grandeur stems from his knowledge of his own misery.*
> *A tree does not know itself to be miserable.*
> —Blaise Pascal

9. **wry** wit rī A wry person's humor is a little twisted, a little perverse. From Old English, *writhan* = to twist.

> *Wit is educated insolence.*
> —Aristotle

10. **xenophobic** racist zē-nə-fo'bik Xenophobes are fearful of strangers or contamination from the outside, or they have contempt for foreigners. From Greek, *xeno* = stranger, foreign + *phobos* = a fear.

> Likely comment:
> *You from 'round here?*
> Your response:
> *Why yes! I'm your mother.*

QUIZ 85

Match the definitions with the words on the right.

____ 1. wastrel
____ 2. wheedle
____ 3. whimsical
____ 4. willful
____ 5. wily
____ 6. wince
____ 7. wizened
____ 8. woebegone
____ 9. wry
____ 10. xenophobic

a. capricious, fanciful, odd
b. crafty and sly
c. dried up, shriveled, withered
d. fearful or contemptuous of strangers and foreigners
e. filled with woe, wretched
f. shrink back involuntarily
g. one who has wasted away his/her money, life, and essence
h. stubborn, unreasonable
i. to influence by flattery or guile
j. twisted, perverse

REVIEW 17

MATCH EACH QUOTE WITH THE APPROPRIATE WORD.

1. One should forgive one's enemies, but not before they are hanged.
—*Heinrich Heine*

2. Hunger is a slut hound on a fresh track.
—*Josh Billings*

3. Some guy hit my fender the other day, and I said unto him, "Be fruitful and multiply," but not in those words.
—*Woody Allen*

4. We love a joke that hands us a pat on the back while it kicks the other fellow downstairs.
—*C. L. Edson*

5. It is the characteristic of all movements and crusades that the psychopathic element rises to the top.
—*Robert Lindner*

6. You play the spaniel, and think with the wagging of your tongue to win me.
—*William Shakespeare*

7. Man is not man, but a wolf, to those he does not know.
—*Plautus*

____ a. voracious   ____ e. militant
____ b. vengeful   ____ f. wag
____ c. xenophobic   ____ g. vulgarian
____ d. wheedle

8. A creditor is worse than a master; for a master owns only your person. A creditor owns your dignity and can belabor that.
—*Victor Hugo*, Les Misérables

9. She has a whim of iron.
—*Oliver Herford*

10. A bribe will enter without knocking.
—*English proverb*

11. Words are like leaves; and where they most abound, much fruit of sense beneath is rarely found.
—*Alexander Pope*

12. Lilies that fester smell far worse than weeds.
—*Shakespeare*

13. To the last I stab at thee; from hell's heart I stab at thee; for hate's sake I spit my last breath at thee.
—*Herman Melville,* Moby Dick

14. The weak in courage is strong in cunning.
—*William Blake*

____ h. vagarious

____ i. venal

____ j. usurious

____ k. verbose

____ l. wily

____ m. vitiated

____ n. vindictive

ANSWER KEY FOR REVIEWS

REVIEW 1

a. 3 & 7	b. 2	c. 1	d. 4	e. 9
f. 10	g. 8	h. 5	i. 6	

REVIEW 2

a. 2	b. 3	c. 1	d. 4	e. 8
f. 7	g. 6	h. 5	i. 10	j. 9
k. 11	l. 12	m. 14	n. 13	

REVIEW 3

a. 2	b. 4	c. 3	d. 1	e. 8
f. 9	g. 7	h. 5	i. 6	j. 11
k. 10	l. 13	m. 12		

REVIEW 4

a. 1	b. 3	c. 4	d. 2	e. 9
f. 5	g. 7	h. 6	i. 8	j. 14
k. 13	l. 12	m. 11	n. 10	

REVIEW 5

a. 2	b. 3	c. 1	d. 4	e. 7
f. 8	g. 5	h. 6	i. 11	j. 9
k. 12	l. 10			

REVIEW 6

a. 4	b. 1	c. 2	d. 3	e. 8
f. 7	g. 5	h. 6	i. 9	j. 14
k. 11	l. 12	m. 10	n. 13	

REVIEW 7

a. 3	b. 2	c. 4	d. 1	e. 6
f. 5	g. 7	h. 8	i. 12	j. 9
k. 10	l. 11			

REVIEW 8

a. 3	b. 4	c. 5	d. 2	e. 1
f. 8	g. 6	h. 7	i. 10	j. 12
k. 11	l. 9			

REVIEW 9

a. 4	b. 3	c. 2	d. 1	e. 8
f. 7	g. 6	h. 9	i. 5	j. 13
k. 14	l. 10	m. 12	n. 11	

REVIEW 10

a. 2	b. 1	c. 3	d. 4	e. 5
f. 6	g. 7	h. 9	i. 8	j. 13
k. 10	l. 11	m. 12		

REVIEW 11

a. 4	b. 2	c. 3	d. 1	e. 6
f. 5	g. 7	h. 8	i. 11	j. 9
k. 10	l. 12			

REVIEW 12

a. 4	b. 3	c. 6	d. 2	e. 1
f. 5	g. 9	h. 8	i. 11	j. 12
k. 10	l. 7			

REVIEW 13

a. 2	b. 3	c. 1	d. 4	e. 7
f. 5	g. 8	h. 6	i. 10	j. 9
k. 12	l. 11			

REVIEW 14

a. 4	b. 5	c. 3	d. 1	e. 2
f. 7	g. 11	h. 9	i. 6	j. 8
k. 10				

REVIEW 15

a. 1	b. 2	c. 3	d. 5	e. 4
f. 9	g. 8	h. 7	i. 6	j. 12
k. 11	l. 13	m. 10		

REVIEW 16

a. 2	b. 3	c. 1	d. 4	e. 6
f. 7	g. 5	h. 12	i. 11	j. 10
k. 9	l. 8			

REVIEW 17

a. 2	b. 1	c. 7	d. 6	e. 5
f. 4	g. 3	h. 9	i. 10	j. 8
k. 11	l. 14	m. 12	n. 13	

ANSWER KEY FOR QUIZZES

QUIZ 1
1. B	2. A	3. B	4. A	5. C
6. E	7. B	8. D	9. D	10. F

QUIZ 2
1. C	2. C	3. D	4. B	5. H
6. E	7. A	8. F	9. I	10. G

QUIZ 3
1. B	2. I	3. B	4. A	5. D
6. G	7. C	8. E	9. F	10. H

QUIZ 4
1. F	2. A	3. G	4. H	5. E
6. D	7. B	8. I	9. J	10. C

QUIZ 5
1. A	2. B	3. F	4. B	5. H
6. E	7. D	8. I	9. G	10. C

QUIZ 6
1. I	2. E	3. E	4. C	5. A
6. D	7. G	8. B	9. F	10. H

QUIZ 7
1. I	2. J	3. F	4. E	5. G
6. H	7. C	8. D	9. B	10. A

QUIZ 8
1. H	2. J	3. E	4. F	5. D
6. C	7. B	8. G	9. A	10. I

QUIZ 9
1. I	2. D	3. E	4. G	5. B
6. H	7. A	8. C	9. J	10. F

QUIZ 10
1. G	2. B	3. F	4. D	5. J
6. A	7. E	8. C	9. H	10. I

QUIZ 11
1. H	2. I	3. J	4. B	5. C
6. D	7. G	8. E	9. A	10. F

QUIZ 12
1. C	2. F	3. G	4. H	5. D
6. B	7. I	8. E	9. A	10. J

QUIZ 13
1. A	2. E	3. C	4. G	5. H
6. D	7. B	8. F	9. G	10. I

QUIZ 14
1. E	2. G	3. H	4. D	5. I
6. J	7. F	8. C	9. B	10. A

QUIZ 15
1. B	2. J	3. C	4. D	5. I
6. E	7. G	8. H	9. A	10. F

QUIZ 16
1. F	2. G	3. I	4. H	5. F
6. C	7. J	8. D	9. B	10. A

QUIZ 17
1. H	2. G	3. I	4. F	5. E
6. C	7. B	8. A	9. E	10. D

QUIZ 18
1. G	2. A	3. D	4. H	5. B
6. C	7. E	8. F	9. F	10. G

QUIZ 19
1. A	2. F	3. J	4. E	5. D
6. G	7. I	8. B	9. H	10. C

QUIZ 20
1. D	2. I	3. G	4. B	5. A
6. I	7. E	8. C	9. H	10. F

QUIZ 21
1. H	2. B	3. F	4. E	5. D
6. A	7. G	8. A	9. C	10. C

QUIZ 22
1. A	2. I	3. E	4. C	5. D
6. B	7. H	8. G	9. B	10. F

QUIZ 23

1. E	2. A	3. I	4. H	5. D
6. J	7. B	8. C	9. G	10. F

QUIZ 24

1. J	2. D	3. H	4. G	5. F
6. E	7. I	8. B	9. A	10. C

QUIZ 25

1. H	2. J	3. E	4. D	5. A
6. F	7. C	8. I	9. B	10. G

QUIZ 26

1. B	2. E	3. G	4. A	5. I
6. C	7. H	8. F	9. D	10. D

QUIZ 27

1. I	2. E	3. G	4. F	5. B
6. H	7. C	8. D	9. A	10. J

QUIZ 28

1. G	2. D	3. B	4. H	5. C
6. F	7. E	8. A	9. I	10. J

QUIZ 29

1. C	2. J	3. A	4. I	5. F
6. G	7. D	8. B	9. H	10. E

QUIZ 30

1. C	2. F	3. J	4. E	5. A
6. H	7. I	8. G	9. B	10. D

QUIZ 31

1. J	2. E	3. F	4. H	5. D
6. A	7. C	8. G	9. B	10. I

QUIZ 32

1. D	2. G	3. C	4. A	5. E
6. H	7. I	8. B	9. F	10. I

QUIZ 33

1. J	2. I	3. H	4. F	5. B
6. C	7. G	8. E	9. D	10. A

QUIZ 34

1. A	2. G	3. C	4. F	5. H
6. D	7. I	8. E	9. B	10. J

QUIZ 35

1. B	2. G	3. D	4. I	5. H
6. F	7. E	8. C	9. A	10. J

QUIZ 36

1. C	2. A	3. D	4. B	5. I
6. J	7. E	8. H	9. G	10. F

QUIZ 37

1. G	2. E	3. B	4. C	5. G
6. D	7. A	8. F	9. H	10. F

QUIZ 38

1. F	2. C	3. J	4. E	5. I
6. A	7. G	8. H	9. D	10. B

QUIZ 39

1. C	2. H	3. J	4. A	5. F
6. B	7. I	8. G	9. E	10. D

QUIZ 40

1. H	2. D	3. B	4. I	5. C
6. D	7. E	8. A	9. G	10. F

QUIZ 41

1. F	2. I	3. H	4. A	5. D
6. I	7. E	8. C	9. G	10. B

QUIZ 42

1. G	2. C	3. A	4. I	5. E
6. F	7. H	8. D	9. J	10. B

QUIZ 43

1. E	2. J	3. A	4. D	5. B
6. I	7. G	8. F	9. C	10. H

QUIZ 44

1. D	2. F	3. E	4. B	5. G
6. B	7. A	8. H	9. B	10. C

QUIZ 45

1. D	2. D	3. G	4. C	5. B
6. E	7. I	8. A	9. F	10. H

QUIZ 46

1. C	2. E	3. H	4. F	5. D
6. B	7. A	8. G	9. G	10. G

QUIZ 47

1. J	2. F	3. D	4. H	5. G
6. C	7. A	8. B	9. E	10. I

QUIZ 48

1. H	2. G	3. C	4. E	5. A
6. J	7. F	8. B	9. D	10. I

QUIZ 49

1. I	2. H	3. G	4. G	5. C
6. F	7. A	8. B	9. E	10. D

QUIZ 50

1. E	2. H	3. I	4. I	5. C
6. G	7. B	8. D	9. A	10. F

QUIZ 51

1. G	2. D	3. H	4. E	5. B
6. C	7. A	8. I	9. F	10. J

QUIZ 52

1. C	2. G	3. I	4. E	5. F
6. H	7. J	8. B	9. A	10. D

QUIZ 53

1. D	2. D	3. E	4. G	5. B
6. A	7. C	8. D	9. F	10. H

QUIZ 54

1. B	2. C	3. A	4. J	5. H
6. G	7. F	8. E	9. D	10. I

QUIZ 55

1. E	2. B	3. C	4. F	5. H
6. J	7. A	8. D	9. G	10. I

QUIZ 56

1. E	2. C	3. I	4. F	5. G
6. J	7. B	8. H	9. A	10. D

QUIZ 57

1. G	2. A	3. C	4. H	5. E
6. I	7. B	8. J	9. F	10. D

QUIZ 58

1. C	2. B	3. G	4. H	5. J
6. E	7. F	8. D	9. I	10. A

QUIZ 59

1. H	2. I	3. A	4. D	5. B
6. C	7. C	8. F	9. E	10. G

QUIZ 60

1. J	2. F	3. C	4. E	5. I
6. H	7. G	8. B	9. A	10. D

QUIZ 61

1. C	2. F	3. D	4. A	5. E
6. H	7. G	8. B	9. J	10. I

QUIZ 62

1. A	2. H	3. E	4. C	5. I
6. F	7. J	8. G	9. D	10. B

QUIZ 63

1. I	2. B	3. B	4. G	5. D
6. F	7. E	8. H	9. A	10. C

QUIZ 64

1. A	2. E	3. D	4. H	5. C
6. G	7. I	8. F	9. J	10. B

QUIZ 65

1. D	2. B	3. C	4. I	5. E
6. F	7. A	8. H	9. G	10. J

QUIZ 66

1. J	2. H	3. I	4. F	5. C
6. G	7. E	8. B	9. D	10. A

QUIZ 67

1. H	2. D	3. C	4. I	5. A
6. G	7. J	8. E	9. B	10. F

QUIZ 68

1. E	2. F	3. I	4. B	5. D
6. A	7. C	8. G	9. H	10. J

QUIZ 69

1. B	2. H	3. D	4. C	5. G
6. F	7. I	8. A	9. E	10. E

QUIZ 70

1. I	2. B	3. H	4. G	5. F
6. D	7. C	8. E	9. J	10. A

QUIZ 71

1. E	2. E	3. D	4. A	5. G
6. I	7. C	8. B	9. F	10. H

QUIZ 72

1. I	2. D	3. B	4. C	5. E
6. H	7. F	8. A	9. I	10. G

QUIZ 73

1. C	2. F	3. I	4. G	5. E
6. J	7. A	8. H	9. D	10. B

QUIZ 74

1. I	2. F	3. B	4. A	5. J
6. E	7. H	8. C	9. D	10. G

QUIZ 75

1. I	2. J	3. D	4. A	5. H
6. B	7. G	8. E	9. C	10. F

QUIZ 76

1. H	2. E	3. F	4. I	5. D
6. J	7. A	8. B	9. G	10. C

QUIZ 77

1. B	2. G	3. E	4. H	5. C
6. A	7. J	8. I	9. D	10. F

QUIZ 78

1. D	2. F	3. J	4. H	5. I
6. E	7. B	8. G	9. A	10. C

QUIZ 79

1. I	2. G	3. F	4. D	5. I
6. B	7. C	8. E	9. H	10. A

QUIZ 80

1. B	2. A	3. F	4. H	5. H
6. I	7. E	8. D	9. G	10. C

QUIZ 81

1. D	2. H	3. A	4. F	5. G
6. I	7. C	8. C	9. B	10. E

QUIZ 82

1. F	2. E	3. A	4. G	5. A
6. B	7. D	8. I	9. C	10. H

QUIZ 83

1. H	2. D	3. G	4. A	5. C
6. F	7. B	8. H	9. D	10. E

QUIZ 84

1. H	2. D	3. F	4. A	5. B
6. G	7. E	8. I	9. C	10. J

QUIZ 85

1. G	2. I	3. A	4. H	5. B
6. F	7. C	8. E	9. J	10. D